53

January
2008

ECONOMIC POLICY

SENIOR EDITORS
GEORGES DE MÉNIL
RICHARD PORTES
HANS-WERNER SINN

MANAGING EDITORS
GIUSEPPE BERTOLA
PHILIPPE MARTIN
JAN VAN OURS

Published in association with the European Economic Association

Blackwell Publishing Ltd for Centre for Economic Policy Research,
Center for Economic Studies of the University of Munich, and
Paris-Jourdan Sciences Economiques (PSE)
in collaboration with the Maison des Sciences de l'Homme.

STATEMENT OF PURPOSE

Economic Policy provides timely and authoritative analyses of the choices which confront policy-makers. The subject matter ranges from the study of how individual markets can and should work to the broadest interactions in the world economy.

Economic Policy is a joint activity of the Centre for Economic Policy Research (CEPR), the Munich-based Center for Economic Studies (CES) and the Paris-based Maison des Sciences de l'Homme (PSE). It offers an independent, non-partisan, European perspective on issues of worldwide concern. It emphasizes problems of international significance, either because they affect the world economy directly or because the experience of one country contains important lessons for policy-makers elsewhere.

All the articles are specifically commissioned from leading professional economists. Their brief is to demonstrate how live policy issues can be illuminated by the insights of modern economics and by the most recent evidence. The presentation is incisive and written in plain language accessible to the wide audience which participates in the policy debate.

Prior to publication, the contents of each volume are discussed by a Panel of distinguished economists from Europe and elsewhere. The Panel rotates annually. Inclusion in each volume of a summary of the highlights of the Economic Policy Panel discussion provides the reader with alternative interpretations of the evidence and a sense of the liveliness of the current debate.

Economic Policy is owned by the Maison des Sciences de l'Homme, CEPR and CES. The 45th panel meeting was held in Frankfurt and was hosted by the Deutsche Bundesbank. We gratefully acknowledge this support, without implicating any of these organizations in the views expressed here, which are the sole responsibility of the authors.

5

January 2008

CONTENTS

Editors' introduction

The papers published in this issue of *Economic Policy* were presented at the April 2007 Panel meeting, hosted in Frankfurt by the Bundesbank. In this introduction we highlight, and relate to each other and to wider issues, their novel insights into highly topical international trade patterns and productivity dynamics.

The type of competition that industrialized countries face from new trading partners has important implications for the income distribution implications of globalization. Analysis of imports from China and other countries brings a mix of worrisome and reassuring news in this regard.

CHINESE EXPORTS

On the one hand, using very detailed information about countries' international trade with the United States, Peter Schott's paper presents convincing evidence that the overlap of China's exports to the US with exports of OECD countries has strongly increased over time. This suggests that manufacturing in industrialized countries is more exposed to direct competition from China. Another implication is that wages in OECD countries should be increasingly influenced by the level of wages in China as workers compete to sell and export goods in the same industries.

On the other hand, however, the paper finds that Chinese exports sell at a discount relative to other countries, particularly those from the OECD, and the price difference has been growing over time. If prices are a good indicator of product quality, and if goods of different quality are poor substitutes, this suggests that rich countries may be able to compete with China on terms other than price. In particular, it suggests that developed economies compete with developing economies like China by raising the quality of their exports. If this is the case, this should help insulate industrialized labour markets from Chinese direct competition.

Given the importance that these issues have acquired in political debates, the original findings that this paper presents attracted a considerable amount of interest

Economic Policy January 2008 pp. 1–4 Printed in Great Britain
© CEPR, CES, MSH, 2008.

at the panel. Some questions were raised on the role of the Chinese exchange rate policy as an alternative to relative lower quality in explaining the low Chinese prices on world markets. Some panel members also questioned how representative Chinese exports to the US are and therefore the extent to which Schott's results could be generalized to other OECD countries. However, most of the debate centred on the interpretation of the results and the overall optimism of Schott's own interpretation of the effect of Chinese competition on income distribution in the OECD. That several economic interpretations to Schott's findings are possible shows that there is a rich research agenda ahead. This paper will certainly attract attention as the first quantification of these important issues.

The paper by Peter Schott uncovers and analyzes very intriguing features of trade patterns between the US and China, and the US and other countries. But what is more generally the character of challenges posed by newly industrialized countries to established producers? And are different members of the latter group similarly equipped to meet those challenges?

NORTH–SOUTH COMPETITION IN QUALITY

Lionel Fontagné, Guillaume Gaulier and Soledad Zignago's paper answers these important questions. Using a vast set of trade quantity and price data, they slice each product category in segments according to the values of units shipped. This procedure uncovers interesting and sharp cross-sectional and time series patterns. Not surprisingly, and consistently with Schott's results, not only the US but also other advanced countries tend to produce and export higher-value items than China and other newly industrializing countries. This pattern strengthens over time, as new producers gain ground in the low-value segments of each market and established producers retrench in higher-value segments. However, and even more interestingly, not all industrialized countries appear to be equally successful in repositioning their product lines in the face of new competition. Readers familiar with German car producers' craftsmanship will not be surprised to learn from the paper that German trade patterns, for example, reveal a strong specialization in high-value products in a broad range of manufacturing sectors, and are very resilient to competition from developing countries. Generally, Europe is overall more successful than the US and Japan in maintaining high-quality market shares. However, important differences can be observed within Europe. Italy's traditional specialization in relatively low-price segments of various sectors, for example, makes it difficult for its producers both to resist Chinese competition in similar products, and to reposition in higher-value market segments.

The quality and depth of the paper's analysis was very much appreciated by the panel. Its findings will be an essential reference for further work aimed at fleshing out the implications of quality-specialization patterns for wages and other factor prices and for income distribution, and through these for the sources and remedies of political tensions arising in a world of increasingly deep, but perhaps unstable, trade liberalization processes.

ANTIDUMPING LAWS

Do countries react to such tensions, and how? The starting point of the paper by Hylke Vandenbussche and Maurizio Zanardi is the observed proliferation of anti-dumping laws, especially in developing countries. The fact that antidumping laws are no longer adopted only by industrialized countries is a source of concern for anybody who favours further efficiency-enhancing trade liberalization, because antidumping actions are viewed by most economists as a new form of protectionism against efficient competition, rather than a tool against poorly defined predatory or 'unfair' practices. Vandenbussche and Zanardi analyze empirically why countries adopt antidumping (AD) laws, and what causes them to start using the law actively. They bring to bear on these issues an interesting set of data from 108 countries that did not have an AD law in 1980 and either adopted an AD law at some point between 1980 and 2003, or never did within that period. One of their main results is that AD law proliferation seems to be driven by 'retaliation motives': countries that were the target of more AD measures in the past are more likely to adopt an AD law themselves, suggesting that AD may indeed be abused for strategic purposes. Another finding is that substantial trade liberalization in the past raises the probability that a country will adopt an AD law. Hence countries seem to substitute tariffs by narrower protection instruments, like AD laws.

The authors conclude that their results call for the urgent need to renegotiate the AD procedure at the multilateral level. The paper was appreciated by the panel as professionally executed and providing interesting results on a relevant policy subject. The discussion centred on the interpretation of some of the results, which was not as clear as it would be if the hypotheses were based on more precise theoretical considerations. A more structural approach, based on political economy and industrial organization models, would be very interesting indeed, and will certainly need to refer to the highly original approach and findings of this paper.

In fact, the patterns of trade and competition among countries are ultimately and intimately linked with technological and organizational features determining pro-ductivity. Ultimately, each country's ability to support its citizens' economic wellbeing boils down to how efficiently it can make use of available resources. We close the issue with a paper that focuses precisely on this important issue, again bringing novel data to bear on it.

MARKET SERVICES PRODUCTIVITY

Much has been written in our journal and elsewhere about the US productivity boom of the late 1990s, about the role of Information and Communication Technology

(ICT) in fuelling it, and about the possible role of institutional rigidities in causing the comparatively poor productivity performance of most European countries. More food for thought and writing has been provided by data revisions, which have tended to downplay somewhat the initially astonishing American performance, and by subtle definitional issues (such as the treatment of software expenditures as investment or current cost). Robert Inklaar, Marcel P. Timmer and Bart van Ark analyze a new dataset that remedies an important shortcoming of the data used in previous comparative work. For the first time, it is possible to account for the quality of inputs (such as the education achievements of workers) on a comparable basis when assessing productivity across sectors not only of the American economy, but also of many European countries. Focusing on services sectors where the gap in productivity levels and growth appeared particularly large in previous work, the paper documents that accounting for input quality does make a difference. Intriguingly, the results of the paper's more refined analysis are mostly negative: productivity differences are less significant and less easily explained here than in previous work. Broadly speaking, the dataset's input quality indicators turn out to imply that US producers really use better inputs than their European counterparts. Hence, unexplained ('multifactor') productivity gaps are smaller than in previous work or even switch sign, with European sectors the more efficient producers. The paper also assesses whether country- and sector-level institutional rigidity and ICT use indicators and may account for such multifactor productivity patterns, and fails to find significant evidence of their relevance.

The Panel appreciated the much needed effort to improve statistical measures of productivity in Europe, but could not avoid feeling that the data's inability to detect sharp patterns may be due to a poor signal/noise ratio. Many panel members felt that the paper's data and results are not yet accurate and robust enough to support unconventional policy implications, such as for example a lesser need to foster productivity by flexibility-oriented reforms in light of apparently excellent productivity performance by many services sectors of the most rigid countries. An important lesson of the paper is that productivity is not as easy to measure, and certainly not as easy to improve by reforms, as some earlier contributions indicated. But another important lesson is that data quality is very important and, as the paper itself acknowledges, further improvements in that respect may yet overturn the results of early measurement efforts.

Chinese exports

SUMMARY

China's exports have grown dramatically over the last three decades in large part due to its rapid penetration of new product markets. To help address the implications of this growth for developed economies, this paper gauges the relative sophistication of Chinese exports along two dimensions. First, I measure China's export overlap with developed countries by comparing the set of products China exports to the United States with the bundle of products exported by the OECD. Second, I compare Chinese and other countries' exports within product markets in terms of the price they receive in the US market. While China's export overlap with the OECD is much greater than one would predict given its low wages, the prices that US consumers are willing to pay for China's exports are substantially lower than the prices they are willing to pay for OECD exports. This fact, as well as the increase in the 'OECD premium' over time, suggests that competition between China and the world's most developed economies may be less direct than their product-mix overlap implies. It may also reflect efforts by developed-country firms to compete with China by dropping their least sophisticated offerings and moving up the quality ladder.

— Peter K. Schott

Economic Policy January 2008 Printed in Great Britain
© CEPR, CES, MSH, 2008.

The relative sophistication of Chinese exports

Peter K. Schott

Yale School of Management and NBER

1. INTRODUCTION

Speculation about the impact Chinese growth will have on developed and developing countries over the coming decade varies widely. Some observers predict the imminent end of manufacturing in developed economies like the United States and Europe, while others believe low- and middle-income countries are most at risk.

This paper analyzes very detailed information about countries' international trade with the United States to gain a better understanding of developed countries' susceptibility to competition from China. It considers both the breadth of product markets China has entered over the last three decades as well as changes in the relative prices of Chinese products within these product markets. The data show that China's penetration of the US market has been substantial and that its export bundle overlaps significantly with that of developed economies. On the other hand, Chinese

I thank Keith Chen, Amit Khandelwal, Philippe Martin, Kevin O'Rourke, Clemens Fuest, members of the 2004 NBER China Working Group and the April 2007 Economic Policy panel for helpful comments, suggestions and insights. This research is based upon work supported by the National Science Foundation under Grant No. 0241474. Any opinions, findings, and conclusions or recommendations expressed in this material are those of the author and do not necessarily reflect the views of the National Science Foundation.

Economic Policy January 2008 pp. 5–49 Printed in Great Britain
© CEPR, CES, MSH, 2008.

exports sell at a discount relative to other countries, particularly the advanced economies that are members of the OECD. The existence of these price differences, as well as their increase over time, suggests that developed and developing economies may compete on terms other than price. In theory, such competition may help insulate workers in developed economies from the relatively low wages earned by workers in developing economies.

Conventional models of international trade imply that developed countries like the United States and those in the EU have little to fear and much to gain from the emergence of China. In these models, comparative advantage drives countries to specialize in unique subsets of goods that do not compete directly on world markets. In models where comparative advantage flows from countries' relative endowments of capital, skill and labor, extremely labor-abundant countries like China are expected to produce and export relatively labor-intensive goods such as toys and t-shirts. More capital- and skill-abundant countries like Germany, on the other hand, ought to manufacture and export capital- and skill-intensive goods such as pharmaceuticals and electron microscopes.

The extent to which countries specialize in different sets of goods influences how directly their workers compete, and is therefore a key determinant of the distributional implications of globalization. When all countries produce the same products, price-wage arbitrage implies that reductions in the world price of goods influences wages in all countries: if China's entry into the world toy market leads to a sharp reduction in the price of toys, then the wages of the low-skill workers that make toys will be driven down in every country. On the other hand, if China produces toys and Germany does not, low-skill German workers only gain from the emergence of a toy industry in China: their nominal wages are unaffected by the surge in toy exports, and the decline in toy prices leads to an increase in the amount of income they can spend on other products.

Though the intuition for these outcomes is motivated by specialization that takes place across industries, specialization might also be expected within industries or even within products. One reason for this is aggregation. If the product codes used to measure international trade are 'too' aggregate, they will erroneously place goods that are essentially different into the same product classification: 'Televisions', for example, might capture both high-definition flat panel displays as well as receivers with conventional cathode ray tubes.

On the other hand, differences in countries' exports within the very narrow product classifications examined in this paper may also reflect a more subtle phenomenon – vertical differentiation: Japan and China might both produce and export high-definition televisions, but the Japanese televisions might employ more sophisticated technology, be of much higher quality, or contain a richer set of attributes than the ones exported by China. These vertical differences should manifest in prices, with Japanese televisions fetching a much higher price in the US market than Chinese televisions due to consumers' willingness to pay for them. As with across-industry specialization, within-industry specialization based on vertical differentiation can influence the degree to which workers in developed economies are insulated from workers in developing countries. Intuitively, the less substitutable goods of greater and less sophistication are, the less strong is price-wage arbitrage and the more insulated the workers in the two types of countries will be.

To learn more about the potential impact of Chinese competition on developed country outcomes, this paper uses US import data to assess the relative sophistication of the Chinese export bundle both across and within products over a very long time horizon. I first compare the range of manufacturing product categories China exports to the United States between 1972 and 2005 with the range of manufacturing product categories exported by other countries, notably the developed economies in the OECD. I assume that the more similar a non-OECD country's export bundle is to the OECD, the more sophisticated its exports are revealed to be in the across-product dimension.

I find that China's overlap with the OECD *across* products is substantial and increasing over time. This result is surprising given China's level of development, but it is consistent with its size. Recent models of international trade stress consumers' love of variety and the impact of countries' size on their ability to supply that variety. In these models, larger economies produce and export broader ranges of goods. China had the fourth largest economy measured in terms of World Bank real GDP in 2005, up from a rank of eighteen in 1972.

Over the same period, China's export-bundle similarity with the OECD jumped from a rank of nineteen to four, just behind Korea, Mexico and Taiwan. This increase was driven by China's very rapid penetration of US product markets. Indeed, while China was present in just 9% of all manufacturing product categories in 1972, it was present in 85% of categories by 2005. No other country's growth in product penetration comes close to this increase. Even groups of countries have a hard time matching progress on this dimension. Product penetration for all of Latin America, for example, increased from 38% in 1972 to 69% in 2005.

To get a sense of how closely China and developed economies compete *within* product markets, I examine export prices (i.e. unit values) within product categories for evidence of vertical differentiation. It is well known in the international trade literature that countries' export prices vary positively with their level of development, that is, with their per capita GDP or their relative endowments of capital and skill versus labor (Schott, 2004). This relationship is consistent with the idea that countries use their endowment or technological advantages to embed higher levels of sophistication in their goods, and that consumers pay a higher price for this higher sophistication.

In the analysis below, I compare the prices China receives for its exports in the US market to those received by other countries as well as those received by the composite OECD. I find Chinese export prices to be consistently lower than the prices of countries at a similar level of development, and that this disparity increases over time in most industries. In a direct comparison with the OECD, I show that Chinese export prices are on average 23% lower in Chemicals, 40% lower in Manufactured Materials and 60% lower in Miscellaneous Manufactures and Machinery from 1980 to 2005. These discounts have widened over the past five to ten years.

The gap between Chinese and OECD export prices suggests that competition between China and the world's most developed economies might be less direct than their overlap in product markets implies. Indeed, the competition in differentiated manufactured goods analysed here contrasts markedly with the often stark price competition found in undifferentiated commodities such as wheat documented by Kevin O'Rourke in his discussion of this paper. Furthermore, it is possible that increases in the China-OECD price gaps over time are a reflection of developed economies 'moving up' or 'moving out' in response to trade with low-wage countries, that is, their tendency to either raise the sophistication of their incumbent varieties or drop the least-sophisticated varieties from their export bundle. Upgrading of this sort would be consistent with theoretical models of product cycling as well as evidence emerging from micro-studies of firms' reactions to globalization. It would support the view that the world's most skill- and capital-abundant economies will specialize in the most sophisticated varieties within product markets even as production of low-end varieties is ceded to less-developed economies. If that is the case, there is hope that manufacturing in high-wage developing countries will continue to survive competition from low-wage countries like China.

The remainder of this paper is structured as follows. Section 2 provides a brief description of relevant theories of international trade that stresses the intuitions relied upon in the analysis; Section 3 provides a short overview of China's position in terms of its relative size and level of development; Sections 4, 5 and 6 describe the major results of the paper; Sections 7 and 8 provide an interpretation of these results; and Section 9 concludes with a discussion of where future research might be most helpful.

2. A BRIEF SUMMARY OF INTERNATIONAL TRADE THEORY

My comparison of countries' export mix and export prices is guided by several strands of international trade theory. This section provides a brief introduction to the basic assumptions and intuitions of these models.

The Heckscher–Ohlin model, which has countries' product mix varying with relative factor endowments, can be used both to understand why countries specialize according to comparative advantage and to gain insight into the relationship between specialization and the distributional implications of international trade. So-called 'new' trade theory models, on the other hand, articulate a connection between country size and the range of goods a country will produce. Finally, models of international product cycling provide intuition for the movement of once cutting-edge goods from developed to developing economies over time.

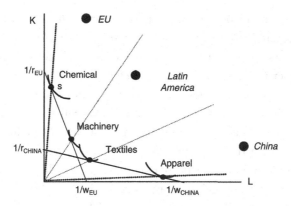

Figure 1. International specialization according to relative factor endowments

2.1. The Heckscher–Ohlin model ('old' trade theory)

The Heckscher–Ohlin model connects countries' resources to the mixes of goods they can profitably produce. A two-factor version of the Heckscher–Ohlin model, where the two factors are capital (K) and labor (L), is displayed in the Lerner diagram in Figure 1. This diagram features dollar-value isoquants for four industries – apparel, textiles, machinery and chemicals – that differ in terms of their capital intensity. Each isoquant traces out the amounts of capital and labor that can be combined to produce one dollar's worth of output in the noted industry. Given their relative positions in the figure, apparel is the most labor-intensive industry while chemicals is the most capital intensive: it takes relatively more capital to produce a dollar's worth of chemicals than a dollar's worth of apparel. Under standard assumptions, the four industries' unit-value isoquants carve out three 'cones of diversification', that is, three sets of relative endowment vectors selecting a unique mix of two industries. Dixit and Norman (1980) and Leamer (1984) provide detailed discussions of these assumptions and their implications.

A country's endowments of capital and labor determine the cone in which it resides. In the figure, the capital-abundant countries of the EU inhabit the most capital-abundant cone, while relatively capital scarce China is in the most labor-abundant cone. The countries of Latin America are assumed to reside in the middle cone.

Because production of an industry outside of the cone in which a country resides results in negative profit, GDP-maximizing countries specialize in the two industries anchoring their cones of diversification, i.e. the two industries whose input intensities are most closely related to their endowments. Leamer (1987) provides a generalization of these implications to higher-dimensional settings.

The negative profits that the relatively capital-abundant countries of the European Union would earn in labor-intensive apparel and textiles, for example, can be seen by comparing the amount of capital and labor that can be bought for one dollar in the EU (via the downward sloping isocost line defined by r_{EU} and w_{EU}) with the amount of capital and labor needed to produce one dollar's worth of output (via the dollar-value isoquants). A key message of Figure 1 is that relatively high production costs keep industries out of industries at odds with their comparative advantage.

The Heckscher-Ohlin model provides useful insight into the relationship between specialization and relative wages across countries. In the endowment-driven specialization depicted in Figure 1, for example, workers in the EU are insulated from goods-price changes caused by the emergence of China. If China's entry into world markets drives down the price of labor-intensive apparel, the relative returns to capital and labor in any country producing these goods will also change. In the figure, this is because of 'price-wage' arbitrage, that is, the fact that relative wage lines are defined by goods prices: when the price of a good falls, it takes more capital and labor to produce one dollar's worth of output, so the isocost lines tangential to the dollar-value isoquants adjust.

In Figure 1, relative wages in the EU are unaffected by China's entry into the apparel market. That is because its specialization breaks wage-price arbitrage: its participation in industries other than those produced by China means that its relative wages are determined solely by prices in those other industries. Indeed, if China were to drive down the price of apparel, EU workers would benefit by having more income available to spend on other products.

Trade barriers, of course, can provide incentives for countries to act against their comparative advantage. Import tariffs (which are assumed to be zero in Figure 1) drive a wedge between the price of a good inside a country and its price on world markets, that is, the prices displayed in the figure. If the EU were to impose sufficiently high import tariffs on apparel, then production of apparel in the EU would be profitable because the distorted EU price would cover its relatively high production costs. In that case, trade liberalization would necessitate the loss of apparel industry jobs and the lowering of their tariff-protected wages. As tariffs are removed, EU firms that found it profitable to produce apparel under tariff protection would drop those products or fail outright. Resources freed up from these adjustments would move towards firms producing chemicals and machinery, that is, the industries that are consistent with the EU's comparative advantage. As discussed in greater detail below, evidence in favour of such reallocations has been found in examinations of US firms' responses to trade liberalization.

In a similar way, trade policies that promote exports in China can increase the range of products Chinese firms export to the United States. Under those circumstances, the observed export overlap between China and the OECD would be 'artificially' high.

The specialization displayed in Figure 1 provides intuition for the first dimension of across-product sophistication developed in this paper. Because countries' product mix is a function of the relative similarity of their endowments, China and the EU are predicted to have few industries in common. In the figure, Latin America occupies the middle cone of diversification, with the labor-intensive portion of its product mix overlapping that of China and the capital-intensive portion of its product mix overlapping that of the EU. I return to a potential implication of such a setting in the discussion of Figure 4 in Section 7 below. In a more general, three-factor setting, these overlaps might be less extreme given Latin American land abundance. Leamer et al. (1999) offer a more detailed discussion of the potential effects of Latin American resource abundance on development, in particular, how the attractiveness of using low-cost resources provides a disincentive for capital accumulation.

This discussion highlights one method for gauging the 'closeness' of competition between China and the OECD: looking across industries and asking how many they export in common to a third country like the United States.

A slight change in perspective renders Figure 1 useful for understanding the second dimension of export sophistication relied upon in this paper – vertical differentiation. For that intuition, one should reinterpret the industry isoquants in Figure 1 as representing vertically differentiated products in a single industry. Instead of apparel, textiles, machinery and chemicals, consider four different types of televisions: cheap black-and-white tube televisions, colour tube televisions, rear-projection televisions and plasma displays. These vertically differentiated products might each be located on a separate dollar-value isoquant in the figure, and countries would choose to produce a different level of quality in the television market depending upon their relative endowments. Empirically, if such vertical differentiation takes place within the product classification codes used to track countries' international trade, it might be discerned by examining the relative prices of countries' exports within these product categories. That is the strategy I rely upon below.

2.2. New trade theory

A key implication of the Heckscher–Ohlin model is that trade between two countries increases with the disparity in their comparative advantage. This implication is at first sight hard to reconcile with the observation that a large share of international trade takes place within industries between relatively similar trading partners (Grubel and Lloyd, 1975). Germany and the United States, for example, carry on a robust two-way trade in automobiles.

This dissonance between theory and data has led to the development of 'new' trade theory models that emphasize consumer love of variety and horizontal product differentiation as drivers of international trade (see, for example, Krugman, 1980). In these models, firms 'specialize' in distinct horizontal varieties (e.g. Volkswagens and Fords), and consumers' love of variety induces countries to engage in intra-product trade. An important implication of these models is that the number of horizontal varieties a country produces is predicted to be a function of the resources at its disposal – that is, the overall size of its economy or labor force. Hummels and Klenow (2005), for example, find a positive correlation between country size and the number of product categories countries export.

Though China is relatively skill scarce, its labor force and economy are quite large. Thus, a key implication for China from new trade theory models is that China will produce a greater number of varieties than smaller countries, all else being equal. To the extent that the industry or product classifications used to track international trade capture such horizontal differentiation, one would expect it to have greater product penetration in the US market than smaller countries. Note that to the extent horizontal product differentiation takes place *within* narrow product categories – for example red shoes versus black shoes – it is much more difficult to detect using existing trade datasets. In the results below, I find that larger countries have greater overlap with the range of products exported by the OECD, a feature of the data that fits this model well.

A related literature in international trade that provides insight into how the relative sophistication of countries' export can be measured considers the impact of economic growth on countries' terms of trade. The classical argument (e.g. Johnson, 1958) is that economic growth depresses a countries' terms of trade because the greater supply of exports associated with this growth leads to a decline in export prices. As noted above, this effect might be moderated or overturned by vertical differentiation, as the capital and skill deepening that occurs concomitant with development leads countries into cones of diversification anchored by more sophisticated products. Results in Schott (2004), for example, offer support for the view that emerging economies on relatively fast development tracks experience relatively rapid growth in export prices.

A negative correlation between economic growth and export prices might also be mitigated by horizontal differentiation: by increasing exports via variety proliferation rather than by exporting more and more of a given variety, downward pressure on export prices can be averted (Krugman, 1989, Corsetti *et al.*, forthcoming). As noted above, identifying this outcome in international trade datasets is difficult if horizontal differentiation occurs within product categories.

2.3. International product cycles

In models of international product cycling, developed countries invent and export the most sophisticated goods to developing countries until the latter figure out how to replicate them (Posner, 1961; Vernon, 1966, 1979). At that point, owing to their lower labor costs, developing countries drive developed countries out of the market and become the sole suppliers. A 'quality ladder' variant of this model has developed and developing countries trading dominance in varieties of a particular good over time, as developed countries re-enter the markets of existing goods by innovating and offering a more sophisticated version (Grossman and Helpman, 1991).

These models can provide intuition for how globalization influences relative incomes as well as the location of production. Zhu and Trefler (2005), for example, examine a model in which countries' comparative advantage is derived from differences in both productivity and factor-endowments. In the model, relatively fast productivity growth in developing countries allows them to catch up to developed countries. As a result of these gains, the least skill-intensive industries in the developed economies move to developing economies, where they become the most skill intensive. This movement raises the demand for skill in all countries, pushing up the skill premium and therefore income inequality. Productivity growth in developing economies also pushes up the skill premium via a more subtle channel: by raising the amount of output a given low-skilled worker can produce, relatively fast productivity growth in developing economies increases the world's effective supply of unskilled labor.

3. A BRIEF SUMMARY OF CHINA'S RELATIVE ENDOWMENTS

There is no doubt that China is labor abundant. Tables 1 and 2 provide complementary views of this labor abundance relative to other countries in Asia, the Caribbean, Latin America and the OECD. (A mapping of countries to regions is provided in Table 5 and discussed in the next section.) Table 1 compares China's relative endowments to the mean relative endowments of other countries, by region. The first four columns summarize educational attainment as estimated by Barro and Lee (2000). They reveal that highly skilled workers – that is, those with more than a secondary school education – are relatively scarce in Asia compared to Latin America, and scarcer still in China. While 13% of Latin America's population had attained a post-secondary education by 1999, the numbers are 8% and 3% for Asia and China, respectively. China also has a higher share of workers without any schooling than Latin America or the Caribbean: 21% of its population, versus 18% for both the Caribbean and Latin America, have never received formal schooling.

Table 2 reports the location of China in the distribution of other regions' relative endowments. A value of 50 in this table, for example, indicates that China's relative endowments are equal to the median of the noted region. China's skill scarcity ranks it below the median of the Asian, Latin American and Caribbean distributions. As indicated in the table, China's post-secondary education attainment places it in the 32nd percentile in Asia (behind Pakistan and India), in the 5th percentile of Latin America (just behind Guyana) and in the 33rd percentile of the Caribbean (between Haiti and Jamaica). It has relatively more unschooled citizens than 58% of Asian countries, 68% of Latin American countries and 67% of Caribbean countries. By comparison, China's location in the World Bank PPP-adjusted real GDP distribution increases from the 94th to the 99th percentile from 1972 to 2005.

In addition to being relatively skill scarce, China is relatively capital and land scarce. As of 2000, it has 0.10 hectares of arable land per person versus 0.25 hectares per person in Latin America, placing it in the 19th percentile of the Latin American distribution (between El Salvador and Venezuela). It's median capital per capita in 1990 (from Nehru and Dhareshwar, 1993) of US$ 2274 is also relatively low, placing it at the 21st percentile of the Latin American distribution (between Ecuador and Honduras). I compare regions' capital per capita in Tables 1 and 2 using the median

Table 1. Relative endowments by region

Region	No schooling (%)	Primary attainment (%)	Secondary attainment (%)	Post-secondary attainment (%)	Arable land per person (hectares)	Capital per capita ($)
Asia	32	32	27	8	0.14	3339
Carribean	18	44	31	7	0.08	6212
Latin America	18	49	20	13	0.25	5590
OECD	5	34	40	21	0.38	67688
China	21	42	36	3	0.10	2274

Notes: Cells report mean (columns 2 through 5) or median (column 6) values across all countries by region for which data is available. Education measures are for 1999 and are from Barro and Lee (2000). Land abundance data are for 2000 and are from the World Bank's World Development Indicators database. Capital per population data is for 1990 and are from Nehru and Dhareshwar (1993). Per capita capital values are adjusted for purchasing power parity using World Bank PPP conversion factors; they are expressed in 1987 dollars.

Table 2. Where China fits in other regions' relative endowments

Region	No schooling	Primary attainment	Secondary attainment	Post-secondary attainment	Arable land per person (hectares)	Capital per capita ($)
Asia	58	84	68	32	52	27
Carribean	67	50	50	33	75	20
Latin America	68	26	89	5	19	21
OECD	95	64	41	5	26	9

Notes: Cells report the percentile of each region's distribution that would be occupied by China if it were part of the region. See the notes to Table 1 for information on the source of each relative endowment variable. Education measures are for 1999 and are from Barro and Lee (2000). Land abundance data are for 2000 and are from the World Bank's World Development Indicators database. Capital per population data is for 1990 and are from Nehru and Dhareshwar (1993).

rather than the mean because of significant outliers (for Mexico and Uruguay among others) in the dataset.

Though China as a whole is extremely labor abundant, its provinces vary substantially in terms of their levels of development. This internal heterogeneity is noteworthy given the theoretical models discussed above. It implies that coastal Shanghai's relative skill- and capital-abundance may provide it with the resources to produce a more sophisticated range of goods than the much more labor-abundant inland province of Guizhou. As discussed above, such an outcome depends on factor immobility: if labor were freely mobile in China, workers in provinces with relatively low wages like Guizhou would have an incentive to move to provinces like Shanghai where wages are higher. These movements would lead to convergence in factor prices, relative endowments and product mix.

There is, of course, ample reason to believe that labor is not freely mobile within China. As documented in Bannister (2005), the Chinese government explicitly controls the ability of workers from the inland provinces to migrate and seek employment in

Table 3. Inter-regional relative endowment disparities within China

Province or region	PCGDP (CNY mill)	Illiteracy (%)	Province or region	PCGDP (CNY mill)	Illiteracy (%)
Shanghai Municipality	30 805	8.7	Hunan	5105	11.1
Beijing Municipality	19 846	6.5	Henan	4894	16.3
Tianjin Municipality	15 976	8.0	Chongqing Municipality	4826	4.0
Zhejiang	12 037	15.7	Shanxi	4727	9.1
Guangdong	11 728	9.2	Anhui	4707	20.3
Fujian	10 797	18.5	Qinghai	4662	30.5
Jiangsu	10 665	16.8	Jiangxi	4661	13.2
Liaoning	10 086	7.2	Ningxia Hui AR	4473	23.3
Shandong	8673	20.2	Sichuan	4452	24.3
Heilongjiang	7660	9.8	Yunnan	4452	16.8
Hebei	6932	11.4	Xizang (Tibet) AR	4262	66.2
Hubei	6514	15.0	Guangxi Zhuang AR	4148	12.4
Xinjiang Uygur AR	6470	9.8	Shaanxi	4101	18.3
Hainan	6383	14.6	Gansu	3668	25.6
Jilin	6341	6.8	Guizhou	2475	24.5
Neimongu (Mongolia) AR	5350	16.4			

Notes: The official CNY per USD exchange rate for 1999 is 8.27. Using this exchange rate, per capita GDP (PCGDP) ranges from US$3725 to US$299. Regions are sorted according to PCGDP. AR=Autonomous region.
Source: China Statistical Yearbook, 2000. Quoted from OECD (2001).

coastal provinces. As a result, the Chinese economy as a whole may be able to profitably produce a larger range of goods than would be expected of a country with a more uniform distribution of endowments at a similar aggregate level of development.

Unfortunately, data comparable to Tables 1 and 2 on the distribution of factors within China are unavailable. In its place, Table 3 compares Chinese provinces, Autonomous Regions and Municipalities along two dimensions in 1999 using data on (non-PPP-adjusted) per capita GDP and illiteracy from the Chinese government quoted in OECD (2001). Regions in the table are sorted according to per capita GDP, which ranges from US$ 3275 (CNY 30 805) in Shanghai to US$ 299 (CNY 2475) in the inland province of Guizhou. To put this variation in perspective, note that comparable World Bank PCGDP figures for Korea, Mexico and Brazil are US$ 10 855, US$ 5934 and US$ 3538, respectively, and that China's aggregate per capita GDP in that year is US$ 856. The final column of Table 3 reports Chinese regional illiteracy rates. These range from a high of 66% in Tibet to a low of 4% in Chonqing Municipality. By comparison, World Bank illiteracy rates in the over-15-year-old population in Mexico, Brazil and China as a whole are 9, 14 and 14%, respectively. Intra-national PCGDP and illiteracy in China have a correlation of −0.33.

Though these comparisons are by no means rigorous, they and anecdotal evidence suggest that some regions of China may be able to produce products with skill and capital intensity approaching that of countries with much greater skill and capital abundance than China overall.

4. PRODUCT-LEVEL TRADE DATA

Product-level trade data provide much sharper resolution of the sophistication of countries' export bundles than traditionally available industry-level trade data for two reasons. First, while all countries generally export in all industries (e.g. 'machinery'), they exhibit substantial heterogeneity in their product participation within industries. Second, product-level international trade data permit examination of trading-partner heterogeneity within product markets via unit values (e.g. 'dollars per dozen shirts').

The data used in this paper are drawn from Feenstra *et al.* (2002) for 1972 to 1989 and the US Customs Service for 1990 to 2005. They record the customs value of all US imports by exporting country and year from 1972 to 2005 according to thousands of finely detailed categories, which I refer to as 'products' or 'goods'. Imports are classified according to the seven-digit Tariff Schedule of the United States (TSUSA) codes from 1972 through 1988 and according to the ten-digit Harmonized System (HS) codes from 1989 through 2005. As discussed further below, this break in the use of product codes in 1989 places some limits on our ability to track countries' exports at the product-level over time. I refer to imports at higher levels of aggregation, such as the one- or five-digit Standard International Trade Classification (SITC) system, as 'industries'. Note that SITC industry codes at the one-digit level are defined consistently throughout the sample period. I refer to country-specific imports within product categories as 'varieties'.

Table 4 lists the number of product categories by one-digit SITC industry in both 1972 and 2005. SITC codes beginning with 0 through 4 comprise resource products, while those beginning with 5 through 8 encompass manufacturing goods, which are the focus of this study. Two of the manufacturing industries, Manufactured Materials (SITC 6) and Miscellaneous Manufactures (SITC 8) – which include textiles (SITC 65) and apparel (SITC 84), respectively – account for the largest share of products in both periods. Machinery (SITC 7), on the other hand, experiences the largest increase in the number of product categories over the sample period. Because of their idiosyncrasy, I exclude products from SITC 9 (Not Elsewhere Classified) from the analysis.

To facilitate the comparison of countries' export bundles and unit values, I make use of the country-region assignments provided in Table 5. Three aspects of how countries are assigned to regions deserve mention. First, Latin America includes all of the countries of Central and South America, plus Mexico. Second, I define the OECD as the 23 members in place as of 1974 in order to exclude Korea, Mexico and other, more recent entrants. The resulting set of countries captures a more uniform mix of high-wage, developed economies during the sample period. Even so, the 1974 cohort still includes Ireland and Turkey.

It should also be noted that my mapping of countries into regions places Japan in the OECD group rather than the Asia group. Finally, the actual set of countries

Table 4. TSUSA and HS products by one-digit SITC industry

One-digit SITC	Two-digit SITC examples	Product examples	Number of five-digit SITC	Number of products (1972/2005)
0 Food	Meat, Dairy, Fruit	Live Sheep	197	704/1954
1 Beverage/Tobacco	Wine, Cigarettes	Carbonated softdrinks	17	77/166
2 Crude Materials	Rubber Cork, Wood, Textile Fibers	Silkworm cocoons suitable for reeling	175	646/820
3 Mineral Fuels	Coal, Coke, Petroleum	Unleaded gasoline	26	49/114
4 Animal/Vegetable Oils	Lard, Soybean Oil	Edible tallow	24	60/80
5 Chemicals	Organic Chemicals, Dyes, Medicines, Fertilizer, Plastics	Chloroform	251	758/2108
6 Manufactured Materials	Leather, Textile Yarn, Paper, Steel	Diaries and address books of paper or cardboard	445	2868/4727
7 Machinery	Generators, Computers, Autos	Ultrasonic scanning apparatus	298	648/3071
8 Misc Manufacturing	Apparel, Footwear, Scientific Equipment, Toys	Boys' shorts cotton playsuit parts, not knit	258	1870/3738
9 Not Elsewhere Classified	Special Transactions, Coins, Gold	Sound recordings for State Department use	9	51/84

Notes: Number of products refers to seven-digit TSUSA categories for 1972 and ten-digit Harmonized System (HS) categories for 2005. SITC industries are consistently defined across the sample period and are therefore the same in both 1972 and 2005.

Source: US Customs Service; author's calculations.

Table 5. US trading partners, by region

Country	Region	Country	Region	Country	Region
Afghanistan	AS	Bahamas	CAR	Suriname	LA
American Samoa	AS	Barbados	CAR	Uruguay	LA
Bangladesh	AS	Dom Rep	CAR	Venezuela	LA
Cambodia	AS	Guadeloupe	CAR	Australia	OECD
China	AS	Haiti	CAR	Austria	OECD
Fiji	AS	Jamaica	CAR	Belgium	OECD
Hong Kong	AS	Neth Antilles	CAR	Canada	OECD
India	AS	St. Kitts and Nevis	CAR	Denmark	OECD
Indonesia	AS	Trinidad	CAR	Finland	OECD
Kiribati	AS	Argentina	LA	France	OECD
Korea	AS	Belize	LA	Germany	OECD
Lao	AS	Bolivia	LA	Greece	OECD
Macao	AS	Brazil	LA	Iceland	OECD
Malaysia	AS	Chile	LA	Ireland	OECD
Mongolia	AS	Colombia	LA	Italy	OECD
Myanmar	AS	Costa Rica	LA	Japan	OECD
Nepal	AS	Ecuador	LA	Netherlands	OECD
New Caledonia	AS	El Salvador	LA	New Zealand	OECD
Pakistan	AS	Guatemala	LA	Norway	OECD
Papua New Guinea	AS	Guyana	LA	Portugal	OECD
Philippines	AS	Honduras	LA	Spain	OECD
Singapore	AS	Mexico	LA	Sweden	OECD
Sri Lanka	AS	Nicaragua	LA	Switzerland	OECD
Taiwan	AS	Panama	LA	Turkey	OECD
Thailand	AS	Paraguay	LA	UK	OECD
Vietnam	AS	Peru	LA		

Notes: Countries sorted alphabetically by region. Region affiliations are mutually exclusive. AS=Asia. CA=Caribbean; LA=Latin America. OECD definition excludes post-1973 entrants (e.g. Mexico and Korea).

within each region used in computing any given summary statistic may vary depending upon data availability.

My comparison of Chinese and other countries' trade patterns proceeds under the assumption that US trading partners' exports to the US accurately reflect their domestic production as well as their exports to other markets. This assumption is partially justified by the relative openness of the US economy and its attractiveness as an export destination. Nevertheless, variation in countries' demand, the existence of tariff and non-tariff barriers (for example, the global Multifiber Arrangement or the subsequent Agreement on Textiles and Clothing), as well as more general trade costs such as transportation, can be influential in determining which of a country's goods are exported, and to which trading partner they are sent. Deardorff (2004), for example, offers an insightful discussion of how transport costs create and influence countries' 'local' comparative advantage. On the other hand, as Fontagné, Gaulier and Zignago (2007) document in this volume, the basic trends I find in this paper are echoed in the import statistics of other countries, albeit at a higher level of product aggregation.

5. ACROSS-PRODUCT SOPHISTICATION

To provide greater context for understanding US trading partners' export similarity, I briefly compare China's performance in the US market in terms of market share and product penetration to that of other regions. Even cursory analysis reveals that China's performance in these dimensions has been exceptional.

5.1. Chinese market share and product penetration

Table 6 reports the US market share of Asia, Latin America, the OECD and China in terms of import value (V), by industry, for the first and last years of the sample. The market share of region r in year t and industry i is the sum of the regions' exports to the United States as a share of all countries exports to the United States,

$$MS_{tri} = 100 \times \sum_{c \in r} V_{tci} \bigg/ \sum_{c} V_{tci}, \tag{1}$$

where c indexes countries and $c \in r$ captures the set of countries in region r. Recall that the results for Asia exclude China and Japan and that market shares across the columns of Table 6 do not sum to 100% because all US trading partners are not represented.

The market shares displayed in Table 6 convey several messages. First, they show that exports from the world's most developed economies, proxied here by the aggregate OECD, dominate the US market, though less so over time. While the OECD accounted for 83% of manufacturing imports in 1972, this share falls to 48% by 2005. Second, they reveal that China is the main contributor to Asia's overall growth. China's share of manufacturing imports increases steadily from essentially 0% in 1972 to 19% in 2005, driven by a relatively large gain in Miscellaneous Manufacturing (which includes apparel and toys). By comparison, over the same interval, the remaining countries in Asia saw their market share increase from 10% to 16%.

China's 19 percentage point jump in market share dominates all other US trading partners except for Mexico, whose market share rises from 2 to 10%. Table 7 reports

Table 6. US import value market share by region and year

SITC1 industry	China		Asia		Latin America		OECD	
	1972	2005	1972	2005	1972	2005	1972	2005
5 Chemicals	0	4	2	6	6	6	85	76
6 Manufactured Materials	0	15	10	14	5	15	80	48
7 Machinery	0	17	5	17	2	15	93	50
8 Misc Manufacturing	0	36	29	20	4	13	64	27
Overall Manufacturing	0	19	10	16	3	14	83	48

Notes: Cells display the market share of each region's or country's exports to the US. Asia results exclude China.
Source: Author's calculations.

Table 7. Largest gains in market share, 1972 to 2005

Country	1972	2005	Change	% change
China	0.04	19.26	19.22	47 912
Mexico	1.96	10.44	8.47	431
Malaysia	0.42	2.61	2.19	524
Ireland	0.25	2.22	1.97	797
Korea	1.79	3.32	1.53	85
Thailand	0.20	1.38	1.18	601
Brazil	0.50	1.39	0.89	176
Israel	0.53	1.30	0.77	145
Indonesia	0.04	0.74	0.69	1634
India	0.77	1.36	0.59	76
Singapore	0.58	1.11	0.53	92
Average	0.10	0.54	0.44	465

Notes: Table lists US trading partners with the top ten absolute changes in US manufacturing import market share between 1972 and 2005.

Source: Author's calculations.

the countries with the top ten absolute changes in manufacturing market share between 1972 and 2005. China tops the list.

Increases in market share occur through increasing exports of incumbent products and an increase in the number of products exported. Table 8 focuses on regions' performance in the latter by examining manufacturing product penetration by industry over the sample period. Each cell in the table reports the percentage of products in each industry exported by China or the countries in the noted regions. Regional penetration is 100% if every product in the industry is exported by at least one country in the region and 0% if no country in the region exports any of the industry's products to the United States. The total number of products in each industry in 1972 and 2005 is reported in the final column of Table 4. As above, results for Asia exclude China and Japan.

As indicated in the table, product penetration by the OECD is virtually 100% throughout the sample period. This fact, by itself, is puzzling from the standpoint of the Heckscher–Ohlin model: why should the most developed economies in the world export every good? The answer, discussed in more detail below, comes from new trade theory: the most developed economies are among the largest.

Table 8 also shows that product penetration by Asian and Latin American countries, though substantially lower than the OECD in 1972, has increased markedly over time. Finally, Table 8 reveals that China, by itself, has experienced a very large increase in product penetration, from 9% of all products in 1972 to 85% by 2005. Table 9, which ranks countries with the biggest absolute gains in penetration between 1972 and 2005, shows that China's 76 percentage point increase is the largest of any trading partner by a factor of more than two.

Overall, China's nominal manufacturing exports to the United States grew from US$ 9 million in 1972 to US$ 176 billion in 2005. To gauge the relative importance

Table 8. Product penetration by region and year

SITC1 industry	China		Asia		Latin America		OECD	
	1972	2005	1972	2005	1972	2005	1972	2005
5 Chemicals	4	76	16	70	22	51	98	97
6 Manufactured Materials	7	80	45	81	34	70	96	97
7 Machinery	1	83	56	87	51	75	100	99
8 Misc Manufacturing	16	91	72	89	45	74	98	95
Overall Manufacturing	9	85	51	83	38	69	97	97

Notes: Cells display share of products in the industry that are exported to the US by at least one country from the region. Asia results exclude China.

Source: Author's calculations.

Table 9. Largest gains in product penetration, 1972 to 2005

Country	1972	2005	Change	% change
China	9	85	76	853
Korea	19	55	36	195
India	18	53	35	190
Mexico	26	57	31	118
Thailand	6	36	31	544
Taiwan	30	56	26	88
Indonesia	2	28	26	1315
Brazil	14	39	25	183
Malaysia	3	25	22	644
Canada	52	73	21	41
Average	7	13	6	90

Notes: Table lists US trading partners with the top ten absolute changes in US manufacturing import product penetration between 1972 and 2005.

Source: Author's calculations.

of product penetration in this increase, I decompose China's overall manufacturing export growth into that which is attributable to continuously produced goods (the 'intensive' margin) and that which is due to the net adding and dropping of products (the 'extensive' margin). In contrast to Table 8, Table 10 examines the extensive margin according to five-digit SITC industries rather than TSUSA or HS product categories. The reason for this, as noted above, is that TSUSA and HS categories change frequently throughout the sample period. SITC industries have just a single break, in 1988: before 1988, the data are tracked with SITC Revision 2; after 1988, they are tracked with SITC Revision 3. As a result, decompositions are performed for each half of the sample. Results are shown for China's overall manufacturing exports to the United States (final two rows) as well by manufacturing industry.

As indicated in the table, the relative contribution of the extensive versus intensive margins varies across industries and time periods. The extensive margin is relatively more important in the first half of the sample than in the second half, particularly for

Table 10. Decomposing China's US export growth, 1972 to 2005

Industry	Margin	1972–88	1989–2005
5 Chemicals	Intensive Margin	43	77
	Extensive Margin	57	23
6 Manufactured Materials	Intensive Margin	53	79
	Extensive Margin	47	21
7 Machinery	Intensive Margin	1	95
	Extensive Margin	99	5
8 Misc Manufacturing	Intensive Margin	66	99
	Extensive Margin	34	1
Overall Manufacturing	Intensive Margin	55	94
	Extensive Margin	45	6

Notes: Table decomposes nominal Chinese export growth to the United States over the noted intervals according to the net increase due to continuously exported five-digit SITC industries (the 'intensive margin') and the net growth due to the adding and dropping of industries (the 'extensive margin'). Amounts are rounded to the nearest integer. First period tracks products according to SITC revision 2; second period tracks products across SITC revision 3.

Source: Author's calculations.

Machinery. Overall, the extensive margin accounts for 45% of China's export growth from 1972 to 1988 but just 6% of its growth from 1989 to 2005. Note that the results in Table 10 may underestimate the importance of the extensive margin to the extent that they use five-digit SITC industries rather than the more numerous seven-digit TSUSA or ten-digit HS product categories.

5.2. Export similarity with the OECD

This section gauges the relative sophistication of China's manufacturing export bundle in terms of its similarity to that of the aggregate OECD. Two findings stand out. First, China's export similarity with the OECD increases substantially, and far more than for any other US trading partner, over the sample period. Second, though China's export similarity with the OECD is higher than one would expect given relative level of development, it is consistent with its size.

I measure the overlap in countries' export bundles via Finger and Kreinin's (1979) export similarity index (ESI). For any two US trading partners c and d in year t, this index is just the sum of the two countries' minimum presence in each good,

$$ESI_t^{cd} = \sum_p \min(s_{tp}^c, s_{tp}^d), \qquad (2)$$

where presence (s_{tp}^c) is just the share of country c's export value in manufacturing product p relative to all of its exports in year t. This bilateral measure can be computed using all manufacturing products or by manufacturing industry. In either case the index is bounded by zero and unity: ESI_t^{cd} equals zero if countries c and d have no products in common in year t and ESI_t^{cd} equals unity if their exports are distributed

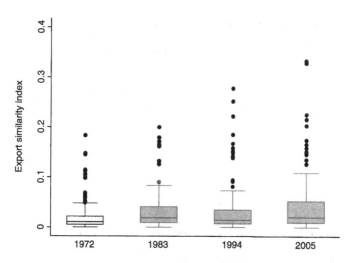

Figure 2. Distribution of countries' export similarity with the OECD, 1972 to 2005

Note: Figure displays the distribution of non-OECD countries' export similarity index (ESI) vis-à-vis the OECD over ten-year intervals between 1972 and 2005. Boxes outline the interquartile range, while lines within each box report the median.

Source: Author's calculations.

identically across products. To compare two regions (or to compare a region with China), I sum exports over all countries in the region first and then use region-level rather than country-level export shares in equation (2).

Figure 2 summarizes the distribution of non-OECD countries' export similarity with the OECD using box-and-whisker plots displayed at eleven-year intervals from 1972 to 2005. The box for each year spans the inter-quartile range of the data, while lines within the boxes record the median observation in each year. Circles above the whiskers represent individual observations that are outliers. A key message of the figure is that non-OECD countries' product-mix overlap with the OECD is increasing with time. This trend can be seen in the boxes' slow rise across the eleven-year intervals.

Perhaps unsurprisingly, China's exports are more similar to the other countries of Asia than with either the OECD or Latin America. This similarity is evident in Table 11, which reports China's ESI with Asia (which excludes China), Latin America and the OECD at eleven-year intervals from 1972 to 2005. The table reveals that China's overlap with countries outside Asia also has grown substantially over time.

China's export overlap with the OECD has increased far more than for any other US trading partner. Table 12 reports the twenty countries whose export bundle most resembles the OECD, at eleven-year intervals over the sample period. As indicated in the table, China's ESI increase from 0.05 to 0.21 results in its rank jumping from 19 in 1972 (near India) to a rank of 4 in 2005 (just behind Taiwan, Mexico and Korea). In the table, China's rank is highlighted and in bold text.

Table 11. Regions' export similarity with China

Region	Export similarity with China			
	1972	1983	1994	2005
Asia	0.14	0.30	0.37	0.46
Latin America	0.05	0.10	0.20	0.26
OECD	0.05	0.08	0.15	0.21

Notes: Table displays each region's export similarity index (see text) with China. Asia excludes China.

Source: Author's calculations.

Table 12. Countries with the highest export similarity to the OECD, 1972 to 2005

1972		1983		1994		2005	
Mexico	0.18	Mexico	0.20	Mexico	0.28	Korea	0.33
Brazil	0.15	Korea	0.18	Korea	0.25	Mexico	0.33
Taiwan	0.14	Taiwan	0.17	Taiwan	0.22	Taiwan	0.22
Israel	0.11	Israel	0.16	Brazil	0.19	**China**	**0.21**
Korea	0.11	Brazil	0.16	Hong Kong	0.17	Brazil	0.20
Argentina	0.11	Hong Kong	0.13	Singapore	0.16	Poland	0.17
Hong Kong	0.11	Singapore	0.13	**China**	**0.15**	Israel	0.17
Czech Republic	0.10	Argentina	0.09	Malaysia	0.15	India	0.16
Poland	0.10	Yugoslavia	0.09	Israel	0.14	Singapore	0.15
Yugoslavia	0.10	Hungary	0.08	Thailand	0.14	Hong Kong	0.15
Colombia	0.07	Poland	0.08	Argentina	0.09	Thailand	0.15
South Africa	0.07	Saudi Arabia	0.08	Poland	0.09	Argentina	0.13
Venezuela	0.06	**China**	**0.08**	India	0.09	Hungary	0.13
Singapore	0.06	South Africa	0.07	Philippines	0.08	Malaysia	0.11
Hungary	0.05	Neth Antilles	0.07	Venezuela	0.08	Indonesia	0.11
Romania	0.05	India	0.07	Hungary	0.07	Philippines	0.10
Cyprus	0.05	Philippines	0.07	Indonesia	0.07	South Africa	0.10
Gibraltar	0.05	Panama	0.06	South Africa	0.07	Panama	0.09
China	**0.05**	Thailand	0.06	Bermuda	0.06	Romania	0.08
India	0.05	Colombia	0.06	Colombia	0.06	Colombia	0.08

Notes: Table displays non-OECD countries with the highest manufacturing export similarity index (ESI) with the OECD at noted intervals from 1972 to 2005.

Source: Author's calculations.

Regression analysis reveals that although China's manufacturing export similarity with the OECD is exceptional in terms of its level of development, it accords with its size. Table 13 reports coefficients from an OLS regression of the log of trading partners' ESI with the OECD on logs of measures of countries' relative development and size as well as a set of four China-decade interactions for the 1970s (i.e. 1972–1979); the 1980s (i.e. 1980–1989); the 1990s (i.e. 1990–1999) and the 2000s (i.e. 2000–2005),

$$\log(ESI_{tc}) = \alpha_t + country\ characteristics + \gamma_d CHINA_d + \varepsilon_{tc}. \tag{3}$$

Table 13. Export similarity with the OECD, all manufacturing

	ESI_{ct}	ESI_{ct}	ESI_{ct}	ESI_{ct}	ESI_{ct}
Log (Real PCGDP$_{ct}$)	0.015***			0.005***	0.020***
	0.003			0.002	0.004
Log (Skill Abundance$_{ct}$)		0.022***			
		0.005			
Log (Real GDP$_{ct}$)			−0.192***	−0.189***	
			0.042	0.043	
Log (Real GDP$_{ct}$)2			0.005***	0.004***	
			0.001	0.001	
Log (Population$_{ct}$)					−0.031
					0.019
Log (Population$_{ct}$)2					0.001**
					0.001
China 70s	0.049***	−0.010	−0.056***	−0.039***	−0.048*
	0.005	0.008	0.012	0.012	0.025
China 80s	0.070***	0.016**	−0.059***	−0.043**	−0.033***
	0.003	0.007	0.017	0.017	0.027
China 90s	0.134***	0.086***	−0.028	−0.014	0.027
	0.003	0.009	0.026	0.025	0.028
China 00s	0.164***	0.146***	−0.028	−0.016	0.055*
	0.005	0.009	0.033	0.032	0.029
Constant	−0.073***	−0.019	2.023***	1.961***	0.013
	0.021	0.011	0.469	0.472	0.146
Year fixed effects	Yes	Yes	Yes	Yes	Yes
Observations	3405	555	3405	3405	3405
R^2	0.24	0.21	0.63	0.65	0.48

Notes: Table reports OLS regression results of non-OECD countries' manufacturing export similarity with the OECD (ESI) on countries' real per capita GDP (PCGDP), skill abundance, real GDP and population from 1972 to 2005. Data on GDP and population are from the World Bank. Data on skill abundance are from Barro and Lee (2000). Explanatory variables include China dummies interacted with dummies for the 1970s (i.e., 1972–1979), 1980s (i.e., 1980–1989) and 1990s (i.e., 1990–1999) and the 2000s (i.e., 2000–2005). Robust standard errors adjusted for clustering at the country level reported below each coefficient. ***, ** and * denote statistical significance at the 1, 5 and 10% levels, respectively.

The China-decade interactions, indexed by *d*, facilitate examination of the extent to which China's actual export similarity index deviates from what the regression model would predict. Because the variables in the regression are in natural logs, these deviations can be interpreted as percentages. Robust standard errors adjusted for clustering at the country level are reported below each coefficient in the table.

In Table 13, I use PPP-adjusted real GDP as well as population, both from the World Bank's World Development Indicators database, to measure countries' size. For countries' level of development, I employ World Bank PPP-adjusted real per capita GDP and skill abundance, defined as the share of the population attaining a secondary or higher level of education according to Barro and Lee (2000). The latter data are available at five-year intervals rather than annually, a feature of the data accounts for the large difference in the number of observations across the columns of Table 13. To increase the sample size, I use the 1970 value for 1972 and the 2000 variable for 2005, so that there are two observations per decade; this change does not affect results in any substantial way. I use per capita GDP rather than an explicit measure of capital abundance to assess countries' level of development because the latter are unavailable for a large set of countries or for the full 1972 to 2005 sample period.

Results for four different specifications are reported. The first two columns indicate that countries' export similarity with the OECD increases with their level of development, that is, their per capita GDP or skill abundance. At the same time, the China-decade interactions reveal that China is a positive outlier relative to countries at a similar stage of development, and increasingly so over time: in column one, the coefficients for the China-decade dummies increase from 4.9% for the 1970s to 16.4% for the 2000s. These coefficients indicate that China exhibits significantly greater overlap with the OECD than one would expect from a country with its per capita GDP. Note that the magnitudes of the coefficients on the China-decade interactions are consistent with the unconditional export similarity indexes reported in Table 12. Though I also examined quadratic relationships in the first two specifications, they are statistically insignificant and are therefore omitted from the table.

The third column of Table 13 reveals that a substantially larger share of the variation in countries' export similarity indexes can be explained by a quadratic in country size than by relative levels of development. The R^2 in column three, at 63%, is three times higher than the R^2 in columns one and two. Moreover, the results in column three demonstrate that once one controls for country size, the coefficients on the China-decade interactions are negative and significant in the 1970s and 1980s and statistically indistinguishable from zero in the last two decades. This trend indicates that China overlapped less with the OECD than one would have expected early on, when its economy was more-or-less closed to the world, but that this situation reversed once it began entering world markets.

The fourth column of Table 13 demonstrates that simultaneously controlling for countries' level of development with per capita GDP contributes little additional explanatory power but results in China-decade coefficients that are closer to zero in magnitude across all four decades. Thus, after one jointly controls for size and level of development, China looks less like an outlier than it does after controlling for size alone.

As a check on the results in columns one through four, the final column of Table 13 repeats the specification in column four but uses population rather than GDP to measure countries' size. Results are very similar, though China's export similarity to the OECD is now significantly *larger* than one would expect in the final years of the sample. The China-decade interactions for the 1990s and 2000s are a statistically insignificant 2.7 and a statistically significant 5.5%, respectively. This outcome suggests China's PPP-adjusted GDP attributes relatively larger size to the country than its population, which seems reasonable.

A similar pattern of results is evident across the one-digit SITC industries within manufacturing. Table 14 reports the results of regressing ESI indexes specific to each industry on the specification from column four of Table 13. Coefficients for per capita GDP and GDP reveal that export similarity rises with both level of development and size.

Table 14. Export similarity with the OECD, by manufacturing industry

	5 – Chemicals ESI_{ct}	6 – Manuf Materials ESI_{ct}	7 – Machinery ESI_{ct}	8 – Misc Manuf ESI_{ct}
Log (Real PCGDP$_{ct}$)	0.006**	0.005**	0.008***	0.011***
	0.003	0.002	0.002	0.003
Log (Real GDP$_{ct}$)	−0.163***	−0.213***	−0.214***	−0.137***
	0.029	0.044	0.044	0.028
Log (Real GDP$_{ct}$)^2	0.004***	0.005***	0.005***	0.003***
	0.001	0.001	0.001	0.001
China 70s	−0.035***	−0.055***	−0.047***	0.003
	0.009	0.013	0.011	0.012
China 80s	0.030***	−0.043**	−0.028*	−0.014
	0.011	0.018	0.016	0.014
China 90s	0.037**	−0.023	−0.013	0.001
	0.016	0.024	0.024	0.019
China 00s	0.042**	−0.004	−0.047	0.011
	0.020	0.03	0.031	0.024
Constant	1.698***	2.221***	2.214***	1.314***
	0.325	0.493	0.497	0.303
Year fixed effects	Yes	Yes	Yes	Yes
Observations	2695	3286	2975	3359
R^2	0.60	0.66	0.67	0.62

Notes: Table reports OLS regression results of non-OECD countries' manufacturing export similarity with the OECD (ESI) on countries' real per capita GDP (PCGDP) and GDP from 1972 to 2005. Explanatory variables include China dummies interacted with dummies for the 1970s (i.e., 1972–1979), 1980s (i.e., 1980–1989) and 1990s (i.e., 1990–1999) and the 2000s (i.e., 2000–2005). Robust standard errors adjusted for clustering at the country level reported below each coefficient. ***, ** and * denote statistical significance at the 1, 5 and 10% levels, respectively.

Coefficients for the China-decade interactions for Machinery and Manufactured Materials follow the same pattern as they do for aggregate manufacturing. For Miscellaneous Manufactures, the interactions are statistically indistinguishable from zero in all four decades. In Chemicals, however, China has greater overlap with the OECD than one would expect given *both* its level of development and size. As demonstrated below, this industry is the one in which China's export prices most closely resemble those of the OECD.

6. WITHIN-PRODUCT SOPHISTICATION

This section measures the relative sophistication of Chinese export varieties within products in terms of relative prices. I find that Chinese varieties exhibit relatively low prices compared to countries with similar per capita GDP, and that this 'China discount' widens with time. *Vis-à-vis* the OECD, I find that Chinese relative export prices are low throughout the sample period and that they have decreased over the last five to ten years.

An extremely useful feature of the product-level US trade data is the inclusion of both quantity and value information for a large number of goods and countries. This renders possible the calculation of unit values as a measure of price. I compute the unit value of product p from country c (u_{pc}), by dividing the free-on-board (fob) import value by import quantity (Q), $u_{pc} = V_{pc}/Q_{pc}$. Examples of the units employed to classify products include dozens of shirts in apparel, square meters of carpet in textiles and pounds of folic acid in chemicals. For some years and products, there are multiple country observations of value and quantity in the raw data. In those cases, I define the unit value to be a value-weighted average of the observations. Availability of unit values ranges from 77% of product-country observations in 1972 to 84% of observations in 2005.

It is important to note that the unit values are measured with error. A study by the US General Accounting Office (1995), for example, identified classification error and underlying product heterogeneity as two major sources of unit value error in an in-depth analysis of eight products. Of course, identifying potential heterogeneity within product categories is a goal of this section.

To assess the price of Chinese exports relative to similarly developed countries, I regress country-product log unit values on country characteristics, a set of controls for distance and trade costs and, as above, a set of China-decade interactions for the 1970s, the 1980s, the 1990s and the 2000s,

$$\log(u_{tpc}) = \alpha_{tp} + country\ characteristics + controls + \gamma_d CHINA_c + \varepsilon_{tpc}. \qquad (4)$$

The regression also includes year-product fixed effects (α_{tp}) that account for the fact that units vary markedly across different kinds of goods. Note that although I do not screen the data in the regressions presented below, I get substantially similar results if I eliminate potentially suspect observations, that is, those where just a single unit are shipped or where total value is low. Robust standard errors adjusted for clustering at the country level are displayed below coefficients.

Unit values are known to increase with transportation costs (Hummels and Skiba, 2004). This relationship has been interpreted as capturing Alchian and Allen's (1964) idea that firms have an incentive to ship their highest quality goods to their furthest customers when facing per unit transport costs. As a result, in all specifications I control for US trading partners' great circle distance from the United States, whether or not a trading partner is landlocked, and *ad valorem* measures of tariff and transport costs. Inclusion of these variables follows Harrigan (2005). I compute *ad valorem* tariff and transport rates as the share of duties and customs, insurance and freight (cif) charges per import value, respectively, at the product-country-year level. Data on distance and being landlocked are from the Centre D'Etudes Prospectives et D'Informations Internationales (CEPII) website. Data on duties and cif charges are from Feenstra *et al.* (2002) and the US Customs Service.

The first two columns of Table 15 examine the quadratic relationship between unit values and per capita GDP, while the latter two columns focus on skill abundance. Both sets of results indicate that higher levels of development are associated with larger unit values over the ranges of per capita GDP and skill abundance observed

Table 15. China's relative export prices, all manufacturing, 1972 to 2005

	Log(uv$_{pct}$)	Log(uv$_{pct}$)	Log(uv$_{pct}$)	Log(uv$_{pct}$)
Log (Real PCGDPct)	−0.685**	−0.723**		
	0.299	0.328		
Log (Real PCGDP$_{ct}$)2	0.056***	0.057***		
	0.019	0.020		
Log (Skill Abundance$_{ct}$)			−1.300**	−0.952**
			0.554	0.455
Log (Skill Abundance$_{ct}$)2			0.265***	0.210***
			0.087	0.072
China 70s		−0.080		−0.190**
		0.176		0.081
China 80s		−0.162*		−0.186***
		0.084		0.066
China 90s		−0.403***		−0.659***
		0.041		0.088
China 00s		−0.480***		−0.758***
		0.065		0.079
Log (Distance$_c$)	2.536***	2.494***	4.282***	3.992***
	0.737	0.742	0.827	0.790
Log (Distance$_c$)2	−0.158***	−0.155***	−0.268***	−0.249***
	0.049	0.049	0.052	0.052
Landlocked$_c$	0.303***	0.298***	0.312***	0.316***
	0.070	0.069	0.073	0.074
Ad Valorem Tariff Rate$_{pct}$	−0.334**	−0.293**	−0.113	−0.066
	0.147	0.146	0.110	0.097
Ad Valorem Trade Cost$_{pct}$	−0.065	−0.067	−0.215***	−0.217***
	0.04	0.042	0.068	0.069
Constant	−5.270*	−4.859*	−12.492***	−11.903***
	2.825	2.871	3.218	3.133
Product-year fixed effects	Yes	Yes	Yes	Yes
Observations	3 745 640	3 745 640	811 498	811 499
R^2	0.80	0.80	0.80	0.80

Notes: Table reports OLS regression results of country-product unit values on country and product characteristics from 1972 to 2005. Explanatory variables include four China-decade dummies for the 1970s (i.e., 1972–1979), 1980s (i.e., 1980–1989) and 1990s (i.e., 1990–1999) and the 2000s (i.e., 2000–2005). Robust standard errors adjusted for clustering at the country level reported below each coefficient. Data on per capita GDP (PCGDP), GDP and population are from the World Bank. Data on unit values, duty and transport costs are from the US Customs Bureau. ***, ** and * denote statistical significance at the 1, 5 and 10% levels.

in the sample. Consistent with the literature, the controls for distance indicate that countries that are further from the United States or without access to ports export goods whose unit values are higher within product categories. Coefficients for *ad valorem* tariff and freight rates indicate that unit values decline with policy barriers and shipping costs and are in accord with results reported by Harrigan (2005).

Results for the China-decade interactions in the second and fourth columns of Table 15 show that Chinese products sell at an increasing discount relative to countries at similar levels of development over time. In the per capita GDP regression, this discount declines from a statistically significant −8% in the 1970s to a statistically

Table 16. Countries exhibiting the largest *conditional* unit value discounts

1970s		1980s		1990s		2000s	
Japan	−0.59	Hong Kong	−0.69	Hong Kong	−0.96	Hong Kong	−1.08
Hong Kong	−0.57	Mexico	−0.52	Mexico	−0.62	Oman	−0.77
UAE	−0.51	Japan	−0.45	UAE	−0.61	Mexico	−0.59
Guyana	−0.45	Costa Rica	−0.37	Oman	−0.55	Kuwait	−0.50
Costa Rica	−0.41	Macao	−0.33	Mongolia	−0.49	UAE	−0.49
Oman	−0.35	Dom Rep	−0.32	Haiti	−0.46	**China**	**−0.48**
Mexico	−0.31	Haiti	−0.30	Guatemala	−0.43	Syrian	−0.48
Dom Rep	−0.29	UAE	−0.30	Nepal	−0.43	Korea	−0.45
Mali	−0.28	Cyprus	−0.29	**China**	**−0.40**	Haiti	−0.44
Haiti	−0.27	Venezuela	−0.27	Japan	−0.37	Malawi	−0.43
Burkina Faso	−0.24	Guyana	−0.26	Honduras	−0.35	Macao	−0.37
Honduras	−0.23	Guatemala	−0.25	El Salvador	−0.35	Nepal	−0.35
Korea	−0.22	Bolivia	−0.21	Korea	−0.33	Mongolia	−0.35
El Salvador	−0.19	Korea	−0.19	Nicaragua	−0.33	Pakistan	−0.34
Trinidad	−0.16	Bangladesh	−0.19	Venezuela	−0.32	Japan	−0.33
Iceland	−0.15	Paraguay	−0.18	Czech Republic	−0.32	Guatemala	−0.31
Spain	−0.11	Iceland	−0.18	Syrian	−0.32	El Salvador	−0.26
Italy	0.10	Switzerland	−0.18	Macao	−0.30	Paraguay	−0.25
Cote d'Ivoire	0.10	**China**	**−0.16**	Bahrain	−0.28	Bahrain	−0.21
Brazil	0.11	Romania	−0.12	Bangladesh	−0.24	Benin	−0.21

Notes: Table displays countries with the top 20 largest unit value discounts conditional on level of development and trade costs, in log points. Estimates are derived from estimation of equation (4), where each country's country-decade dummies are estimated in a seperate regression. Estimates insignificant at the 10 percent level, including China in the 1970s, are omitted. Estimates for China are highlighted.

Source: Author's calculations.

significant −48% in the 2000s. For skill abundance, deviations are also statistically significant in all four decades and decline from −19% to −76% between the 1970s and the 2000s.

China is not alone in exhibiting such *conditional* unit value discounts, that is, discounts that deviate from what one would predict given relative levels of development and trade costs. Other outliers are reported in Table 16. This table ranks countries according to the largest average negative deviations observed in each decade. The coefficients listed in the table are derived from a separate estimation of the regression in column two of Table 15 for each country in the sample, where the China-decade interactions are replaced with interactions specific to the country. In Table 16, I exclude country-decade coefficients that are statistically insignificant at the 10% level.

Overall, China's conditional discounts receive ranks of 19, 9 and 6 in the 1980s, 1990s and 2000s. (China's 8% discount for the 1970s does not appear in the table because it is statistically insignificant.) Two other countries with relatively large conditional discounts are Hong Kong – the perennial leader – and Macao, both of which are notable as transhipment points for Chinese exports.

Other countries with relatively large conditional discounts include Mexico, Korea and Japan. Japan, whose conditional discounts fall over time, is notable in that it, like China, is often accused of maintaining a relatively low nominal exchange rate in

Table 17. China's relative export prices, by industry, 1972 to 2005

	5-Chemicals Log(uv_pct)	6-Manuf Materials Log(uv_pct)	7-Machinery Log(uv_pct)	8-Misc Manuf Log(uv_pct)
Log (Real PCGDP_ct)	−1.020***	−0.868***	−0.935	−0.607**
	0.294	0.271	0.725	0.289
Log (Real PCGDP_ct)²	0.072***	0.064***	0.067	0.052***
	0.018	0.017	0.045	0.018
China 70s	−0.483***	−0.055	−0.560	−0.051
	0.138	0.188	0.379	0.188
China 80s	−0.305***	−0.221**	−0.446**	−0.118
	0.071	0.087	0.171	0.09
China 90s	−0.246***	−0.332***	−1.120***	−0.242***
	0.039	0.050	0.072	0.053
China 00s	−0.395***	−0.344***	−1.162***	−0.363***
	0.067	0.060	0.110	0.062
Log (Distance_c)	1.180*	2.288***	3.523**	2.177***
	0.586	0.613	1.374	0.785
Log (Distance_c)²	−0.061	−0.138***	−0.230**	−0.137***
	0.038	0.040	0.091	0.051
Landlocked_c	0.591***	0.305***	0.216	0.261**
	0.079	0.052	0.138	0.099
Ad Valorem Tariff Rate_pct	−0.131*	−0.329	0.122	−0.389*
	0.073	0.268	0.424	0.206
Ad Valorem Trade Cost_pct	−0.095*	−0.379***	−0.010	−0.517***
	0.053	0.036	0.008	0.058
Constant	−0.456	−5.156**	−5.048	−3.380
	2.184	2.363	5.397	3.052
Product-Year Fixed Effects	Yes	Yes	Yes	Yes
Observations	423 328	1 247 031	756 866	1 318 415
R²	0.64	0.71	0.79	0.73

Notes: Table reports OLS regression results of country-product unit values on country and product characteristics from 1972 to 2005. Explanatory variables include four China-decade dummies for the 1970s (i.e., 1972–1979), 1980s (i.e., 1980–1989) and 1990s (i.e., 1990–1999) and the 2000s (i.e., 2000–2005). Robust standard errors adjusted for clustering at the country level reported below each coefficient. Data on per capita GDP (PCGDP), GDP and population are from the World Bank. Data on unit values, duty and transport costs are from the US Customs Bureau. ***, ** and * denote statistical significance at the 1, 5 and 10% levels.

order to stimulate exports. Conditional discounts for Mexico are relatively stable over time, while those for Korea increase. Switzerland's presence in the table in the 1980s is interesting and perhaps due to it having better infrastructure than the typical landlocked country. Unconditionally, Switzerland has among the highest unit values in the sample. For the most part, the most developed OECD countries have negligible (e.g. Germany) or significantly positive (e.g. France) conditional deviations across decades.

Unit value regressions for one-digit SITC manufacturing industries are reported in Table 17. Here, too, the China discount becomes more negative over time in all sectors except Chemicals. Across industries, discounts are greatest in Machinery.

A more direct comparison of Chinese and OECD manufacturing export prices reveals that Chinese goods sell at an increasing discount *vi-à-vis* the OECD across manufacturing industries. I compare Chinese and OECD export unit values according to log unit value ratios,

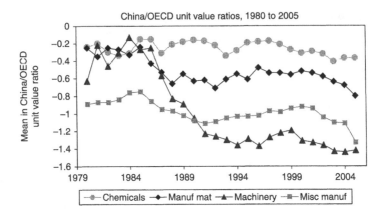

Figure 3. OECD/China log unit value ratios, 1980 to 2005

Note: Figure displays mean natural log China/OECD unit value ratio across products in noted industry, by year. Log unit values for each year and industry are significantly different from zero at the 1% in almost all cases.

Source: Author's calculations.

$$\log(UVR_{tp}) = \log(u_{tp}^{China})/\log(u_{tp}^{OECD}),\tag{5}$$

where u_{tp}^{China} and u_{tp}^{OECD} are the unit values of product p in year t for China and OECD countries, respectively. As above, log unit value ratios less than zero indicate a China discount.

Figure 3 reports the mean log unit value ratio between the OECD and China by manufacturing industry between 1980 and 2005. Two features of the data are noteworthy. First, the fact that all ratios are less than zero indicates that OECD exports generally sell for more than Chinese exports in all years. The China discount is greatest in Machinery and Manufactured Materials and lowest in Chemicals, perhaps because that manufacturing industry contains relatively more goods (chloroform, for example) that are commodities. Chinese machinery varieties in 2005, for example, are priced at a 25% discount ($e^{-1.4}$) relative to OECD machinery varieties. T-tests of these log unit value ratios (not reported) indicate that virtually all are statistically significantly different from zero at the 10% level.

The second noteworthy feature of the results in Figure 3 is that the Chinese price discount generally declines over the last five to ten years in all four industries. This trend is most pronounced in Manufactured Materials and Miscellaneous Manufactures.

7. INTERPRETATION OF RESULTS: HOW CLOSE IS CHINA TO THE OECD?

This paper highlights two facts. First, China's manufacturing export bundle increasingly overlaps with that of the world's most developed economies. Second, within product markets, China's exports sell at an increasing discount relative to the exports of the OECD.

The first fact implies that competition between the OECD and China is heating up, as China enters more and more product categories in which the OECD is present. On the other hand, the substantial price disparities observed between Chinese and OECD exports within product markets suggests Chinese exports may be of lower quality than OECD exports. To the extent that consumers view goods of low and high quality as poor substitutes, competition between China and the OECD might be less extreme than their growing overlap in terms of export bundles would otherwise imply.

The fact that the price gap between Chinese and OECD varieties is widening over time may be an indication of international product cycling, that is, that developed countries are specializing in ever-more sophisticated varieties as a response to globalization. Such a response would be consistent with more direct evidence of quality upgrading observed in firm-level data. Bernard, Jensen and Schott (2006), for example, examine US manufacturing plants' reactions to increased import penetration from low-wage countries as tariff rates and transportation costs fall from 1972 to 1997. Changes in exposure to low-wage countries varied substantially across industries, with firms in labor-intensive industries like apparel facing far greater low-wage country import penetration than firms manufacturing in more skill- and capital industries like scientific equipment. In their study, the authors find that firms in industries experiencing greater exposure to low-wage country imports are more likely to shrink or die, suggesting that firms 'move out' of products inconsistent with their country's comparative advantage during trade liberalization.

On the other hand, Bernard, Jensen and Schott (2006) also find evidence of firms' 'moving up' in response to trade liberalization. First, plants with higher exposure to low-wage country imports are more likely to switch into industries that are more skill and capital intensive, and less exposed to low-wage country exports, than the industries they leave behind. Second, within industries subject to the same level of low-wage country exposure, plants that are more capital intensive are more likely to survive and grow. To the extent that plants' capital intensities within industries rise with the sophistication of the goods they produce in those industries, this finding implies US firms adjust their product mix in line with US comparative advantage. Both of these adjustments can be interpreted as a reallocation of economic resources within and across plants towards the manufacture of more sophisticated goods.

These adjustments provide intuition for why trade with developing countries will not necessarily lead to the elimination of all manufacturing jobs in the developed world. Even though increased trade with China may cause the OECD to abandon the production of its less-sophisticated goods, production of more-sophisticated goods (or the research, design, etc. services associated with them) is in principle always waiting to take its place. Indeed, as is often pointed out, the creative destruction associated with these reallocations should be encouraged: allowing countries to produce according to their comparative advantage enhances the efficiency of production and encourages the availability of a wider variety of products at lower prices to all consumers in all countries, raising standards of living. In a theoretical model, Bernard, Redding and Schott (2006) demonstrate that trade liberalization forces firms to focus on their 'core competencies' by dropping relatively unproductive goods that are at odds with their comparative advantage. In doing so, aggregate productivity rises due to gains in efficiency that occur both within and across firms. For the United States between 1972 and 2001, Bernard Jensen and Schott (2004) show that although industries exposed to the highest levels of low-wage competition have experienced the largest declines in employment, their real output nevertheless increased.

As these facts and the theoretical discussion in Section 3 make clear, all workers do not fare equally well under trade liberalization. In developed countries, low-skill workers are disproportionately likely to be dislocated from their jobs, and they may also have the hardest time finding matches with new employers. Not every apparel worker that loses their job in Germany can find immediate employment with a pharmaceutical firm manufacturing the latest biotechnology drugs. In a study of displaced workers in the United States, Kletzer (2001) finds that manufacturing workers dislocated by import competition accept an average pay cut of 13% in moving to their next job. Across workers, one third of respondents report earning the same wage or more in their new job, while one fourth report earning at least 30% less.

It is precisely such losses to workers, and not jobs, which should be the focus of trade policy. Temporarily shielding certain jobs from import competition merely postpones an inevitable reallocation that becomes more painful the longer it is delayed. Instead, trade policy should facilitate the ability of workers to find new employment when existing occupations disappear. As Denmark's 'flexicurity' program reveals, this goal can be achieved in part by providing workers with incentives to undergo retraining necessary for re-employment in viable sectors. But trade policy must also encompass broader support for the primary, secondary and tertiary educational institutions that provide workers with human capital before they even enter the workforce. It should also consider how these institutions should evolve in a fast-paced global economy. Obviously, it is only by maintaining their relative human capital abundance that developed economies will retain production of the world's most sophisticated goods.

Other proposals to reduce labor-market frictions might also be considered. Davidson and Matusz (2006) compare several such policies – including wage subsidies, employment subsidies, trade adjustment assistance, and training subsidies – in terms of their ability to transfer some of the aggregate gains from trade to those whose jobs are displaced by it. A well-designed wage insurance plan, for example, might give dislocated workers an incentive to accept a job where the wage is initially low but where the wage may increase with time, retraining and experience (Kletzer, 2004). These policies may also reduce the time displaced workers spend unemployed. Though the cost of such assistance is not trivial, they can also aid in gathering support for trade liberalization at the outset: as reported by Scheve and Slaughter

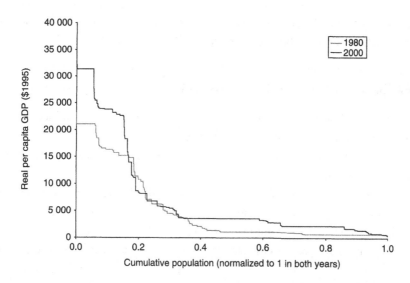

Figure 4. Per capita GDP and population, 1980 versus 2000

(2001), public opinion about free trade increases when it is linked to worker adjustment programs.

In many ways, speculation today about the impact on developed economies of trade with China mirrors the debate over trade with Japan that took place in the 1980s. Back then, it was the Japanese who were poised to take over the world's manufacturing, and it was the Yen rather than the Yuan that was under-valued. It turned out that although competition with Japan was painful for developed countries, firms in these economies were able to adjust.

One manifestation of this adaptability is displayed in Figure 4, which is drawn from Leamer and Schott (2005) and which compares countries' per capita GDP and population in 1980 and 2000. Each country is represented by a horizontal line segment, with the height of the segment indicating the country's per capita GDP and its length measuring the country's share of the world's population. The area enclosed by the rectangle extending up from the x-axis therefore represents each country's total GDP. The United Kingdom, with a small population and high per capita GDP appears as a short (unlabelled) horizontal line high up on the left while China and India, with a large populations and low per capita GDP appear as long lines near the bottom.

Trade barriers were relatively high in the 1980s compared with today, and many critics warned that if they were lowered outsourcing would reduce wages in developed economies. In the language of Figure 4, it was feared that the line for 2000 would be flatter and somewhere nearer the world average for per capita GDP than the line for 1980. That did not occur. As indicated in the figure, the 20% of the world's population living in wealthy economies have experienced substantial earnings growth since 1980, and so, incidentally, have the 60% who live in the world's poorest countries. It is the middle-income countries, whose goods occupy the middle cone of Figure 1 and are perhaps insufficiently differentiated from those exported by the lowest-wage countries, whose incomes have stagnated.

8. CAVEATS: DOES PRICE EQUAL QUALITY?

This paper – in line with much of the literature on export unit values – interprets differences in countries' export prices within product categories as evidence of quality gaps. This assumption is reasonable when products possess only vertical attributes, that is, attributes for which all consumers agree to pay more. It is unlikely that the price differences observed between the OECD and China are solely a reflection of production costs, though this interpretation does appear to be on many policy makers' minds. If that were true, it would only be a matter of time before OECD countries, with their very high (quality-adjusted) prices, are driven from the market entirely. Indeed, if Chinese and OECD varieties were perfect substitutes, demand for OECD exports would cease immediately absent any supply constraints allowing them to retain customers in the short run. O'Rourke and Willamson (2005) provide a stark demonstration of such competition in the market for (undifferentiated) wheat during the late 1800s and early 1900s, where very soon after low-cost United States entered the market, world prices plummeted. This does not appear to have occurred in present-day manufacturing.

A more rigorous assessment of quality could be accomplished in two ways. The first would be to accumulate very detailed information on the hedonic attributes of goods exported by US trading partners. Because such information is very expensive to collect, it is generally unavailable. On the other hand, pilot studies of a handful of industries do exist. Sutton (2007a,b), for example, documents detailed 'benchmarking' of manufacturing plants in the automobile-component and machine-tool industries to assess China and India's attempts to catch up to developed economies.

An alternate approach, pursued by Hallak and Schott (2006) and Khandelwal (2006), proposes the use of empirical techniques to recover information on countries' export quality using information on export quantities as well as prices. Hallak and Schott focus on countries' global net trade, while Khandelwal takes account of their US market share. The basic intuition behind their procedures is straightforward. For example, a country observed to have rising net trade in the presence of constant prices is assumed to have rising quality: if demand is a function of quality-adjusted prices, stable observed prices and growing net trade imply rising quality. Though identification is more difficult if one allows for both horizontal and vertical differentiation within product categories, preliminary estimates from Hallak and Schott indicate that China's export quality is significantly lower than that of the OECD.

Exporters' efforts to promote sales abroad can also influence the trends observed in this paper. Policies such as export subsidies and explicit or implicit exchange rate management can both inflate the range of products a country like China exports to the United States as well as lower their prices. China's efforts in this regard are well known (Naughton, 1996). It would be quite useful to examine the extent to which such policies influence the major findings of this paper, but comprehensive datasets tracking their extensiveness across both countries and time do not yet exist.

A related issue concerns the more fundamental question of where exporters' quality originates. In the theoretical models discussed above, export sophistication emanates from relative endowments in capital and skill. This line of thinking – as well as the use of unit values to proxy for quality – ignores the potential contribution of imported intermediate inputs. China, of course, has been the recipient of a staggering level of foreign direct investment, much of it to make use of the country as an export platform. Rodrik (2006), for example, argues that the attractiveness of China's export processing zones has exerted an important affect on the sophistication of its exports. Decomposing countries' export quality according to the relative contributions of its factor endowments versus its imported inputs would be a very valuable exercise. Unfortunately, it too, is hampered by the general unavailability of data mapping countries' imports into their exports.

9. CONCLUSION

This paper documents the extent to which developed economies are exposed to China in terms of both the breadth of products they export and the range of prices those products command. It finds that China and developed economies overlap considerably in terms of export mix, but much less so, and less over time, in terms of export prices. It interprets these findings as being consistent with other evidence suggesting that developed economies compete with developing economies like China by raising the quality of their exports. It points out that such competition offers hope to workers in developed economies who fear their standards of living will fall as a result of globalization. On the other hand, the paper highlights the difficulties associated with identifying quality competition and acknowledges that alternate interpretations of the evidence are not unreasonable.

Though the results in this paper provide insight into how China and developed economies compete, it raises a number of questions requiring further research. First, what factors govern developed-country firms' ability to move up the quality ladder and thereby 'escape' competition from low-wage countries? Research by Khandelwal (2006), for example, finds that products vary widely in terms of the 'length' of their quality ladders. As a result, developed-country firms in high-ladder industries may have more 'room' to 'move away' from competition from low-wage countries than firms in low-ladder industries, but they may also have greater incentives to invest in increasing the length of the ladder. We need a better understanding of these dynamics.

Second, how substitutable are high- and low-end product varieties within export markets? When specialization takes place across wholly different products, say t-shirts and electron microscopes, it is relatively easy to be sanguine about the inability of declining t-shirt prices to influence the wages of electron-microscope manufacturers.

One suspects that price-wage arbitrage is much more likely when developed and developing economies specialize in vertically differentiated varieties: price declines in conventional televisions may influence the price of high-end plasma displays. Though estimating such substitutability is beyond the scope of this paper, research in Khandelwal (2006) suggests that the within-product substitutability of imports is lower for products characterized by long quality ladders. If this is true, the quality gaps discerned above will help insulate workers in high-wage countries from the low labor costs of developing countries.

Third, to what extent will China's internal heterogeneity in relative factor endowments, as well as differences in the rates of skill and capital deepening across provinces, lead some regions of the country to raise the sophistication of their products more quickly than others? Quality variation across Chinese provinces cannot be discerned in the international trade data used in this paper; it merely reflects the value-weighted average unit value of exports from all regions of the country. When data for Chinese exports by region become available, it would be useful to determine whether the exports of the more developed coastal provinces are closer substitutes for OECD exports than the exports of provinces in the interior.

A final question for further research involves investigating the speed of product cycling. Is globalization hastening the migration of varieties from developed to developing economies? What are the implications of this acceleration?

Discussion

Clemens Fuest
Universität zu Köln

China's emergence as an important actor on international markets is one of the most interesting economic developments of the last decades. Peter Schott's paper focuses on a central aspect of this development: China's breathtaking export performance. The analysis addresses a number of highly interesting and relevant questions and concerns: Will competition from China eventually eliminate manufacturing in industrialized countries? Are developed or developing countries more affected by competition from China? Can the export performance of China in terms of export similarity with the OECD be explained on the basis of differences in country size and factor endowments, as standard models of trade theory would suggest? What are the policy implications of Chinese export growth? The answer to the first question is good and bad news at the same time: The 'bad news' is that China's export similarity with OECD countries, measured on the basis of standard product classification, is higher than that of other non-OECD countries, given China's relative level of development. This suggests that manufacturing in industrialized countries is exposed to intensive competition from China. But a comparison of export prices within

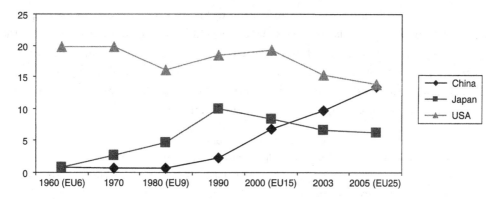

Figure 5. European Union impact market shares 1960–2005

Source: Eurostat.

product varieties reveals that Chinese products are selling at a considerable discount relative to goods produced in OECD countries. This discount seems to increase over time. If prices are seen as an indicator of product quality, and if goods of different quality are poor substitutes, this finding suggests that OECD countries have been able to avoid competition by moving up the quality ladder, i.e. by producing more sophisticated goods.

A first question which naturally arises in this context is whether the Chinese exports to the US are similar to the exports to other developed countries, in particular the EU. Figure 5 illustrates the development of European imports from China, compared to the imports from other major trading partners.

The numbers show that the development of EU imports from China is similar to that of the US. The market share of China in EU imports, which was negligible in 1980, has grown quickly over the last two decades, overtook that of Japan a few years ago and is currently equal to the market share of imports from the US. No other trading partner has experienced a similar development.[1] Although these numbers are aggregates, which tell us nothing about the similarity of the goods imported from China to those imported from the US or those produced by European firms for the home market, it seems that the unique export performance of China is not a phenomenon which is particular to the US. The bilateral trade deficit with China, however, is larger in the US than in Europe. In 2005, the EU bilateral trade deficit with China was €106 bn, compared to $202 bn deficit for the US. Of course, one should take into account that the economic interpretation of bilateral trade deficits is difficult. In the political debate they do play an important role, though.

Another question raised by Peter Schott's analysis is whether the composition of exports can really be interpreted as a good indicator of the development of the

---

[1] The number of EU member countries included in these numbers has changed. But imports to individual large EU countries like Germany or France show similar patterns.

Chinese export industry and the underlying technological and economic development
of the country as a player in world markets. In their recent survey paper on the
economic development of China, Branstetter and Lardy (2006) point to two reasons
why this may be problematic. Firstly they argue that the large high tech product share
in Chinese exports should not be interpreted as evidence that Chinese firms are able
to compete in human capital intensive high technology sectors:

> 'China is able to export huge quantities of electronic and information technology products only
> because it imports most of the high value added parts and components that go into these goods.
> China, in short, does not in any real sense manufacture these goods. Rather it assembles them
> from imported parts and components.' (ibid., p. 38).

As an example, Branstetter and Lardy (2006) point to China's exports and imports
of electronics and information technology products. In 2003, China exported $142 bn
in this product group, but it imported $127 bn in the same group, mostly parts and
components. If China's contribution to the production of these goods just consists
of low productivity assembly services provided by unskilled workers, this seems to be
well in line with what is usually perceived as the country's comparative advantage.
This suggests that export similarity may be a misleading indicator of the degree of
competition to which workers of industrialized countries are exposed. It could be the
case that industrialized countries export the high tech components to other countries,
where these parts are essentially assembled. Of course, it remains to be demonstrated
that this is really the case. Peter Schott is aware of this caveat and points to the fact
that there are currently no data available which would allow this issue to be explored.

Secondly, Brandstetter and Lardy (2006) point to the fact that most of the exported
electronics and information technology products are not manufactured by Chinese-
owned firms but by foreign firms which operate in China and use the country as an
export platform. For instance, in 2003, foreign firms accounted for 92% of China's
exports in computers, components and peripherals and 74% of exports of electronics and
telecommunications equipment. Most of these firms are wholly foreign-owned firms,
rather than joint ventures (Gilboy, 2004), so that diffusion of technological knowledge
will proceed only slowly. Moreover, many domestically-owned Chinese-owned firms seem
to spend little on research and development and networks for research and innovations
seem to be poorly developed (Gilboy, 2004). This suggests that the growing share of
high tech products in exports should not be interpreted as evidence that 'genuinely'
Chinese firms are closing the technological gap to firms from industrialized countries.

The key role of foreign firms for the development of the Chinese export industry
has its roots in the way foreign trade policy evolved. Naughton (1996) argues that
'China ... embarked on the process of transition with a highly centralized, monopolistic
foreign trade regime. ... Since 1978 China has gradually ... established a system in
which most trade is governed by market forces' (p. 295). '... by 1986–87 China had
established two separate trading regimes ... One is an ... export promotion regime
... most domestic firms are excluded while foreign firms can participate ... the other

is the traditional import substitution regime' (p. 298). He further reports that at least up to the mid-90s, there was a strong geographical correlation between foreign direct investment and foreign trade in China. For instance, in 1994, the export to GDP ratio of the province of Guandong was 106%. Almost 40% were produced by foreign firms. The export to GDP ratio in the rest of China was only 14%, and less than 25% was produced by foreign firms.

From the perspective of the industrialized countries and in particular the workers in the manufacturing sector, it is an open question whether the dominance of foreign firms in the Chinese export industry is a reason for optimism, though. For instance, in 2003, among the 200 of China's largest exporters 28 were Taiwan owned firms.[2] All were electronics manufacturers. If workers in the electronics industry in the US or in Europe lose their jobs, it is probably of secondary importance to them whether they do so because of competition from China or from Taiwan. Moreover, even if US or European firms were key players in the Chinese export industry, European and US workers might lose because they are replaced by Chinese workers.

There are two further issues which question the ability of China to maintain its growth in exports in the years to come. The first issue is the impact of this performance on the trade policy debate in the US and in other industrialized countries. Messerlin (2004) reports that since 1995, an average share of 15% of all anti-dumping measures in force in the US were directed against China. It is possible if not likely that trade policy measures against imports from China will play a role in the 2008 presidential elections.

The second issue is the exchange rate regime. For some time, the Chinese exchange rate policy has been criticized for subsidizing exports through undervaluation. There is an ongoing debate on whether or not the undervaluation of the Yuan is a recent phenomenon, but there is no doubt that it has been undervalued at least since 2002, when the Chinese authorities had to build up unrecorded currency reserves to sustain the exchange rate of the Yuan to the dollar. This undervaluation gives rise to a serious misallocation of resources. Part of the current Chinese export industry is likely to lose its competitiveness if the exchange rate is corrected.

In summary, this paper represents an important contribution to the analysis of China's economic development and its impact on the industrialized world. The fact that the economic interpretation of indicators like export similarity and export pricing faces several difficulties shows that there is a fascinating research agenda ahead.

Kevin O'Rourke
Trinity College Dublin

This is a difficult paper to comment on. It is tightly argued and tightly focussed. It provides compelling evidence documenting two stylized facts, both of which are

---

[2] China Economic News Service, June 28, 2004, cited in Brandstetter and Lardy, 2006, p. 40.

interesting, and possibly even important. All of this is good news for the reader, but not such good news for the discussant. In my remarks I will thus place this paper in a somewhat longer-run context, before going on to make two minor comments, and one major one, regarding the author's argument.

The big issue which this paper implicitly addresses is the long-run political sustainability of the current phase of globalization. Although the author provides us with both good and bad news, on the whole the paper is meant to be reassuring. It thus seems worth noting that the historical evidence is *not* reassuring as regards the ease with which markets can be kept open in the face of large-scale trade in 'competing' goods between world regions with very different factor endowments.

Prior to the 19th century, inter-continental freight rates remained high, and such trade as did occur between continents involved goods with a very high value to weight ratio. In 1608–10, more than a century after da Gama, fully 80% of Portuguese imports from Asia involved pepper and other spices. As late as the 1750s, the majority of British and Dutch imports from Asia and the Americas consisted of tea, coffee, pepper and spices, sugar, tobacco, and other goods which could either not be produced in Europe at all, or only with great difficulty (Findlay and O'Rourke, 2007, Table 5.8). This of course implied that there were no European producers of these goods who felt threatened by these imports. The politics of trade during the mercantilist era thus involved inter-state competition over which country would get the rents thought to be associated with successfully monopolizing such trades.

All of this changed some time during the 19th century, as a result of the new steam-driven transport technologies associated with the Industrial Revolution. Harley's (1988, Figure 1) evidence on ocean freight rates suggests that 1840 is as good a candidate for a turning point as any other, since his data show British freight rates fluctuating around a fairly steady trend up to that date, and collapsing thereafter. Not coincidentally, the period after 1840 also saw the beginnings of a mass trans-Atlantic trade in such bulk commodities as wheat, and a collapse in wheat price gaps between land-scarce and land-abundant continents (Figure 6). Intercontinental trade now impacted on domestic producers of such goods, and began to have the effects on income distribution predicted (retrospectively) by two Swedish observers of the period, Heckscher and Ohlin. The politics of trade now involved intra-state distributional conflict, and there soon followed a backlash against the grain trade across Continental Europe driven by discontented farmers, with barriers to agricultural trade being erected that remain with us to this day (O'Rourke, 1997; O'Rourke and Williamson, 2005).

The fact that the GATT liberalized trade fairly successfully in the aftermath of 1945 is not as reassuring as it might be, since the Western countries that were primarily involved were prosperous and shared similarly high capital–labor and human-capital–labor ratios. Notably, they did differ in terms of their land–labor ratios, and agriculture was an exception to the generally liberal trend. With the spread of communism, and decolonization, the South was for decades largely absent from this process, and insofar as it exported goods to the North, these were largely

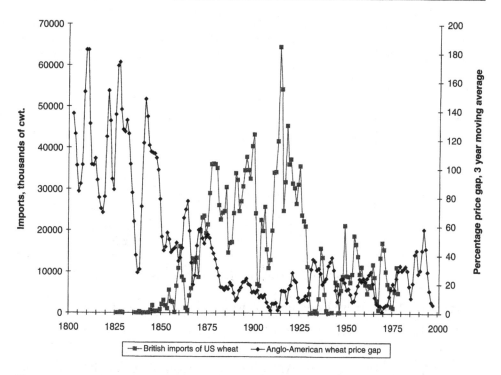

Figure 6. Anglo–American wheat trade, 1800–2000

Source: O'Rourke and Williamson (2005), Figure 3, p. 10.

non-competing primary products. Since the 1980s, however, the South has massively liberalized, and as Figure 7 shows, this has coincided with a dramatic shift in the structure of its exports to the North, as the Industrial Revolution spreads across the globe, and the Great Specialisation that Dennis Robertson (1938) memorably described unravels. While this is good news for the South, one has to query whether current trends will last, since once again rich European markets are mass importing competing goods – manufactures on this occasion – from continents with very different factor endowments. Will European (and North American) unskilled labor demand protective tariffs, as did European farmers over a century ago? Presumably this will in part depend on how badly European labor is hurt by Chinese competition.

Schott's paper contains bad news and good news for these workers. The bad news is that China's exports overlap with OECD exports a lot, and that this overlap has been increasing over time. The paper succeeds in establishing this stylized fact in convincing fashion, which is worrying since this makes it more likely that OECD wages will be influenced by Chinese competition.

The good news, for Schott, is that the prices obtained by Chinese exporters for their products are unusually low given China's size and endowments, and that they have been falling relative to OECD prices. Schott assumes that price differentials reflect quality differences between products. The price data thus suggest that Chinese exports remain relatively unsophisticated, and that OECD manufacturers have been

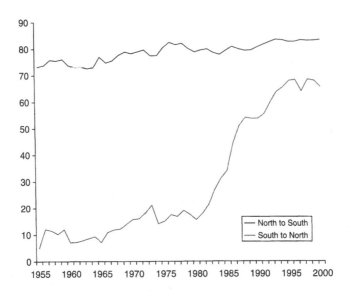

Figure 7. Manufactured products' share of exports, 1955–2000

Source: UNCTAD.

engaged in quality upgrading within product categories. All of this may limit the extent to which Chinese and OECD firms compete head-on, thus shielding OECD workers in a way that 19th century European farmers could not have been.

My minor comment on this argument is as follows. The empirical strategy relies on the assumption that Chinese exports to the US are representative of Chinese exports and production generally. Is this necessarily the case? As Schott points out, Harrigan (2005) has recently provided evidence that the quality of goods transported varies with distance. Not surprisingly, the further you are from the US, the higher will be the unit values of the goods you ship there, *ceteris paribus*, a finding which this paper confirms. To be sure, Schott finds that Chinese export prices are low, even controlling for distance from the US market, but it would still be of interest to see if Schott's findings for the US can be generalized to OECD markets closer to China, such as Japan.

The major comment is that Schott's evidence for optimism is largely to be found in his Figure 3. What that seems to show, however, is that the fall in relative Chinese unit values was largely limited to the late 1980s and early 1990s (although there was another important dip after 1999 or 2000). Figure 8 below shows that this was also a period in which the real value of the Chinese renminbi fell dramatically. In a careful study taking account of the dual nature of China's exchange rate system during 1998–93, Wang (2004) finds that the Chinese manufacturing unit-labor-cost-based real exchange rate depreciated by roughly 85% between 1984 and 1993. A worried Western worker might well interpret Schott's relative price evidence quite differently than does Schott. According to such a pessimistic reading, it was this real depreciation that lowered relative Chinese prices, not a deterioration in relative Chinese quality,

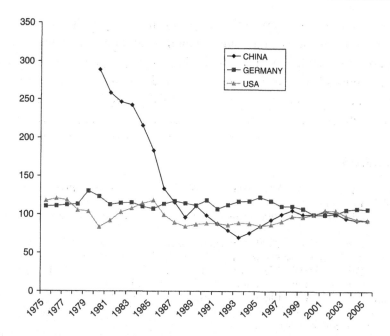

Figure 8. Real exchange rates, 1975–2005

Source: World Development Indicators.

and this relative price fall then spurred a massive growth in Chinese exports, with potentially adverse consequences for unskilled OECD workers.

Schott's benign conclusions may well be valid, but without firmer evidence linking prices and quality I fear that they won't sway wavering protectionists. Having said this, the issues raised in this paper are of major importance for the future of the international trading system. I look forward to seeing future work by Schott and others on the subject.

Panel discussion

Much of the discussion focussed on the identification of price and quality changes. Carlin, for example, asked how much of market share increase was driven by changes in cost competitiveness. Once the cost change is taken into account, any positive value of the China dummy (influencing the value of products) can be assumed to come from an improvement in product quality. Similarly any negative value of the China dummy can be interpreted as a decrease in quality. Several panel members were also interested in the results on the terms of trade. Redding pointed out China's export growth has a positive terms of trade impact on countries that are not competing in the same products, for example the US, and that the closest competitors such as

Mexico are the real losers. Some panel members were also uncertain about the interpretation to give to the China dummy and would have liked to see how it compares, for example, with an India dummy. Some panel members also thought that the optimistic tone of the introduction and conclusion on the impact of Chinese competition on income distribution in the OECD could not be fully justified by the results of the paper.

REFERENCES

Alchian Armen, A. and W.R. Allen (1964). *University Economics*, Belmont, CA: Wadsworth Publishing Company.
Bannister, J. (2005). 'Manufacturing Earnings and Compensation in China', *Monthly Labor Review*, 128(8), 22–40.
Barro, R.J. and J.-W. Lee (2000). 'International Data on Educational Attainment: Updates and Implications', *Center for International Development Working Paper 42*, Harvard University.
Bernard, A.B., J. Bradford Jensen and P.K. Schott (2004). 'Facing the Dragon: Prospects for US Manufacturers in the Coming Decade', Yale University, *mimeo*.
Bernard, A.B., J. Bradford Jensen and P.K. Schott (2006). 'Survival of the Best Fit: Exposure to Low-Wage Countries and the (Uneven) Growth of US Manufacturing Plants', *Journal of International Economic Studies*, 68, 219–237.
Bernard, A.B., S.J. Reddings and P.K. Schott (2006). 'Multi-Product Firms and Trade Liberalization', *NBER Working Paper 12782*, Cambridge, MA: NBER.
Branstetter, L. and N. Lardy (2006). 'China's Embrace of Globalization', *NBER Working Paper No. 12373*, Cambridge, MA: NBER.
Centre D'Etudes Prospectives et D'Informations Internationales (CEPII), http://www.cepii.fr/anglaisgraph/bdd/distances.htm.
Corsetti, G., P. Martin and P. Pesenti, 'Productivity Spillovers, Terms of Trade and the Home Market Effect', *Journal of International Economics*, forthcoming.
Davidson, C. and S.J. Matusz (2006). 'Trade Liberalization and Compensation', *International Economic Review*, 47(3), 723–747.
Deardorff, A.V. (2004). 'Local Comparative Advantage: Trade Costs and the Pattern of Trade', University of Michigan, *mimeo*.
Dixit, A. and V. Norman (1980). *Theory of International Trade*, New York, NY: Cambridge University Press.
Feenstra, R., J. Romalis and P.K. Schott (2002). 'US Imports, Exports and Tariff Data, 1989 to 2001', *NBER Working Paper 9387*, Cambridge, MA: NBER.
Findlay, R. and K.H. O'Rourke (2007). *Power and Plenty: Trade, War, and the World Economy in the Second Millennium*, Princeton, NJ: Princeton University Press.
Finger, J.M. and M.E. Kreinin (1979). 'A Measure of "Export Similarity" and Its Possible Uses', *Economic Journal*, 89, 905–912.
Fontagne, L., G. Gaulier and S. Zignago (2007). 'Specialisation Across Varieties Within Products and North–South Competition', *mimeo*, Paris: CEPII,.
Gilboy, G.J. (2004). 'The Myth behind China's Miracle', *Foreign Affairs*, 83, 33–48.
Grossman, G.M. and E. Helpman (1991). *Innovation and Growth in the Global Economy*, Cambridge, MA: MIT Press.
Grubel, H.G. and P.J. Lloyd (1975). *Intra-Industry Trade: The Theory and Measurement of International Trade in Differentiated Products*, New York: Wiley.
Hallak, J.-C.s and P.K. Schott (2006). 'Estimating Cross-Country Differences in Product Quality', Yale University, *mimeo*.
Harigan, J. (2005). 'Airplanes and Comparative Advantage', *NBER Working Paper 11688*, Cambridge, MA: NBER.
Harley, C.K. (1988). 'Ocean Freight Rates and Productivity, 1740–1913: The Primacy of Mechanical Invention Reaffirmed', *Journal of Economic History*, (48), 1–14.
Hummels, D. and P. Klenow (2005). 'The Variety and Quality of a Nation's Exports', *American Economic Review*, 95, 704–723.

Hummels, D. and A. Skiba (2004). 'Shipping the Good Apples Out? An Empirical Confirmation of the Alchian-Allen Conjecture', *Journal of Political Economy*, 112, 1384–1402.

Johnson, H. (1958). *International Trade and Economic Growth: Studies in Pure Theory*, London: Allen and Unwin.

Khandelwal, A. (2006). 'The Long and Short (of) Quality Ladders', Yale University, *mimeo*

Kletzer, L. (2001). 'What are the Costs of Job Loss from Import-Competing Industries?' Washington, DC: Institute for International Economics.

Kletzer, L. (2004). 'Trade-related Job Loss and Wage Insurance: A Synthetic Review', *Review of International Economics*, 12(5), 724–748.

Krugman, P. (1980). 'Scale Economies, Product Differentiation, and the Pattern of Trade', *American Economic Review*, 70, 950–959.

Krugman, P. (1989). 'Income Elasticities and Real Exchange Rates', *European Economic Review*, 33, 1031–1054.

Leamer, E.E. (1984). *Sources of International Comparative Advantage*, Cambridge: MIT Press.

Leamer, E.E. (1987). 'Paths of Development in the Three-Factor, n-Good General Equilibrium Model', *Journal of Political Economy*, 95, 961–999.

Leamer, E.E., H. Maul, S. Rodriguez and P.K. Schott (1999). 'Why Does Natural Resource Abundance Increase Latin American Income Inequality?' *Journal of Development Economics*, 59(1), 3–42.

Leamer, E.E. and P.K. Schott (2005). 'The Rich (and Poor) Keep Getting Richer', *Harvard Business Review*, 83(4), 20.

Messerlin, P.A. (2004). 'China in the World Trade Organization, Antidumping and Safeguards', World Bank Economic Review, 18, 105–130.

Naughton, B. (1996). 'China's Emergence and Future as a Trading Nation', *Brookings Papers on Economic Activity*, 2, 273–344.

Nehru, V. and A. Dhareshwar (1993). 'A New Database on Physical Capital Stock: Sources, Methodology and Results', *Revista de Analisis Economico*, 8(1), 37–59.

O'Rourke, K.H. (1997). 'The European Grown Invasion, 1870–1913', *Journal of Economic History*, (57), 775–801.

O'Rourke, K. and J.G. Williamson (2005). 'From Malthus to Ohlin: Trade, Industrialisation and Distribution Since 1500', *Journal of Economic Growth*, 10, 5–34.

OECD (2001). 'Regional Disparities and Trade Investment Liberalisation in China', http://www.oecd.org/dataoecd/58/12/2369981.pdf

Posner, M.V. (1961). 'International Trade and Technical Change', *Oxford Economic Papers* 41, 323–341.

Robertson, D.H. (1938). 'The Future of International Trade', *Economic Journal*, (48), 1–14.

Rodrik, D. (2006). 'What's so Special about China's Exports?', *mimeo*, Harvard.

Scheve, K.F. and M.J. Slaughter (2001). *Globalization and the Perceptions of American Workers*, Washington, DC: Institute for International Economics.

Schott, P.K. (2004). 'Across-Product versus Within-Product Specialization in International Trade', *Quarterly Journal of Economics*, 119(2), 647–678.

Sutton, J. (2007a). 'The Globalization Process: Auto-component Supply Chains in China and India', *mimeo*, London School of Econmics.

Sutton, J. (2007b). 'The Indian Machine-Tool Industry: A Benchmarking Study', London School of Economics, *mimeo*.

US General Accounting Office (1995). 'US Imports: Unit Values Vary Widely for Identically Classified Commodities', Report GAO/GGD-95-90, http://www.gao.gov/archive/1995/gg95090.pdf

Vernon, R. (1966). 'International Investment and International Trade in the Product Cycle', *Quarterly Journal of Economics*, 80, 190–207.

Vernon, R. (1979). 'The Product Cycle Hypothesis in a New International Environment', *Oxford Bulletin of Economics and Statistics*, 41, 255–267.

Wang, T. (2004). 'China: Sources of Real Exchange Rate Fluctuations', *IMF Working Paper*, WP/04/18.

Zhu, S. and D. Trefler (2005). 'Trade and Inequality in Developing Countries: A General Equilibrium Analysis', *Journal of International Economcs*, 65, 21–48.

North–South competition in quality

SUMMARY

Analyzing a new database that makes it possible to disaggregate trade flows across many countries according to unit values, we show that international specialization in terms of quality within industries and product categories plays an important role in the dynamics of North–South competition. The different specialization of countries at different levels of development within products and across varieties is mirrored in the recent shifts in world market shares, which are very different across quality segments: the South is not gaining market share in high-value portions of trade pattern. In this respect Europe's specialization pattern appears to be different from that of the US and Japan, and may allow it to better resist the competitive pressure of the South.

— *Lionel Fontagné, Guillaume Gaulier and Soledad Zignago*

Specialization across varieties and North–South competition

Lionel Fontagné, Guillaume Gaulier and Soledad Zignago

Paris School of Economics, Université Paris 1 and CEPII; Banque de France and CEPII; CEPII

1. INTRODUCTION

Empirical work on trade data (see especially Schott, 2004, and references therein) has documented considerable variation in prices of traded products at the most detailed level of product classification. More precisely, such observation pertains to unit values, since prices are not directly observable in trade statistics. Unit values are defined as values of shipments (Free On Board), divided by quantities shipped. On average, Japanese unit values are 1.43 times higher than for Brazil, 1.80 times higher than for India, and 2.89 times higher than for China, for the *same* products, shipped to the *same* markets, within the *same* year (2004). Similarly, US export unit values are on average 1.55 times higher than for India and 2.44 times higher than for China.

To illustrate this phenomenon, and this paper's research strategy, let us split international trade prices into three market segments (low, medium, high), using the world distribution of unit values (see Appendix A2). In Figure 1 we plot the share of down and up-market varieties, in US imports from each exporter, by development level

We acknowledge helpful comments and suggestions from three anonymous referees on an earlier draft, and by the Economic Policy panel held in Frankfurt. We also thank Rodrigo Paillacar for his excellent research assistance, as well as Louise Curran for her comments on the previous draft. We thank participants to the seminar held at the INSEE & CEPII for their suggestions. The Managing Editor in charge of this paper was Giuseppe Bertola.

Economic Policy January 2008 pp. 51–91 Printed in Great Britain

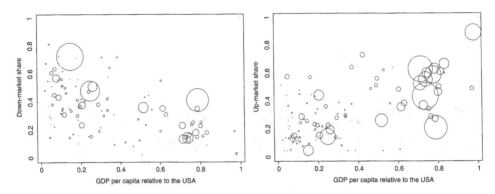

Figure 1. Share of down- and up-market varieties, in US imports from each exporter, by development level of the exporter

Note: Horizontal axis: GDP per capita of the exporter, relative to the US. Vertical axis: share of market segment in US imports. The size of the bubble is proportional to the value of US imports by country of origin. Import data below USD 1bn are not plotted.

Source: BACI-CEPII, and authors' calculations.

(GDP per capita relative to the US) of the latter. The size of the bubble is proportional to the value of US imports from each country. In the case of down-market varieties, there is a negative relationship between the development level of the exporter to the US market and its specialization. In the case of up-market ones, the relationship is positive.

Accordingly, in a given market, countries at different development levels do sell differentiated varieties of the same products, at very different prices; these countries do not compete directly since they are not positioned in the same market segment. The policy implications of such a simple stylized fact are considerable and such a shift in our understanding of international specialization should prevent us from drawing hasty conclusions on the competitive pressures faced by high income countries coping with competition from emerging economies.

On the one hand, the North is now in competition with the South on a wide range of products. Nearly the whole spectrum of the headings of the international product classification are covered by Chinese exports. Out of 5041 products traded at the international level in 2004, 4898 were exported by China, compared with 4932 for Germany. Moreover, when one takes as a benchmark the number of pairs of destination markets and exported products, China was exporting on 335 720 such 'elementary markets' in 2004 (but only 163 250 in 1995), compared with 352 855 in 2004 for Germany. All in all, China is exhibiting specialization patterns at the most detailed level corresponding to countries three times as rich (Rodrik, 2007). Accordingly, workers in the North could fear that direct competition from the South on the whole range of products will induce downward pressure on their wages.

However, although China may well export as many products as Germany, varieties exported by Germany and China seem too different to be in direct competition. This implies that workers in the two countries do not compete in production of the same varieties, and if the different varieties are not very substitutable, there will be only a weak link between trade and factor prices.

Of course, it might be the case that such broad brush evidence as that reported above hides large differences among sectors or countries. And it is also important to consider dynamic aspects, because such large differences in unit values could well be only transitory. To shed further light on these phenomena, we adopt a fact-oriented approach and systematically scan world trade data, in order to establish the precise patterns of specialization across varieties of countries of the North and the South, and to detect their determinants. We aim at assessing policy challenges posed by the emergence of competitors in the South covering the whole range of traded products, and we focus particularly on similarities and differences across the US, Japan, and the EU as regards the character of competition from the South.

To measure the within products specialization of countries and their market positioning, we use a newly developed database of world trade flows: BACI.[1] It covers the largest available set of countries over a decade and reconciles the declarations of trading partners, extracting trade costs from unit values of imports, and correcting for the quality of the declarations. Relying on this exhaustive set of more than 200 countries and 5000 products in the database, we address differences in unit values for the same *manufactured* products. These unit values are used to calculate the relative prices of the varieties exported, as well as to allocate the shipped varieties in the three different market segments we referred to above. Importantly, we do find that Europe differs from other developed regions of the world. The EU appears to be less specialized than the United States or Japan in hi-tech industries, and has a very resilient market share in the upper segment of the unit value distribution.

2. POLICY QUESTIONS

Policy makers are concerned by the increasing range of sectors facing the competition of emerging countries. Considering differentiated varieties of products rather than sectors sheds new light on the perceived similarity in specialization between North and South, and contrasts with the classical view of the trade theory (see Box 1).

2.1. Trade impacts revisited

Since the pioneering work of Finger (1975), a series of contributions have confirmed that specialization is taking place within products across varieties as well as across products or across industries. Torstensson (1991) provided early evidence of Sweden's specialization on quality vis-à-vis countries at different levels of per capita income. But the major breakthrough was Schott's (2004) finding that US imports are exhibiting a large variance in unit values within product categories; it has launched a new series

---

[1] BACI is the French acronym for 'Base pour l'Analyse du Commerce International', the new CEPII Database for International Trade Analysis. See Appendix A1 and http://www.cepii.fr/anglaisgraph/bdd/baci.htm.

Box 1. Predictions of trade theory contradict empirical evidence

According to the standard theory of international trade, and using a multi-products setting, countries will not specialize in products exhibiting relative factor contents at odds with their relative endowments. Hence different countries should have different bundles of exported products.

In contrast, the 'new' trade theory basically relies on trade in varieties having the same production function. In the latter framework using a single factor, countries advantaged in terms of productivity should ship low price varieties. This is the very framework synthesized by Helpman and Krugman (1985), where different countries specialize in different industries, while similar countries specialize in different varieties shipped at the same price.

Both predictions are conflicting with the repeated empirical evidence of trade in varieties at dissimilar prices among countries at different levels of development. Countries advantaged in terms of productivity do not export low price but rather high price varieties. Exporters to a given market do not specialize in a limited subset of products exhibiting production functions in coherence with their factor endowments, but on the contrary manage to specialize in a wide range of products. Lastly, countries actually import only a subset of all available varieties, while all varieties should enter symmetrically in preferences.

Hence, one is not facing an endowment-driven specialization across products, but on the contrary an endowment-driven specialization across varieties within products. This finding led Schott to suggest that 'our thinking about international specialization must shift away from industries (. . .) and toward varieties within industries (. . .)' (Schott, 2004, p. 649).

Such specialization may be the result of a double selection process: in a theoretical framework allowing for heterogeneous multi-product firms, not only does trade select among firms: there is also a self-selection within firms among products, as trade costs induce firms to ship mostly the best products of their portfolio (Bernard, Redding and Schott, 2006).

of works on the actual patterns of trade specialization. For instance, the International Monetary Fund's explanation of increasing world market shares of eight Central and Eastern European Countries, in spite of an appreciation of their real exchange rate, invokes an upgrading of the quality of exported varieties (IMF, 2006). Similarly, using 1995 import data for 59 countries from 110 exporters at the 6-digit level of the harmonized classification of traded goods (HS6 hereafter), as well as 10-digit data on US imports, Hummels and Klenow (2005), find that large countries do export higher quality goods (the 'quality margin' that may be interpreted as one component of the intensive margin), and not only more varieties (the extensive margin).

In total, we face a situation where countries are completely specialized within products, on varieties with different market positioning. In terms of the traditional factor price equalization mechanism, the North and the South are not directly competing and this should smooth the perception of the impacts of globalization.

We provide in the following convincing evidence that this new approach of international specialization helps to better understand the dynamics of North–South competition and its implications for advanced countries.

Firstly, we show that this dissimilarity in the specialization of countries at different levels of development within products and across varieties is mirrored in the recent shifts in world market shares. These shifts may profoundly differ among market segments, and different countries may be differently affected; hence, the popular view that the South is gaining market shares inexorably must be better qualified if one aims at drawing sound policy conclusions on the consequences of emergence for advanced economies.

Secondly, specific policy concerns arise with the hi-tech sector. Presumably, this is the very last refuge of industries of advanced economies, or at least the very place where rents are extracted. Hence, it is worth considering recent shifts in market shares and the presence of emerging economies as competitors. Here again, we observe that the diagnosis must take into account the differentiation of the varieties traded.

Thirdly, we identify a specific pattern of Europe's specialization that may allow it to better resist the competitive pressure of the South.

Our evidence calls for further analysis of the distributive impacts of such specialization across varieties: the need to climb the ladder of vertical differentiation of products may well profoundly impact on advanced economies. A first and obvious channel is that the production function of goods is accordingly changing. Instead of producing a consumption good with inputs of blue collar workers, capital and raw materials, what is needed is a combination of highly skilled designers, market analysts, engineers, etc. Accordingly, such a shift in production technologies may well have a similar impact to biased technical progress, detrimental to low-skilled, less adaptable workers. These arguments shed new light on the roles of technical progress and international competition in the relative worsening of the position of unskilled labor in the North, which may result not from product market competition directly but from the labor market implications of up-market positioning strategies by firms in the North. Similarity between North and South is limited at the variety level.

There is necessarily arbitrariness in the definition of what a product, versus a variety of a product, is. We rely here on the distinction proposed by Schott (2004). Two different headings of the most detailed level of the international trade classification represent two different products (HS6). Two different market segments represents two different varieties of a product having different unit values (see Box 2).[2]

---

[2] This departs from the vocabulary of the literature on intra-industry trade, which would use 'varieties' to refer to products shipped under the same heading but having similar unit values (horizontal differentiation), as opposed to 'qualities' having different unit values (vertical differentiation).

Box 2. Unit values and quality of the traded varieties

Using detailed trade data, Hummels and Klenow (2005) point to differences in quality to explain such differences in unit values. But interpreting differences in unit values of varieties of the same product is rather challenging, and a narrow view based on quality only is not necessarily warranted.

Firstly, consider the case that rich countries export high price varieties. Using cross-sectional bilateral data for 60 countries in 1995, Hallak (2006a) asks whether the correlation of export prices with per capita income, and thus with other factors than quality *per se*, leads to spurious conclusions. Is it quality or other factors tightly linked to income, such as production costs, that determine export prices?

Secondly, Hallak and Schott (2005) challenge the strong association of prices to quality, stressing that differences in unit values may reflect, not only the quality of the product, but also exchange rate misalignments or differences in production costs. Instead of assuming a one-to-one relationship between unit value and quality, they extract the 'comparative advantage' component of the difference in unit values by taking into consideration sectoral global balances of the exporting country. A country running a trade surplus and selling at a low unit value is considered as having a comparative advantage, rather than selling low quality products.

Thirdly, the composition of exports may vary with distance if transport costs have a fixed component, i.e. are not simply proportional to prices. In this case, distance should be less relevant for higher-quality products, according to the Alchian-Allen conjecture that 'the better apples are exported' (Hummels and Skiba, 2004).

Our bottom line is that quality and other characteristics differentiating varieties exported lead to the observed differences in relative unit values for the same product exported by two different countries on the same destination market. And inversely, that different export prices for a given product and in a given market, are reflecting differences in the quality perceived by local consumers.

To illustrate how exactly the international division of labor is taking place among countries at different levels of development, let us consider indicators of export similarity between countries, computed alternatively at the level of 26 'sectors', i.e. International Standard Industrial Classification (ISIC) codes; or 'products,' i.e. 4528 headings of manufacturing HS6 codes; or 'varieties,' i.e. the 4528 times 3 categories of export grouped in three price groups within each HS6 classification code. The similarity of export sectoral structures is one minus half the sum of the absolute value of the differences between the sectoral (or product or variety) shares in manufacturing exports of each country (1 is perfect similarity).

Given the heterogeneity of the EU-25, we *include* intra-EU exports in our calculation, and we consider separately the largest member states, France, Germany, Italy and the United Kingdom.

By considering similarity indexes computed at the sectoral level (Table 1, first panel), one might conclude that there is intensive competition between the North and the South. Similarity is however especially high for pairs of countries in the North, like for example an index of 0.77 for the United States and Japan. More interestingly, values near or above 0.50 are obtained for North–South comparisons: the similarity between China and the United States or Japan is comparable to the similarity between China and India. Italy is more similar to China (0.60) than to Japan (0.58).

Using a more aggregated classification of products, the Broad Economic Categories of the United Nations by transformation level, leads, not surprisingly, to an even greater level of similarity (see Appendix A5). Similarity peaks to 0.95 for the pair USA–Japan in 1995, and has very much increased between 1995 and 2004 for Chinese exports and Japanese or US exports. The share of intermediate, consumption or investment products in total exports is accordingly converging, which explains the increasing concerns of advanced economies' exporters, confronted with Chinese exporters in markets where they were not present a decade ago.

A similar calculation can be made at the most detailed level of the classification of the *products* (the 6-digit level of the Harmonized System), instead of using ISIC industries (second panel of Table 1). Certain bilateral relationships exhibit very similar patterns among industrialized countries, even at such a detailed level, as for instance between Germany and France (0.55). However, the similarity indexes are much lower between North and South exporters, indicating that countries at different levels of development are specialized on different products. Still sizeable similarity can be found between China and Japan (0.34) or China and the United States (0.34). With the exception of Italy, export structures of the European member states considered here are less similar with respect to the Chinese ones than the US or Japanese export structures.

Lastly, if we consider *varieties* of products, the similarities decrease again, especially for North–South pairs (third panel of Table 1). Industrialized countries are not competing with emerging countries (or with each other to a lesser extent) on the same varieties, thanks to a clear specialization across varieties within product categories. As Section 4 shows, when China and Northern countries export the same products, Chinese varieties are usually down-market, while Northern varieties are up-market. The similarity index between China and the US falls to 0.24, and to 0.18 vis-à-vis Japan. Here again the United Kingdom, Germany and France exhibit much less similarity with China than the US export structure does.

As a useful summary of common patterns in these data, consider the case of Germany and China. When *industries* are considered, the similarity between Chinese

Table 1. Similarity of export structures at various levels of detail of the classification (2004)

		Brazil	China	France	Germ.	Italy	Japan	Russia	India	UK	USA	Other emerging
Sector level (ISIC headings)	China	0.39	·									
	France	0.61	0.50	·								
	Germany	0.55	0.47	0.76	·							
	Italy	0.55	0.60	0.66	0.70	·						
	Japan	0.52	0.56	0.64	0.82	0.58	·					
	Russia	0.54	0.30	0.47	0.45	0.44	0.37	·				
	India	0.51	0.56	0.54	0.47	0.63	0.38	0.49	·			
	UK	0.62	0.49	0.86	0.82	0.66	0.73	0.51	0.53	·		
	USA	0.59	0.55	0.84	0.81	0.64	0.77	0.48	0.48	0.88	·	
	Oth. Em.	0.46	0.44	0.40	0.34	0.42	0.35	0.38	0.45	0.39	0.38	0.40
Product level (HS 6 headings)	China	0.21	·									
	France	0.32	0.30	·								
	Germany	0.34	0.30	0.55	·							
	Italy	0.29	0.35	0.48	0.51	·						
	Japan	0.29	0.34	0.41	0.56	0.36	·					
	Russia	0.31	0.16	0.24	0.24	0.21	0.20	·				
	India	0.26	0.30	0.29	0.27	0.35	0.23	0.21	·			
	UK	0.29	0.30	0.55	0.57	0.43	0.44	0.25	0.27	·		
	USA	0.33	0.34	0.56	0.59	0.45	0.53	0.26	0.27	0.59	·	
	Oth. Em.	0.18	0.23	0.18	0.17	0.19	0.17	0.14	0.20	0.18	0.19	0.18
Variety level (market segment)	China	0.17	·									
	France	0.24	0.17	·								
	Germany	0.24	0.17	0.50	·							
	Italy	0.22	0.19	0.42	0.43	·						
	Japan	0.22	0.18	0.36	0.43	0.29	·					
	Russia	0.26	0.12	0.18	0.17	0.16	0.15	·				
	India	0.23	0.23	0.24	0.20	0.24	0.16	0.23	·			
	UK	0.20	0.16	0.47	0.51	0.36	0.36	0.18	0.20	·		
	USA	0.25	0.24	0.45	0.46	0.35	0.40	0.21	0.21	0.46	·	
	Other emerging	0.15	0.16	0.13	0.12	0.14	0.13	0.12	0.19	0.13	0.15	0.14

Note: Similarity between country A (column) and B (row) is one minus half the sum of the absolute value of differences between the (e.g.) sectoral shares in manufacturing exports of country A and those of country B. It ranges between 0 (perfect dissimilarity) and 1 (perfect similarity). The 'other emerging' group are defined as the emerging economies less Russia, India, China and Brazil. Any classification of countries is arbitrary. We stick here to CEPII's definition of emerging economies, based on the statistical criterion reproduced in Appendix A4. Note that new member states of the EU-25 are not considered as emerging economies.

Source: BACI-CEPII, and authors' calculations.

and German exports is high (similarity 0.47). When *products* within industries are considered, this similarity is much lower (similarity 0.30). When *varieties* of these products exported at different unit values are considered, the similarity is once again reduced (similarity 0.17).

Beyond this snapshot, one should ask how this similarity has been changing at the most detailed level over the last decade. Do we observe an increasing similarity in exports?

2.2. Similarity between North and South is hardly increasing at the detailed level

The answer to the previous question depends of the aggregation level. At the broad product categories level, the similarity is increasing between North and South. Table 2 shows how the similarity between export structures of selected developed and emerging economies has been changing recently. The largest increase in absolute terms over 1995–2004 in the similarity of exported products is between China and Japan. The similarity between China and the European member states considered here increased greatly too, and Germany, France or the UK have been the most affected. This evolution is slightly smoother in the US case. A similar evolution is observed between Italy or Japan and Brazil. Switching to the similarity of varieties exported, the evolution is more limited, except for India. The similarity between China and

Table 2. Absolute change in similarity of export structures at the broad product categories and variety level (1995 to 2004)

		Brazil	China	France	Germ.	Italy	Japan	Russia	India	UK	USA	Oth. Em.
Broad product	China	15	.									
categories	France	8	21	.								
	Germany	7	20	−1	.							
	Italy	12	12	1	3	.						
	Japan	10	22	1	2	5	.					
	Russia	−6	9	2	3	7	4	.				
	India	7	1	2	0	2	5	4	.			
	UK	10	20	−1	−6	7	−4	4	8	.		
	USA	7	17	−4	−4	1	−1	6	4	−7	.	
	Oth. Em.	5	−5	4	4	3	7	6	−3	8	5	−2
Variety level	China	2	.									
(market segment)	France	3	4	.								
	Germany	4	5	4	.							
	Italy	−1	4	2	4	.						
	Japan	3	7	3	3	2	.					
	Russia	6	1	9	8	8	8	.				
	India	5	−2	9	6	5	3	12	.			
	UK	1	3	5	6	1	5	7	5	.		
	USA	1	5	4	7	2	1	8	5	1	.	
	Oth. Em.	2	−1	2	3	2	3	4	3	3	2	1

Source: BACI-CEPII, and authors' calculations.

Japan has increased three times less than for broad products categories, for instance. Accordingly, the observed evolutions confirm that recent competitive pressures have been much more limited at the variety level.

We now need to go beyond such simple observations and consider in detail how the competitive pressures at stake have led to a redistribution of market share. The next section points to resilience of EU market shares in the upper segment of the world market.

3. EU TRADE EXHIBITS RESILIENCE IN THE UPPER SEGMENT

All developed countries have not been affected similarly by the emergence of new competitors. Despite their specialization in different varieties, the US economy as well as the Japanese one have been losing ground in all segments of the world market. For Japan, the market share loss is even larger in the upper segment of the market than in the lower one. In contrast, the market share of the EU-25 is resilient in the upper segment of the market, where high-priced varieties of consumer goods even slightly improved their positions on the world market.

This general European pattern is the result of an internal specialization of the EU in the production of up-market varieties, detrimental to France and Germany, and beneficial to new member states as well as the UK, Ireland and Italy. The latter result does not imply that Germany has been losing ground in up-market products, but that its gains in market shares have been less important in this segment of the market than in the middle or lower ones.

3.1. Recent shifts in market shares are concentrated in the low segment of the market

The market positioning of exporters and the recent shift in world market shares confirm the diagnosis of tough competition in the lower segment of the market. Let us once again split the world distribution of unit values of trade flows of a given product into three equal market segments (low, medium, high).

World market shares by transformation level and market segment are reported in Table 3. In the lower segment of the world market, the share of EU exporters was limited to 15.3% in 2004. This is to be compared with a 30.6% world market share in the upper segment. A similar pattern is observed for Japan: 14.6% in the upper segment and 7.5% in the lower segment. Such positioning was much less striking for the US economy: 14.4% in the upper segment and 11.9% in the lower market segment. In contrast, China had an impressive market share in the lower segment (20.1% of the world market), but five times less than that in the upper segment. Such differences in market positioning are more apparent for consumer goods, which have the potential to be highly differentiated, where the EU market share in the upper segment peaks to 38.8%, against 5.8% for China.

Table 3. World market shares by transformation level and market segment (intra-EU exports *excluded*, 2004, %)

Market segment	Exporter	Intermediate goods	Consumer goods	Investment goods	All
Lower	EU-25	14.7	13.6	18.4	15.3
	USA	14.4	7.4	11.5	11.9
	Japan	8.1	4.6	9.4	7.5
	Other developed	19.0	19.7	17.8	18.9
	China	14.9	25.0	25.7	20.1
	Brazil	2.1	1.9	1.4	1.9
	Russia	2.1	0.7	0.8	1.4
	India	2.7	3.0	0.3	2.2
	Other emerging	15.0	16.8	11.3	14.6
	Rest of the world	7.1	7.3	3.5	6.2
	All	100	100	100	100
Upper	EU-25	28.7	38.8	26.1	30.6
	USA	14.6	9.9	18.5	14.4
	Japan	15.8	9.9	16.8	14.6
	Other developed	22.3	13.3	20.3	19.5
	China	2.6	5.8	5.6	4.1
	Brazil	0.7	1.0	0.6	0.7
	Russia	1.1	0.3	0.3	0.7
	India	0.8	1.1	0.6	0.8
	Other emerging	9.9	14.3	9.4	10.9
	Rest of the world	3.7	5.7	2.0	3.8
	All	100	100	100	100

Source: BACI, and authors' calculations.

The redistribution of market shares by market segment and transformation level observed over the last decade confirms that European producers have better resisted new competitive pressures in the upper segment, essentially thanks to consumer goods. The EU has lost 2.75 percentage points of world market share in the lower segment, but has *gained* 0.24 percentage points in the upper segment. Japan and the US have lost ground on both market segments, while Chinese gains have been more concentrated in the lower segment (10.98 percentage points, Table 4).

3.2. Competition in high tech sectors

The technological sector, once seen as a safe haven for developed countries, seems to be increasingly contested by emerging countries. Using the by now standard view of international trade, whereby countries compete in terms of technological leadership and extract rents, it is worth isolating hi-tech products in our data. This can be done at the product (rather than sector) level using the OECD-Eurostat classification. According to this classification, a product is either 'hi-tech' or 'standard' and all varieties of a 'hi-tech product', whatever the market segment they belong to, are 'hi-tech'. We focus on the 261 HS6 headings belonging to this list and ask what is the

Table 4. Changes in world market shares by transformation level and market segment (intra-EU exports *excluded*, 1995 to 2004, percentage points)

Market segment	Exporter	Intermediate goods	Consumer goods	Investment goods	All
Lower	EU-25	−3.55	−0.20	−4.34	−2.75
	USA	−3.99	−4.39	−4.35	−4.19
	Japan	−3.94	0.85	−4.62	−2.78
	Other developed	−4.20	−3.77	−6.77	−4.68
	China	9.94	5.83	18.83	10.98
	Brazil	0.18	0.81	0.26	0.34
	Russia	0.60	0.21	0.56	0.46
	India	1.48	0.60	−0.03	0.86
	Other emerging	1.54	−1.32	−1.38	0.05
	Rest of the world	1.96	1.38	1.86	1.70
	All	0	0	0	0

	Upper	Intermediate goods	Consumer goods	Investment goods	All
Upper	EU-25	−0.06	3.00	−1.65	0.24
	USA	−3.02	−0.90	−6.00	−3.19
	Japan	−4.53	−4.22	−5.92	−4.73
	Other developed	0.90	−4.41	0.78	−0.40
	China	1.71	1.99	4.89	2.52
	Brazil	−0.26	0.14	0.21	−0.04
	Russia	0.73	0.00	0.28	0.44
	India	0.29	0.40	0.43	0.35
	Other emerging	3.12	2.41	6.15	3.64
	Rest of the world	1.13	1.57	0.82	1.16
	All	0	0	0	0

Source: BACI, and authors' calculations.

market positioning of technological products exported by the North and the South and how market shares have changed over the last decade.

Table 5 sheds light on how market shares have changed for the upper and lower market segments, for standard versus high-tech products. China has dramatically increased its market share for hi-tech products in the last decade, but Chinese gains are concentrated in the lower segment of the market.

The better resilience of Europe to competition from emerging economies is no longer confirmed as we focus on hi-tech products: while Europe's market share has been improving for standard goods in the upper segment of the market (by 1.1 percentage points), it has shrunk in the same segment of the market for hi-tech products (by 3.1 percentage points).

It is important to investigate reasons why reactions to the emergence of new competition are so different across countries that are basically similar in terms of factor endowments, technological level and factor costs, such as the EU, the US and Japan.

Table 5. World market shares (intra-EU *excluded*) for standard and hi-tech manufactured goods, by market segment (1995 and 2004, %)

	Standard goods		HT goods	
	down-mkt	up-mkt	down-mkt	up-mkt
Exporter		1995		
EU-25	17.9	30.9	19.2	26.7
USA	15.5	15.7	20.4	28.9
Japan	9.5	19.8	15.8	16.2
Other developed	23.8	19.9	21.5	20.3
China	9.5	1.8	6.4	0.4
Brazil	1.7	0.9	0.6	0.2
Russia	1.0	0.3	0.3	0.0
India	1.4	0.5	0.5	0.2
Other emerging	14.7	7.4	13.5	5.9
Rest of the world	5.0	2.8	1.8	1.2
All	100	100	100	100
Exporter		2004		
EU-25	15.0	32.0	16.8	23.6
USA	11.2	13.4	15.7	19.4
Japan	7.2	14.4	8.9	15.3
Other developed	19.0	18.5	18.1	24.7
China	19.3	4.1	24.3	4.1
Brazil	2.2	0.8	0.5	0.5
Russia	1.6	0.7	0.7	0.5
India	2.4	0.9	0.8	0.2
Other emerging	15.0	11.0	12.3	10.2
Rest of the world	7.1	4.2	1.9	1.6
All	100	100	100	100

Note: See Table 1. High-tech goods are identified at the most detailed level by the Eurostat-OECD list.
Source: BACI-CEPII, and authors' calculations.

Let us briefly consider the usual suspects. The observation that countries running a large macroeconomic deficit (USA), or a large surplus (Japan), have similarly been losing ground in both segments of the market (down and up-market), suggests that widening trade imbalances may not be the explanation.

Regarding exchange rates, a period of appreciation of the dollar against the euro (up to 2001) has been followed by the opposite evolution, and the difference in bilateral exchange rates between 1995 and 2004 remains limited. In total, if we exclude intra-EU flows and thus get rid of the associated valuation effect, any observed impact of the exchange rate over the considered period should have led at most to a slightly better relative performance of the EU.[3] In any case the magnitude of such

[3] A 3% variation in the bilateral real exchange rate in favour of Europe's competitiveness has been observed over the period (euro Real Effective Exchange Rate, CPI deflated, vis-à-vis 44 groups of currencies, fixed definition of the euro area (euro-13), as published by the ECB). Guessing a price elasticity equal to 2, the gain in exported volumes should be 6% with a perfect pass through. Converted to US dollars, since the euro (actually compared with the ecu) has depreciated in nominal terms, this leads to 2% additional EU exports in value. Using an elasticity equal to 1, the evolution in value terms is reversed, with a 1% decrease.

effect is too limited to explain the divergence in relative performances of the two regions.

To better shed light on the observed resilience of the EU, we are now interested in checking how individual member states contribute to this European pattern, and if differences among member states have evolved over the last decade.

3.3. Member states contribute differently to the market positioning of the EU-25

The EU-25 is a very heterogeneous area with regards to the market positioning of member states. The common perception is that large and advanced member states, in particular Germany, are exporting mostly up-market products and thus contributing a large part to the observed market positioning of the EU. Such a statement must however be carefully checked, especially when it comes to the recent dynamics of specialization.

In Table 6 we consider the contribution of each member state to the EU-25 exports in 2004, by market segment and in total. The German contribution is the

Table 6. Contribution of individual EU-25 member states to EU exports (intra-EU excluded), by market segment (2004)

	Down	Middle	Up	Total
Austria	2.7	2.6	3.0	2.8
Belgium and Luxembourg	4.6	4.9	4.3	4.5
Cyprus	0.1	0.1	0.1	0.1
Czech Republic	1.3	1.0	0.7	0.9
Denmark	2.6	2.3	2.3	2.3
Estonia	0.2	0.1	0.1	0.1
Finland	2.4	2.8	2.1	2.4
France	12.6	13.3	11.6	12.3
Germany	24.9	29.7	31.2	29.2
Greece	0.7	0.5	0.3	0.5
Hungary	1.3	1.1	0.9	1.1
Ireland	2.4	1.8	6.3	4.1
Italy	14.3	11.9	10.9	12.0
Latvia	0.2	0.1	0.1	0.1
Lithuania	0.4	0.2	0.1	0.2
Malta	0.3	0.3	0.2	0.2
Netherlands	5.8	5.1	4.5	5.0
Poland	2.6	1.6	0.6	1.4
Portugal	0.7	0.7	0.7	0.7
Slovakia	0.5	0.5	0.4	0.5
Slovenia	0.8	0.5	0.3	0.5
Spain	5.3	4.6	3.0	4.0
Sweden	3.7	4.2	4.5	4.2
United Kingdom	9.8	10.3	12.1	11.0
All	100	100	100	100

Source: BACI-CEPII, authors' calculation.

largest overall, (29.2%), and is even larger in the upper segment of the market (31.2%). At the extreme opposite, Latvia is contributing only marginally (0.1%) and mostly for down-market varieties (0.2%). All in all, when we talk about EU exports of high-range varieties, we focus on Germany, France, the UK and Italy, which account for two thirds of the corresponding EU exports.

We must however get rid of the absolute size and the overall trade balance of each exporter, in order to better understand the evolutions at stake: the contribution of Italy is even larger for varieties located at the bottom of the market, and the German gains might be concentrated or not in the upper segment. To shed light on this, a specialization index will help.

3.4. Specialization of EU member states in the three market segments

We now calculate a simple specialization index by normalizing each market segment share by the average contribution of the country to EU exports (total contribution column in Table 6). Accordingly, the index of specialization for Germany in the up-market varieties will be 1.07 (31.2/29.2) in 2004. These specialization indexes are reported in Table 7 for 1995 and 2004 for each member state. The picture is more nuanced, however, since the most specialized European countries in the up-market segment are Ireland (1.54), the UK (1.10), Sweden (1.08) and Austria (1.07). The second interesting observation is the rapid reduction in the heterogeneity of specialization of the different member states with regards to their market positioning. The standard error reported in the last row of the table illustrates this point, as well as the upgrading of new member states varieties.

The Czech Republic, Poland, Hungary or Slovakia are all moving up the ladder. In contrast, and this is the last important information delivered, France and Germany have reduced their specialization in the upper segment over the last decade, while Italy and the UK were specializing in the opposite direction. All in all, while the European specialization in the upper segment of the market has a permanent pattern, we are facing an internal redistribution of up-market specialization where France and Germany on the one hand, new member states and Italy, Ireland and the UK on the other, move in opposite directions.

3.5. A closer look at US comparative advantages

Macroeconomic imbalances strongly impact US trade and might also affect US trade patterns at the detailed level considered here. In order to properly assess the comparative advantages of a country, the calculation of specialization indexes relates sectoral exports to total exports. We accordingly proceed here to the calculation of revealed comparative advantages (a Balassa index calculated by market segment on ISIC sectoral exports), at the market segment level. A glance at Germany and the United States illustrates the differences in the market positioning of the two countries. In

Table 7. Specialization index of individual EU-25 countries, by market segment (1995 and 2004, intra-EU trade excluded)

	1995			2004		
	Down	Middle	Up	Down	Middle	Up
Austria	0.84	0.96	1.13	0.97	0.91	1.07
Belgium and Luxembourg	0.97	1.09	0.96	1.01	1.09	0.94
Cyprus	1.75	1.00	0.50	1.67	0.83	0.83
Czech Republic	1.96	0.82	0.54	1.39	1.08	0.74
Denmark	1.01	0.92	1.06	1.10	0.97	0.97
Estonia	2.38	0.88	0.38	1.58	1.00	0.58
Finland	1.05	1.13	0.87	1.02	1.18	0.89
France	0.90	1.00	1.06	1.02	1.08	0.94
Germany	0.75	0.99	1.17	0.85	1.02	1.07
Greece	1.60	1.00	0.60	1.44	1.13	0.69
Hungary	2.00	0.80	0.53	1.24	1.04	0.84
Ireland	1.11	0.65	1.18	0.60	0.44	1.54
Italy	1.35	0.92	0.83	1.19	0.99	0.90
Latvia	2.30	0.90	0.30	1.70	1.00	0.70
Lithuania	2.18	0.82	0.35	2.00	1.05	0.47
Malta	0.78	0.44	1.56	1.29	1.08	0.83
Netherlands	0.97	1.13	0.92	1.16	1.02	0.90
Poland	2.15	0.93	0.32	1.88	1.15	0.44
Portugal	1.03	1.03	0.97	1.03	1.06	0.96
Slovakia	2.13	0.96	0.26	1.02	1.18	0.89
Slovenia	1.60	1.09	0.57	1.63	1.06	0.61
Spain	1.32	1.09	0.73	1.33	1.15	0.74
Sweden	0.75	1.03	1.13	0.87	0.99	1.08
United Kingdom	1.07	1.04	0.93	0.89	0.94	1.10
Standard Error	0.56	0.16	0.35	0.35	0.15	0.23

Note: Ratio of contribution by market segment and in total (Balassa index taking EU-25 as a reference). Includes intra-EU exports. Market segments are defined with the exclusion of internal EU prices.

Source: BACI-CEPII, and authors' calculations.

Table 8, seven of the ten main German revealed comparative advantages are in the up-market segments and three in the middle one. Germany's specialization in the upper segment is particularly apparent for transport equipment. In contrast, out of the 10 main revealed comparative advantages of the United States, three are in the up-market segments, three in the middle market segment, and four in the lower one.

In order to systematize these observations and better understand the specialization of countries across varieties within products and their determinants, a careful examination of the dynamics of relative prices of exported varieties is done in the next section.

4. PERMANENT DIFFERENCES IN PRICES AND THE NORTH–SOUTH SPECIALIZATION ACROSS *VARIETIES*

We start by calculating ratios of unit values by pair of countries, destination market and product, in order to assess to what extent varieties of products jointly exported

Table 8. Main specialization sectors by market segment, 2004, United States and Germany (intra-EU trade _excluded_)

United States	Market segment	RCA	Germany	Market segment	RCA
Printing and publishing	2	2.34	Transport equipment	3	3.47
Plastic products	2	2.20	Printing and publishing	2	2.02
Tobacco	2	2.02	Rubber products	3	1.93
Printing and publishing	3	1.80	Fabricated metal products	3	1.89
Tobacco	1	1.61	Other chemicals	2	1.83
Paper and products	1	1.55	Pottery china earthenware	3	1.80
Professional and scientific equipment	1	1.53	Machinery except electrical	3	1.80
Tobacco	3	1.52	Professional and scientific equipment	3	1.79
Professional and scientific equipment	3	1.49	Plastic products	3	1.73
Printing and publishing	1	1.45	Professional and scientific equipment	2	1.64

Note: The Revealed Comparative Advantage (RCA) is calculated annually (t), on ISIC sectoral (k) exports of country i, by market segment g: low (1), middle (2) or upper (3). The index is computed as

$$RCA_{i,k,g}^{t} = \frac{X_{i,k,g}^{t}}{\sum_{k,g} X_{i,k,g}^{t}} \cdot \frac{\sum_{i\,k,g} X_{i,k,g}^{t}}{\sum_{i} X_{i,k,g}^{t}} \quad (1)$$

Source: BACI-CEPII, and authors' calculations.

by the two countries in the pair are dissimilar. We take advantage of the time coverage of our sample to compare the results for 1995 and 2004, and thus to check whether a convergence of relative unit values between North and South is taking place.

In a second stage, we examine the relationship between market positioning, as defined by the unit value of exported varieties of each product, and the level of development of trading countries.

4.1. Relative prices between North and South are stable

The North and the South may indeed export the same bundle of products, in contrast to the standard view of international trade, but they will specialize in different varieties shipped at different unit values. A key issue is whether such differences in unit values of varieties exported by the North and the South are only transitory, reflecting delays in market adjustments, or sustainable patterns in the international division of labor.

In order to do this, we rely on our exhaustive set of exporters and importers and ask what the overall evidence is at the world level. We accordingly calculate bilateral _unit-value ratios_ for varieties exported by the North and the South on each destination market at the HS6 level of the nomenclature of traded products.

Table 9. Relative unit values at the product level, 1995

	EU-25	Germany	France	UK	Italy	USA	Japan	China	Brazil	Russia	India
EU-25	.	.	.	.	.	0.90	1.04	0.39	0.76	0.81	0.51
Germany	.	.	0.98	0.84	0.72	0.79	0.87	0.27	0.62	0.75	0.38
France	.	1.02	.	0.88	0.73	0.86	0.95	0.25	0.68	0.57	0.36
UK	.	1.19	1.14	.	0.85	0.87	0.98	0.30	0.70	0.91	0.44
Italy	.	1.39	1.38	1.17	.	1.00	1.43	0.29	0.73	0.64	0.47
USA	1.12	1.27	1.16	1.15	1.00	.	1.11	0.43	0.93	0.85	0.65
Japan	0.96	1.15	1.05	1.02	0.70	0.90	.	0.31	0.76	0.62	0.44
China	2.59	3.74	4.06	3.39	3.46	2.34	3.25	.	1.38	1.00	1.14
Brazil	1.31	1.62	1.48	1.42	1.36	1.07	1.32	0.73	.	0.97	0.89
Russia	1.23	1.34	1.75	1.09	1.57	1.17	1.62	1.00	1.03	.	1.05
India	1.95	2.66	2.75	2.27	2.14	1.54	2.25	0.88	1.13	0.95	.

Note: A weighted geometric median of relative unit values of country A (in column) and B (in row) across common HS6 positions and geographical destinations of exports (weights are the simple averages of the shares of the export flow in the total exports of A and B) is calculated here. The ratio of export unit-value for a country pair (A,B) is the weighted median of $UV_{A,j}^k / UV_{B,j}^k$ where j is the direction of export. The weighting variable is $w = 0.5 \left(V_{A,j}^{hs6} / V_A + V_{B,j}^{hs6} / V_B \right)$ where V_A and V_B are the total exports of A and B. These ratios are computed for each year. Intra-EU trade flows are excluded.

Source: BACI, and authors' calculations.

Following our research approach, we *exclude* intra-EU trade flows from the calculation of relative unit values. (Results including intra-EU trade flows are provided in Appendix A5, available on the journal's website.) These computations can shed light on the phenomena of interest by answering such questions as 'how did the relative unit value of liquid dielectric transformers in a certain category of power handling capacity, shipped to the same destination market by the US and by China, vary over the last decade?' Lastly, we aggregate such information, for each pair of countries, in order to examine the evolution of the price gap between pairs of developed and emerging countries.

The results are given in Table 9 for 1995. The median of the distribution of Brazilian prices relative to Chinese prices is 1.38, meaning that Brazilian prices were 38% higher than Chinese ones in 1995. Reciprocally, the median of the distribution of Chinese prices relative to Brazilian prices is 0.73 (=1/1.38), meaning that Chinese prices were three quarters of Brazilian prices in 1995. Generally speaking, in 1995 Brazil did not exhibit prices so different from those of advanced economies (93% of US prices, 76% of Japanese prices, 62% of German prices). Accordingly, Brazil might well be specialized in certain products, in a traditional way, rather than in varieties within products.

The opposite is true for China. With prices in 1995 representing 27% of German prices, 31% of Japanese prices, 43% of US prices, or even 88% of Indian prices, for the same products, China was clearly specialized on the lower segment of the market for the bulk of its exported varieties. India was exhibiting the same type of specialization, however it was less pronounced: 38% of German prices, 44% of Japanese prices, or 65% of US prices.

Table 10. Relative unit values at the product level, 2004

	EU-25	Germany	France	UK	Italy	USA	Japan	China	Brazil	Russia	India
EU-25	.	.	.	.	.	0.98	1.00	0.40	0.75	0.77	0.61
Germany	.	.	1.01	0.98	0.89	0.94	0.87	0.33	0.62	0.72	0.60
France	.	0.99	.	1.00	0.84	0.95	0.96	0.27	0.69	0.69	0.41
UK	.	1.02	1.00	.	0.84	0.86	0.86	0.28	0.61	0.74	0.32
Italy	.	1.13	1.19	1.20	.	1.00	1.14	0.35	0.70	0.72	0.57
USA	1.02	1.06	1.05	1.16	1.00	.	1.00	0.41	0.87	0.81	0.64
Japan	1.00	1.15	1.04	1.16	0.88	1.00	.	0.35	0.70	0.76	0.55
China	2.51	3.06	3.67	3.53	2.83	2.44	2.89	.	1.20	1.17	1.27
Brazil	1.34	1.62	1.45	1.65	1.42	1.15	1.43	0.84	.	0.99	1.00
Russia	1.30	1.39	1.45	1.35	1.39	1.23	1.32	0.85	1.01	.	1.16
India	1.65	1.67	2.44	3.13	1.77	1.55	1.80	0.79	1.00	0.86	.

Note: See Table 9 for definitions.

Source: BACI, and authors' calculations.

More interestingly, the Chinese market positioning has not changed dramatically within a decade, even if we record a slight increase in its relative prices (Table 10). Over the period considered, Chinese relative prices have gained 4 percentage points vis-à-vis Japan and 6 percentage points vis-à-vis Germany. In contrast, Chinese relative prices have lost 2 percentage points vis-à-vis the US, and are up 9 percentage points vis-à-vis India and 15 vis-à-vis Russia. Accordingly, the outcome of a specialization on varieties within products is a rather stable pattern.

Export prices of varieties of individual products have hardly converged over the last decade, for instance between China and the EU: observed relative unit values have only slightly decreased from 2.59 to 2.51 over a decade, meaning that on average EU exported varieties are steadily 2.5 times more expensive than Chinese varieties *of the same products.*

Were the products homogenous, such difference in prices should have led within a decade to a profound redistribution of market shares, which has not been observed. European exporters are still in the market, despite their high prices, meaning that varieties are considerably (vertically) differentiated.

At first sight, these findings point to a strong rejection of the Law of One Price (LOP). Notice that, in contrast to the literature on departures from the LOP that focuses on prices of narrowly defined goods sold in different locations (e.g. cities in the Economist Intelligence Unit's Worldwide Cost of Living Survey, as in Crucini and Shintani, 2006), our relative unit values bilateral indexes do proxy prices for the same six-digit headings shipped to the *same* locations. Accordingly the LOP is more likely to show up in our case. However, as in other studies of this kind of evidence, the observed price gaps are arguably too large and too persistent to be explained by price differences across very similar goods. They are more likely evidence of the existence of several varieties of the same good, which may be poorly substitutable to each other. Controlling properly for the elements associated to differentiation (brand, design, associated services, etc.) could provide us with evidence of some form of the LOP. Prices cleaned from vertical differentiation would be needed to better assess convergence properties; but the hedonic price methods necessary for this require microeconomic data that are not available, except for very specific sectors (e.g. passenger cars).

4.2. Determinants of the market positioning of varieties

How have such differences in relative prices of varieties among exporters been sustainable during a decade without profound swings in market shares among exporters?

The impact of the level of development of the exporter (here, proxied by its Purchasing Power Parity GDP per capita) on the price of the varieties exported very much depends of the product considered. Whether the product is differentiated or not and the extent to which vertical differentiation is possible, will certainly impact on this relationship. Where varieties are highly differentiated, the upper market segment will correspond to production functions intensive in R&D, skills and organization, and this is where advanced economies will be advantaged. Lastly, when one considers a large market such as the EU, imports of different varieties of each individual group of products (HS6 heading) may reflect matching of foreign countries' individual endowments and production function prerequisites. This is why we must rely on estimates made at the product level, rather than within large industries.

In order to tentatively answer this question, we extend the empirical analysis on US imports by Schott (2004), by using a world sample (see Table 11). Schott regresses unit-values of American imports on proxies of exporter's level of development or factor intensities. We replicate the exercise for the US imports and two other comparable

Table 11. Impact of the level of development on the unit value of products imported by different groups of countries (pooled data)

	World	USA	EU-25	Japan
Intercept	0.004	−0.001	0.002	0.000
	(0.000)	(0.002)	(0.000)	(0.002)
Log GDP per capita exporter	0.356	0.389	0.353	0.340
	(0.000)	(0.002)	(0.001)	(0.002)
Log GDP per capita importer	0.156	–	–	–
	(0.000)	–	–	–
Log dist	0.097	0.182	0.140	0.349
	(0.000)	(0.004)	(0.000)	(0.003)
N	25 158 156	652 964	8 355 338	422 384
R²	0.0611	0.0524	0.047	0.1046
F	545 952	18 062.5	206 252	24 665.8

Note: The following equation is estimated for a sample in which products are sourced simultaneously and significantly in the North and the South and taking into account product * year fixed effects. In the last three columns, the estimated equation is ln $UV_{i,hs6,t} = C_{hs6,t} + \beta \ln GDPPC_{i,t}$, with i the exporter, HS6 the product and t the year.

Source: BACI, and authors' calculations.

importers, the EU and the Japan. Distance is added in the equation in order to account for the Alchian-Allen conjecture. Lastly, we perform the same calculation using a world sample, which introduces importers' income level. Estimations are done at the product level, over 10 years, and we examine the distribution of the estimated elasticity across products, by market. GDP data are taken from the World Bank's WDI database for 2006. Distances are provided by CEPII.

In order to better shed light on the actual patterns of North–South competition, we select the products that are sourced simultaneously and significantly in the North and the South. In order to do so, we take the first quartile of the distribution of market shares of OECD and emerging exporters (referred to as North and South respectively) in each developed market (across all products) as thresholds. We will retain only the 6-digit products for which the market share of the South and the North is larger than the respective thresholds. We exclude intra-EU exports, but the trade flows are considered for member states on an individual basis, since there is no obviously neutral way of aggregating their unit values.

As shown in Table 11, the price of the imported varieties is positively related to the development level of the exporter.[4] This is true for the three large importing markets and we do not notice any specificity of Europe here. However, a potential heterogeneity among member states is to be considered. We accordingly performed the estimation on a (EU) country-by-country basis and found that EU member states are quite heterogeneous as concerns unit-value elasticity to GDP per capita. The median of estimated coefficients ranges from 0.34 (Ireland) to 0.48 (Portugal).

Distance is proved to a have a positive impact on the unit value of the varieties shipped: this confirms the conjecture of the good apples shipped. This result is particularly pronounced for Japan. This might be the result of its peculiar geographical position: Japan trades with poorer Asian neighbours as well as exporting high unit-value varieties to the US or Europe.

Another approach authorized by our exhaustive sampling is to estimate the relationship considered in Table 11 for the whole set of exporters' unit values. We obtain a comparable parameter estimate on the GDP per capita of the exporter (0.35), a positive estimate on the GDP per capita of the importer, and a positive impact of the distance on the unit value of traded products.

In order to confirm this first set of results obtained by pooling data across products for each importer, we estimate one equation by product for each importer and consider the distribution of the estimated elasticity (see Appendix A6). We have more than 5000 products in total within the HS6 classification, but fewer when the sample is restricted to manufacturing (4528) and even fewer when it is restricted to products exported by both the North and the South (3252). We have a window of ten years leading to (e.g. for EU member states considered individually) 420 369 equations

---

[4] We also included in another specification (not reported) a non-linear term on the GDP per capita of the exporter, which proved to be significant and positive but left other results unaffected.

giving the same number of estimated elasticity. For the EU, the median elasticity is 0.36, meaning that a 10% increase in the GDP per capita of the exporter to the EU will translate into a 4% increase in the price of its exported products, for a given product. This distribution validates our explanation despite the inter-product categories and inter-member state countries variance of the estimated coefficient.

These results confirm the remarkable robustness of the underlying relationship: with economic development, as skills, capital intensity, R&D capacity and organizational capacities increase, countries climb the ladder of vertical differentiation between varieties of exported products.

5. SUPPLY AND DEMAND DETERMINANTS OF TRADE IN VARIETIES

Regularities observed in terms of market positioning of traded products are not determined only by the characteristics of the exporting country. Demand-side explanations of such empirical evidence must also be considered: rich countries spend a larger share of their income on top quality products and import products of higher quality (see Box 3). The facts are consistent with this. Table 12 presents the results of a bilateral calculation, indicating how much each exporter is selling in the upper tier segment on each destination market.

On the demand side, we observe a clear difference in the market positioning of the various exporters on their different destination markets, stressing that importers at different levels of development do consume a different bundle of varieties. In 2004, 72.9% of European exports to Japan were up-market varieties, compared with only 46.5% to China.

Table 12. Share of up-market products in manufactured exports, by destination market (2004, %)

Importer	EU-25	USA	Japan	Oth. dev	China	Brazil	Russia	India	Oth. Em.	RoW	Total
Exporter											
EU-25	41.1	60.3	72.9	50.6	46.5	34.0	21.8	49.1	36.0	37.6	43.2
USA	54.5	.	64.4	32.3	40.0	26.0	23.9	50.3	15.4	30.3	36.9
Japan	54.5	43.2	.	46.4	42.1	33.4	5.8	48.6	32.7	18.8	43.0
Oth. dev	46.5	24.4	41.2	34.0	27.1	28.4	16.1	32.2	22.4	27.7	32.1
China	16.6	4.9	20.7	7.2	.	24.4	2.8	20.9	11.6	8.1	11.6
Brazil	22.8	15.5	37.8	16.4	9.1	.	2.2	14.2	10.5	13.7	15.9
Russia	15.6	22.2	23.2	13.0	13.3	31.5	.	42.8	8.9	14.4	16.0
India	22.0	15.1	19.3	16.9	15.6	17.6	9.3	.	17.0	16.7	17.8
Oth. Em.	36.4	19.3	36.9	26.5	25.1	30.1	9.9	25.8	20.4	18.4	25.8
RoW	32.0	19.0	34.7	18.6	6.6	32.4	9.0	28.1	16.5	19.1	22.9
Total	40.5	31.4	43.9	34.0	34.4	30.0	16.7	36.2	23.3	27.9	35.1

Note: The sample covers manufacturing HS6 goods including the food industry.

Source: BACI-CEPII, and authors' calculations.

Box 3. Supply and demand of quality and the specialization across varieties within products

On the supply side, possible explanations of the positive relationship between unit values of exports and exporters' income per capita identified by Schott (2004) in the US case, would be the exploitation of the productivity advantage to specialize in top-range varieties (Melitz, 2000); or, more generally, an old-fashion theoretical framework, where advantage is based on a combination of factor endowments and technological advance (e.g. Falvey and Kierzkowski, 1987).

On the demand side, rich countries trade more with each other, after controlling for inter-sectoral determinants of trade (Hallak, 2006a and 2006b), in line with the Linder hypothesis (Linder, 1961). Flam and Helpman (1987) proposed a framework in which varieties of different qualities were produced at a cost reflected in higher prices for higher qualities. Marginal income is spent by the consumers on quality rather than on quantity. This model, extended by Choi *et al.* (2006) to a multi-product, multi-country framework, allows for high-income countries buying high unit value varieties. However, even when countries have access to the same technology, the quality positioning of their specialization will be determined by domestic conditions: the larger or the more sophisticated the domestic market, the higher the quality of products supplied to the local consumer (Motta *et al.*, 1997).

These facts call for systematic analysis of supply and demand determinants of the market positioning of trade varieties, considering the direction of trade flows. On the supply side, rich countries should be advantaged in exporting up-market products. On the demand side, rich countries should purchase and import more up-market products, and the opposite should be observed for developing economies.

5.1. A gravity equation accounting for the market positioning of varieties

The basic framework of analysis in this section is the workhorse of the empirical analysis in international trade, namely an augmented gravity equation.

The dependent variable is the value of bilateral exports from country i to country j at year t into market segment g. The market segment in which an industry exports is observed at the HS6 level, according to the methodology referred to above. We estimate this relationship both for total exports, by summing over all manufacturing products but keeping the market segment dimension, and at the sector level. Among the three market segments, only two are considered in samples used in regressions: up-market and down-market.

Regarding explanatory variables, the GDPs of exporter and importer are introduced in the equation explaining the total bilateral value of exports in each of the two market segments. When estimating the equation at the sector level, we use available information on sectoral output of the exporter and sectoral demand of the importer, from the new version of the 'Trade and Production' database compiled by the World Bank and completed by the CEPII.[5] Other unobservable patterns of manufacturing industries, that are common to all exporters and importers, are controlled for by using sector fixed effects.

Regarding distance, we use a harmonic average, taking into account internal distances (see Box 4). Distances are measured using city-level data to assess the geographic distribution of population (in 2004) inside each nation.[6] Bilateral distance may have two different effects. Firstly, as a proxy for transport costs, distance increases the relative price of the lower-market segment for the consumer. This should increase the share of the upper-market segment in imports. Secondly, distance is a proxy for the lack of information on products and may reduce the consumption of expensive varieties. Which of the two is the dominant effect is a matter for empirical analysis. Since cultural proximity may play an important role in the demand for up-market products differentiated by brands or other intangible attributes, we introduce a dummy for common language. We also tentatively introduce past colonial links but the results are not reproduced here. The latter are very similar and we preferred a more parsimonious specification: the only affected parameters with the introduction of colonial links are those obtained to common language. Bilateral distances and common language are from the CEPII geographical database.[7]

Besides these standard gravity variables, the GDP per capita of the exporter (supply side determinant) as well as for the importer (respectively demand side) previously used are introduced in order to account for the determinants of specialization.

Interaction variables are finally introduced. We consider the market segment each elementary bilateral trade flow (an HS product exported by country i to market j at year t) belongs to, either the lower or the upper market segment. The corresponding dummy variables are interacted with distance (does one ship the good apples?), with common language (is the upper segment of the market more sensitive to cultural proximity?) and with GDP per capita (what is the role of supply and demand related determinants?).

Results are summarized in Table 13. The first two columns are dedicated to the equation estimated on total bilateral trade flows by market segment. The remaining columns give the results of the estimations done with the panel of sectors. In all regressions, we introduce time fixed effects in order to control for annual changes in the value of world trade (the period is 1995–2004). For estimations at the sectoral level we use the ISIC classification, in which there are 25 manufacturing sectors, which are introduced as fixed effects.[8]

---

[5] Data available at http://www.cepii.fr/anglaisgraph/bdd/tradeprod.htm.

[6] The distance variable taking into account internal distances makes it unnecessary to introduce a control for contiguity.

[7] Data available at http://www.cepii.fr/anglaisgraph/bdd/distances.htm.

[8] In each manufacturing sector the classification of exports in each market segment is made at the product level before summing the values attributed to each segment in each sector.

Box 4. Computation of distances

The idea is to calculate the distance between two countries based on bilateral distances between the biggest cities of those two countries, those inter-city distances being weighted by the share of the city in the overall country's population. This procedure can be used in a totally consistent way for both domestic and international distances. The distance is based on data from the *World Gazetteer* website, which provides current population figures and geographic coordinates for cities, towns and places of all countries. The calculation is based on the general formula developed by Head and Mayer (2002),

$$d_{ij} = \left(\sum_{k \in i} (pop_k / pop_i) \sum_{\ell \in j} (pop_\ell / pop_j) d_{k\ell}^{\sigma} \right)^{1/\sigma} \tag{2}$$

where pop_k (pop_l) denotes the population of agglomeration k (agglomeration l) belonging to country i (country j). σ measures the sensitivity of trade flows to bilateral distance d_{kl} and is set to -1, which corresponds to the usual coefficient estimated from gravity models of bilateral trade flows.

We firstly run OLS regressions of bilateral trade flows, weighted by the log of their value. Working with a very large and heterogeneous dataset, we avoid giving the same importance to tiny trade flows, more likely to be measured erroneously, and very large trade flows between major countries. All variables are in logarithm. The standard gravity equation however includes prices or country fixed effects aimed at controlling for prices. We accordingly include country fixed effects (for exporters and importers) in the second column of Table 13.

A last concern is with zero flows, which cannot simply be ignored since they carry information. If zeros are due to censoring, the estimators are biased, and this is an important concern at the sector level, where zero values are more frequent. A Poisson Maximum Likelihood method can be suitable under such circumstances (see Santos Silva and Tenreyro, 2006). Note that the explained variable is then the value and not the log value of bilateral exports. The Vuong test discriminates between standard Poisson Pseudo-Maximum Likelihood estimates and Zero Inflated Poisson Estimates (large negative values of the test statistic favour the Poisson, while large positive values favour the ZIP). Based on this test we perform estimations of the latter kind at the sectoral level, in order to check the robustness of our results. In a first step, a probit explains the presence of zero values, while in a second step, the parameters of interest are estimated accordingly.

Table 13. Explaining bilateral exports in a panel of 163 countries and 10 years

Model:	Bilateral trade		Sectoral trade		
	OLS, log (1)	OLS, log (2)	OLS, log (3)	OLS, log (4)	ZIP, level (5)
Intercept	-31.08^a	-14.39^a	-13.91^a	-9.37^a	4.07^a
	(0.31)	(1.64)	(0.37)	(0.83)	(0.05)
Low prices	6.34^a	6.45^a	10.60^a	3.70^a	13.80^a
	(0.17)	(0.17)	(0.24)	(0.12)	(0.00)
Distance * low	-1.08^a	-1.37^a	-0.89^a	-1.22^a	-0.93^a
	(0.02)	(0.02)	(0.02)	(0.02)	(0.00)
Distance * high	-1.03^a	-1.31^a	-0.77^a	-1.19^a	-0.72^a
	(0.01)	(0.02)	(0.02)	(0.02)	(0.04)
Language * low	0.79^a	0.71^a	0.87^a	0.61^a	0.33^a
	(0.04)	(0.04)	(0.06)	(0.05)	(0.00)
Language * high	0.97^a	0.87^a	0.96^a	0.69^a	0.07^a
	(0.04)	(0.04)	(0.05)	(0.05)	(0.00)
Exporter GDP	0.95^a	0.01			
	(0.01)	(0.02)			
Importer GDP	0.74^a	0.59^a			
	(0.01)	(0.02)			
Exp. sectoral production			0.73^a	0.75^a	0.89^a
			(0.01)	(0.01)	(0.00)
Imp. sectoral demand			0.60^a	0.27^a	0.34^a
			(0.01)	(0.01)	(0.00)
Exp. GDP PC * low	0.09^a	0.65^a	-0.20	-0.36^a	-0.41^a
	(0.02)	(0.06)	(0.02)	(0.08)	(0.00)
Exp. GDP PC * high	0.43^a	0.99^a	0.49^a	-0.12	0.42^a
	(0.02)	(0.06)	(0.02)	(0.08)	(0.12)
Imp. GDP PC * low	-0.03^b	0.40^a	-0.05^b	0.58^a	0.83^a
	(0.01)	(0.06)	(0.02)	(0.08)	(0.00)
Imp. GDP PC * high	0.24^a	0.68^a	0.26^a	0.69^a	1.25^a
	(0.01)	(0.06)	(0.02)	(0.08)	(0.00)
N	218 981	218 981	890 174	890 174	1 730 322
R^2	0.702	0.793	0.595	0.706	–
RMSE	1.575	1.313	1.707	1.454	–
Country fixed effects	–	yes	–	yes	yes
Sector fixed effects	–	–	yes	yes	yes
Time effects	yes	yes	yes	yes	yes
Vuong test	–	–	–	–	478.30

Note: The estimated equation at the sectoral (ISIC) level is (for column 2):

$$\ln X^t_{ij,k,g} = \alpha + \beta_1 \ln GDP^t_j + \beta_2 \ln GDP^t_j + \beta_3 g_1 \ln GDPPC^t_i + \beta_4 g_3 \ln GDPPC^t_i + \beta_5 g_1 \ln GDPPC^t_j$$
$$+ \beta_6 g_3 \ln GDPPC^t_j + \delta g_1 Z_{ij} + x g_3 Z_{ij} + u_k + u_i + u_j + u_g + u^t + \varepsilon^t_{ij,k} \tag{3}$$

where g indicates the market segment (g_1: low; g_3: high) in which exports of HS6 products take place in ISIC industry k ($k = 1, \ldots, 25$), Z is a vector of bilateral resistance terms (distance and language) between exporter i and importer j. For the Zero Inflated Poisson regression in column (5) we use the value of exports instead of the log value as dependent variable.

Standard errors in parentheses take into account the correlation of the error terms for a given dyad of countries. Superscripts a, b and c denote statistical significance at the 1%, 5% and 10% levels, respectively.

Source: BACI, and authors' calculations.

We report in column (1) results for the whole sample without sectoral dimension (218 981 observations) and excluding country fixed effects. In column (2) country fixed effects are introduced: the meaning of the GDP variables accordingly change, since only the time dimension of the latter variables is then taken into account.

Columns (3) and (4) report the results for the estimations at the sectoral level (ISIC sectors), with sector fixed effects, and differ according to whether country fixed effects are included or not. There are 890 174 observations, which is much fewer than 25 × 218 981 because, firstly, not all countries do trade in every industry, and, secondly, information is not available on trade and production in the same classification for every country.

Column (5) relies on the ZIP estimator. Limiting the sample in column (5) to the bilateral relationships for which trade is recorded at the sectoral level for at least one market segment (either low, middle or upper), we would get 134 199 zero bilateral sectoral flows and 925 385 non-zero values adding up to 1 059 584 observations. But using the full set of censored values, including the ones pertaining to bilateral flows without any trade, we add 804 937 zero values adding up to 1 730 322 observations. We estimate the probability of trading or not in the upper and lower market segments using this second and larger dataset, before explaining bilateral export values of the two types of variety.

5.2. Supply and demand determinants of trade in varieties

Let us firstly consider the estimations performed on total bilateral trade, in columns (1) and (2). The standard gravity variables have the expected sign and order of magnitude, with the exception of the GDP of the exporter when country fixed effects are introduced.

More interestingly, we can now assess the theoretical predictions referred to above. The parameters on distance interacted with the market segment of the exported varieties (low versus high) illustrate the Alchian-Allen conjecture. Low price varieties are slightly more sensitive to transaction costs than high price ones. This result holds in all the specifications here.

Consider next the theoretical predictions concerning the supply and demand effects of the level of development on the unit value of shipped varieties. Do we observe a within product specialization in line with standard trade theory? We do, since the elasticity associated with the interacted variable on the per capita GDP of the exporter is larger for up-market varieties than for low-market ones. Turning to the demand side effects, we ask whether countries import more of those varieties shipped at a higher unit value, when their income increases. We observe a large difference in the parameter estimated on the importer GDP per capita variable, when it is interacted with low and high prices dummies, indicating that marginal income may be spent on quality rather than on quantity.

Turning to estimations at the sectoral level in columns (3) and (4), the previous conclusions hold. The sectoral determinants in terms of supply and demand have the correct sign. Considering our main variables of interest, namely the interacted variables between per capita income and the market segment in which varieties are traded, results are even clearer. In column (3), when the development level of the exporter increases, exports of varieties in the lower segment of the market decrease, and the opposite holds for the upper segment. We observe the same pattern on the importer side. Accordingly, we can conclude that countries having a higher development level are specialized in varieties having a higher unit value, in the different sectors of their specialization. There is a specialization within sectors, across varieties, in line with the central argument of this paper.

We are less confident in the estimations reported in column (4): the introduction of country fixed effects aiming at controlling for unobserved prices has an undesired consequence; the level of economic development of countries is also captured by these effects, and our interacted variable on the GDP per capita accounts only for the change in this variable. Accordingly, while an increase in the income level of the exporter translates into diminishing exports of down-market varieties, the expected increase in exports of high-market varieties is not observed (the parameter is no longer significant).

As mentioned, however, all these estimates may be biased by the presence of zero values in the sample. In order to assess the robustness of our conclusion, we must proceed in two steps, by using a ZIP estimator. In column (5) we report results obtained by using the ZIP estimator and, accordingly, by taking into account the probability of not exporting in a given market segment of a given sector on a given market in a given year. The results are broadly robust to this change. When an exporting country is moving up the ladder of development, it increases its exports of high-price varieties and reduces its shipments of low-price varieties in the same industrial sector. On the import size, when an importing country gets richer, it imports more of all varieties, but this increase is more pronounced for high-price than for low-price ones.

6. CONCLUSION

Analyzing a database of bilateral trade, we have systematized in this paper the repeated finding of the trade literature that there is considerable variation in unit values of traded products at the most detailed level of products classification. Accordingly, international specialization is taking place within products across varieties, rather than across products or industries, especially for trade between advanced and emerging economies. Our results point to four stylized facts.

Firstly, the similarity of exports between North and South is much more limited when we consider differentiated varieties. At the industry level, the similarity between Chinese and EU exports is large. When we consider products this similarity is more limited. When we consider the market positioning of *varieties*, this similarity is further reduced.

Secondly, and this generalizes Schott's findings, the unit value of exported products to a certain market varies with the level of development of the exporter. Moreover, unit value of traded products is also affected by the distance, and this sheds light on plausible determinants on the supply side.

Thirdly, and according to the role played by traditional determinants of speciali- zation now operating across varieties, the observed redistribution of market shares at the world level has been especially detrimental to advanced economies for low price varieties, while the EU has better resisted competition in high price varieties, in particular in consumer goods.

Fourthly, bilateral trade in varieties can be explained by a gravity equation controlling for the supply side and the demand side determinants considered in the literature, as well as for the determinants of their specialization within products across varieties and demand for quality.

On the basis of such detailed and systematic empirical evidence regarding the specialization of countries *within* – rather than *between* – products, the fears raised by North–South competition may be exaggerated. China may be exporting under quite as many product headings as Germany, but, at the most detailed level of the international classification of products, varieties exported, for instance, by Germany and China are not in direct competition. And if workers in the North and the South hardly compete on the same varieties, the link between trade and factor prices is somehow weakened (subject to the degree of substitution between high and low quality goods).

Our analysis confirms that advanced economies are keeping an advantage, or are at least suffering a lesser disadvantage, in the upper market segment. It also indicates that the North and the South are not competing head on within industries. Still, this need not prevent domestic labor market effects, and further research should explore the impact of systematic repositioning on up-market varieties by advanced economies' firms.

Discussion

Stephen J. Redding
London School of Economics

This paper makes a number of important contributions to the growing literature that has emerged following Schott (2004), which establishes that specialization occurs at finer levels of commodity disaggregation than traditionally thought. The paper's find- ings are closely linked to policy debates about the extent to which workers in advanced industrialized countries compete with those in developing countries such as China. In traditional theories of international trade, such as the Heckscher–Ohlin model, international trade can have very different effects on the real income of factors of production depending upon patterns of specialization. If countries produce the same products, reductions in prices due to the integration of developing countries into the world economy imply, via zero-profit conditions, changes in nominal factor prices in advanced countries. In contrast, if countries produce different products, reductions in prices due to international integration constitute a pure terms of trade gain for workers in advanced countries.

One of the key findings of this paper, and of the wider literature on within-product specialization, is that there are large differences in unit values (the ratio of values to quantities shipped) across countries even within narrowly defined products shipped to the same market within the same year. A key challenge for international economics is establishing the reasons for this variation in unit values. A natural explanation, which is considered in this paper, is that the products observed in the data are too aggregated. On this line of thinking, countries are really specializing in different goods, which only appear to be the same product, because of the use of too coarse a commodity classification in international trade statistics.

To delve deeper and identify the nature of the differences in goods across countries within products raises a number of issues. As discussed by the authors, one explanation for the variation in unit values across countries within products is variation in product quality. But distinguishing vertical differentiation in the form of quality differences from horizontal differentiation that sustains differences in quality-adjusted prices is extremely challenging. Recent work has sought to make progress in distinguishing variation in quality from variation in quality-adjusted prices through the structural estimation of demand systems (see e.g. Hallak and Schott, 2005).

This paper finds that bilateral distance has a positive and highly statistically significant effect on unit values, which connects with recent debates about product quality and the Alchian-Allen hypothesis (see, in particular, Hummels and Skiba, 2004). The goods produced by countries within products may vary not only in terms of their demand-side characteristics, such as quality, but also in terms of their supply-side characteristics, such as factor intensity. Schott (2004) presents evidence that within-product variation in unit values is systematically related to countries' capital and skill abundance, and this paper finds that within-product variation in unit values is systematically related to countries' GDP per capita, which is itself likely to be correlated with capital and skill abundance.

The question arises as to how to interpret the rich array of empirical results reported by the authors in terms of international trade theory. Here two very different stances can be taken.

On the one hand, the results appear entirely consistent with traditional trade theory. On this interpretation, comparative advantage operates at the level of individual varieties or qualities within products, perhaps modelled as in Eaton and Kortum (2002). Specialization within products therefore naturally arises. Products are simply aggregations across heterogeneous varieties or qualities chosen by statistical agencies and industries are further aggregations of products. On this view, traditional trade theory was right after all, but existing empirical work may have considerably underestimated the amount of specialization by focusing on variation across products and industries.

On the other hand, recognizing that comparative advantage operates at a finer level of disaggregation than conventionally thought can profoundly change the conclusions of what otherwise appear to be relatively standard trade models. Thus Feenstra and Hanson (1996) show that the outsourcing of activities that are labor-intensive in the North but skill-intensive in the South can lead to a rise in the relative skilled wage in both the North and South. This result stands in marked contrast to the Stolper-Samuelson Theorem of traditional trade theory, in which the relative skilled wage rises in the skill-abundant North and falls in the skill-scarce South. In an influential paper Grossman and Rossi-Hansberg (2006) develop a general equilibrium model of trade in which the outsourcing of tasks within industries can potentially raise the relative wage of unskilled workers in skill-abundant countries. The intuition is that outsourcing acts to raise productivity within industries, which has general equilibrium consequences for relative factor prices. Again this finding stands in marked contrast to conventional wisdom, in which international integration is expected to lead to a fall in the relative wage of unskilled workers in skill-abundant countries. On this interpretation of the evidence, the recognition that specialization occurs at the level of finely-detailed products or production tasks leads to entirely new theoretical results and can overturn standard intuitions.

Therefore the paper's empirical findings are not only of interest in themselves but also provocative and stimulating for international trade theory. This ongoing dialogue between empirical evidence and theoretical modelling promises to considerably enhance our understanding of the causes and consequences of international trade.

Panel discussion

Several panel members were concerned with possible confusion in the data between quality differences, and price differences for given quality. Ray Rees thought that the long-lasting differentials measured and analyzed in the paper should indeed reflect vertical differentiation in terms of quality, because competition should eliminate price differences for goods of the same quality. Christian Schultz however wondered whether price differences and dynamics could be attributable to market power. In particular, a different and changing competitive environment in Europe and the US could explain some of the paper's findings. Hylke Vandenbussche thought that some of the price differences could reflect quality perceptions influenced by advertising or reputation, rather than intrinsic characteristics of the goods traded.

The panel was also intrigued by the difference between European and American trade trends. Josef Zweimueller thought that the aggregate European data might be importantly influenced by catch-up dynamics on the part of new Member States of the EU. Richard Portes was puzzled by the apparent lack of any influence in the paper's data of the large swings in the exchange rate between the euro on the one hand, and the US dollar and the renmimbi on the other hand. Peter Schott suggested that the paper's evidence is consistent with outsourcing to less developed countries of low quality production, while Europe concentrates on production of high quality goods, and that Japanese outsourcing to China of increasingly sophisticated production could also play a role. Allan Drazen was interested in the paper's evidence that competition between old and new industrial countries might not be as sharp as to trigger tough protectionist policies, but thought that expectations of trade pattern dynamics may well induce established producers to pre-empt incipient competition with trade barriers.

APPENDIX A

A1. Data description

The BACI database draws on United Nations' COMTRADE data and covers trade for more than 200 countries and 5000 products, between 1995 and 2004. Only 4528 manufactured products are considered here. Imports and exports flows are reported annually by 140 countries to United Nations in values and quantities at the HS6 level. The HS6 distinguishes more than 5000 different products, out of which 4200 are manufactured products. There are 16 380 products in 2001 in the 10-digit classification used by Schott (2004) for US data. This loss of detail is the price to be paid when one aims at using data covering all the importing countries in the world.

New procedures have been developed in the BACI database in order to provide a disaggregated and rigorous trade dataset for the largest possible number of countries and years, with special care given to the treatment of unit values.

When only one country reports the observed flow, there is no way of assessing the quality of this specific record. When both the exporting and the importing country report, we have two figures for the same flow, which have to be reconciled given the, often huge, discrepancies between them. An evaluation of the reliability of country declarations is then used as a weighting for the average of mirror values, unit-values and quantities.

In order to evaluate the reliability of countries reporting (as exporters or importers) we decompose the absolute value of the ratios of mirror flows using a (weighted) variance analysis. The error variable (absolute value of the natural log of the ratio of mirror flows) is regressed on four sets of fixed effects concerning exporters, importers, products and years. The OLS estimator is used, each trade flow being weighted with the natural log of the sum of the two reports.

$$\left| \ln\left(\frac{VM_{(FOB)}}{VX_{(FOB)}} \right)_{i,j}^{hs6,t} \right| = \sum_i \alpha_i \cdot I_i + \sum_j \beta_j \cdot I_j + \sum_t \gamma_t \cdot I_t + \sum_{hs6} \lambda_{hs6} \cdot I_{hs6} + error \qquad (4)$$

VM and VX are respectively the report by the importer (adjusted to account for transport costs: see below) and by the exporter. I denotes dummy variables for exporters (index i), importers (index j), years (index t) or products (index $hs6$). Estimated country fixed effects give the marginal impact on discrepancies between reported flows that

Table A1. Treatment of intra-EU trade in the text of the article

Issue	Unit values	Trade
Market positioning	Intra-EU trade excluded	Intra-EU trade included
Market shares		
Relative unit values	Intra-EU trade excluded	

can be attributed to country characteristics cleaned from sectoral, temporal and geographical (exporter or importer) effects. We assume they represent the (relative) reliability of a country data report, that will be used, after transformation, as weights in the reconciliation of bilateral flows.[9]

Besides reconciling the data, the aim was to have a matrix of world trade free of freight costs. Import values are reported CIF (cost, insurance and freight) and the exports are reported FOB (free on board). We use a gravity-type equation to get the FOB-FOB data. To allow the comparison between mirror declarations, CIF costs have to be estimated and removed from import values to compute FOB import values. This procedure is not applied when it widens the gap between mirror flows. We use a gravity-type equation to estimate them.

A gravity-type equation, estimated by OLS on pooled data is used to estimate freight costs:

$$\ln(UVM^{kt}_{ij}/(UVX^{kt}_{ij}) = \alpha + \beta \ln dist_{ij} + \chi \ln(dist_{ij})^2 + \delta \ln UV^k + \gamma \ contiguity_{ij}$$
$$+ \phi \ landlocked_i + \eta \ landlocked_j + \sum_{l=1989}^{2004} \varphi_l t_l + \varepsilon^{kt}_{ij} \qquad (5)$$

The right-hand-side variables are bilateral distance ($dist_{ij}$), dummies for adjacent and for landlocked countries (respectively, $contiguity_{ij}$, $landlocked_i$ and $landlocked_j$), dummies for years (t_l), and the world median unitvalues for each product ($UV^{k,t}$). We consider a non-linear relationship between CIF-FOB ratios and distance by introducing also the square distance. UVM and UVX are respectively the unit value reported by the importer (valued CIF) and by the exporter (valued FOB). The dependent variable is the unit-value ratios reported for a given elementary flow, rather than the ratios of mirror values, because we observe a strong positive relationship between values and quantities (errors, or non-documented differences in ways of reporting are likely to affect values and quantities in the same way). For the same reason, we also weight observations by the inverse of the gap between reported mirror quantities, noted QX and QM: $\text{Min}(QX_{ij},QM_{ji})/\text{Max}(QX_{ij},QM_{ji})$, where i is the exporter and j is the importer.[10]

---

[9] For instance, what matters is the share of poor/good reporters in its trade partners and the share of products with frequent report errors, for instance because of lack of homogeneity in the 6-digit position.

[10] As expected, we find that CIF costs increase with distance and decrease with unit value. Notice that, apart from reporting errors, the left-hand-side variables should be only CIF since the net of freight trade value (which depends on distance) is present both in the numerator and the denominator of the ratio of mirror reports variable. Therefore, the effects of distance and other gravity variables on freight and on trade values are identified separately.

Since this gives the higher weight to trade flows equally reported by partners, differences between reported import and export values are then more likely to be freight costs.

A2. Classification of varieties into three market segments

The classification of unit values of exported varieties in three ranges (low, medium, high) which we adopt is suitable when one thinks of a continuum of vertically differentiated products. Indeed, we use data at the 6-digit level, involving different traded goods aggregated under the same HS6 heading, reported by several firms of a given country on several dates by year. We decided not to classify each trade flow in unique single vertical specialization positioning. Instead, we propose a smoother procedure that divides each elementary trade flow into two ranges, either low range and medium range, or medium range and high range.

We proceed as follows. We define the relative unit value ratio for any trade flow s: $r = (UV_s / UV_{world})$, where the reference group is the trade weighted (geometric) average of UV over all flows in the world.

If $r < 1$ then the value of flow s is divided into low and medium ranges as follows: the share of low range is $(1 - r^{\alpha})$ and the share in medium range is the complement (r^{α});

If $r > 1$ then the value of flow s is divided into high and medium ranges as follows: share in top range is $(1 - 1/r^{\alpha})$ and share in medium range is $(1/r^{\alpha})$;

Table A2. Manufacturing exports of emerging countries

Country	Share in emerging countries manufacturing exports, 2004, %
China	49.4
Malaysia	9.0
Thailand	6.8
Brazil	5.6
India	5.3
Russia	4.9
Indonesia	4.2
Philippines	3.5
South Africa	2.7
Argentina	1.6
Chile	1.5
Vietnam	1.3
Pakistan	1.0
Bangladesh	0.7
Tunisia	0.7
Costa Rica	0.6
Egypt	0.4
Sri Lanka	0.4
Ecuador	0.2
Mauritius	0.1
Mozambique	0.1
Uganda	0.0
Sudan	0.0

If $r = 1$ the whole flow is ascribed to medium range.

This procedure prevents the threshold effects that would be present if each trade flow were assigned to a single positioning: a small change in α implies a small change in quality classification. The lower α, the higher the share of trade in the medium range. In the calculations here, the parameter α that regulates the smoothness of the market segment allocation function is set at 4 to have around the same value in average in each range for total trade in all products.

However, one shortcoming of this method is that it does not ensure stability of the shares of the three segments for the world total. As a robustness check, we applied a more simple method: market segments were simply defined by percentiles in each year (down-market under the 33th percentile of unit-values, up-market above the 67th percentile, middle-market in the middle of the distribution). Our conclusions are robust to such a change.

An additional problem is that the matrix of world trade is not completely filled, even when mirror reports are taken into account. In particular, quantities are not systematically reported for certain reporters. For instance, if India does not report the quantity shipped of a given product to a given market and if the importer is not reporting its trade at all, then the quantity will not be available. When the quantity is missing, we calculate bilateral market shares for up-market varieties, assuming that non-allocated flows are distributed by market segment in the same way as allocated flows. As concerns world market shares by market segment, dropping non-allocated flows would minimise the world market share of countries having more missing quantities. Therefore, we attribute missing flows to market segments in proportion of the allocated flows, for each pair of countries before computing market shares.

A3. How intra-EU trade and associated prices are taken into account

A specific issue arises with prices (unit values) observed within the Single European Market. As a result of the fragmentation of this market, one might observe a specificity of the varieties shipped within Europe. We may include or exclude trade among member countries. However, excluding trade flows that represent the lions share of member states' trade might bias our judgement with regards to their market positioning. At the same time, using world unit values, comprising intra-EU trade flows, to determine market segments in which Member states are specialized, would not be satisfactory either.

In order to bypass this difficulty, world unit values are computed by *excluding* intra-EU flows throughout this article. Intra-EU trade flows are taken into account for the determination of market positioning but excluded when it comes to market shares in order to avoid artificially boosting the European market share in the upper segment of the market as a result of higher European prices. Lastly, relative unit values are computed by excluding intra-EU trade flows. These methodological choices are summarized in Table A1. Alternative choices are provided for the sake of comparison in an appendix available on the journal website.

A4. The CEPII list of emerging countries

Countries in the CEPII's list of emerging countries have been selected according to two criteria: GDP per capita of less than half the average of industrialized countries; rate of export growth at least 10% higher than the average for industrialized countries. These criteria must be fulfilled either during two of the three sub-periods (1985–90, 1990–95, 1995–2002) or in the latest only (1995–2002).

We obtain a list that includes three members of the EU and Korea. Those four countries are dropped, Korea being considered as an industrialized country. This list could have been updated by taking into account more recent data. However we preferred to keep the original list unchanged, in order to favour comparability with previous work (Fontagné *et al.*, 2004). Furthermore, actualizing the list would have very little consequence for small countries.

Table A2 reports the share of each emerging country in the total of manufacturing export in 2004. China represents about half the total exports by emerging countries, while countries as Mozambique, Uganda and Sudan are marginal exporters.

A5. Additional detail tables

Available at http://www.economic-policy.org.

Table A5. Similarity of export structures at the *transformation* level (within BEC categories, 1995 and 2004)

1995	Brazil	China	Japan	Russia	India	USA	EU-25	Oth. Em.
Brazil	.							
China	0.65	.						
Japan	0.80	0.62	.					
Russia	0.80	0.45	0.65	.				
India	0.81	0.77	0.74	0.68	.			
USA	0.85	0.62	0.95	0.70	0.76	.		
EU-25	0.81	0.74	0.83	0.62	0.80	0.84	0.85	
Oth.Em.	0.72	0.76	0.63	0.59	0.81	0.64	0.73	0.71

Source: BACI-CEPII. Authors' calculations.

2004	Brazil	China	Japan	Russia	India	USA	EU-25	Oth. Em.
Brazil	.							
China	0.8	.						
Japan	0.91	0.84	.					
Russia	0.74	0.54	0.69	.				
India	0.88	0.79	0.79	0.71	.			
USA	0.92	0.78	0.94	0.76	0.81	.		
EU-25	0.89	0.84	0.88	0.67	0.82	0.85	0.88	
Oth. Em.	0.77	0.71	0.71	0.65	0.78	0.7	0.76	0.7

Source: BACI-CEPII. Authors' calculations.

A6. Distribution of the median elasticity of export prices to GDP per capita of the exporting country

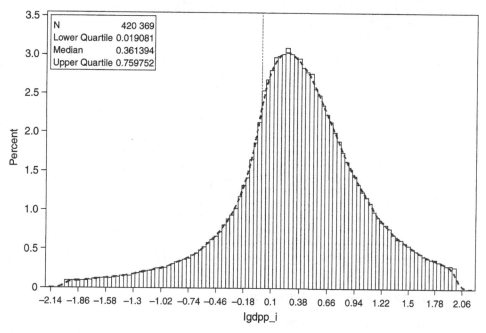

Figure A6.1. EU imports, 1995 to 2004, Member states considered individually

Source: BACI, and authors' estimation using a log linear specification.

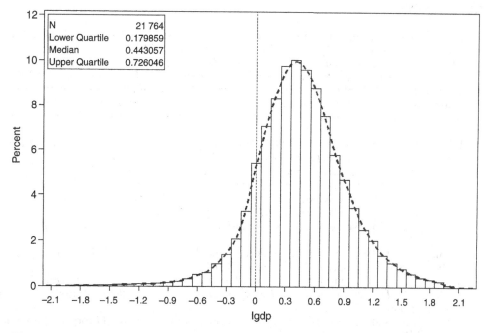

Figure A6.2. Japanese imports

Source: BACI, and authors' estimation using a log linear specification.

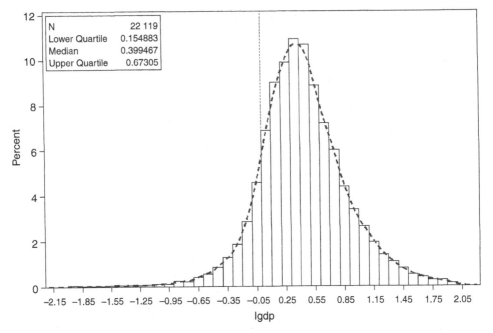

N	22 119
Lower Quartile	0.154883
Median	0.399467
Upper Quartile	0.67305

Figure A6.3. US imports, 1995 to 2004

Source: BACI, and authors' estimation using a log linear specification.

REFERENCES

Bernard, A.B., Redding S.J. and P.K. Schott (2006). 'Multi-Product Firms and Trade Liberalization', *NBER Working Paper No. 12782*, Cambridge, MA: NBER.

Choi, Y.C., Hummels, D. and C. Xiang (2006). 'Explaining Import Variety and Quality: The Role of the Income Distribution', *NBER Working Paper 12531*, Cambridge, MA: NBER.

Crucini, M.J. and M. Shintani (2006). 'Persistence in Law-of-One-Price Deviations: Evidence from Micro-data', *Department of Economics, Vanderbilt University Working Paper 06-W16*, July.

Eaton, J. and S. Kortum (2002). 'Technology, Geography, and Trade', *Econometrica*, 70(5), 1741–1779.

Falvey, R.E. and H. Kierzkowski (1987). 'Product Quality, Intra-industry Trade and (Im)perfect Competition', in H. Kierzkowski (eds.), *Protection and Competition in International Trade: Essays in Honor of M. Corden*, Oxford & New York: Basil Blackwell, pp. 143–161.

Feenstra, R. and G.H. Hanson (1996). 'Foreign Investment, Outsourcing and Relative Wages', in (eds.) R.C. Feenstra, G.M. Grossman, and D.A. Irwin, *Political Economy of Trade Policy: Essays in Honor of Jagdish Bhagwati*, MIT Press, pp. 89–127.

Finger, J.M. (1975). 'Trade Overlap and Intra-Industry Trade', *Economic Inquiry*, 13(4), December, 581–589.

Flam, H. and E. Helpman (1987). 'Vertical Product Differentiation and North–South Trade', *American Economic Review*, 77(5), December, 810–822.

Fontagné, L., M. Fouquin, G. Gaulier, C. Herzog and S. Zignago (2004). *European Industry's Place in the International Division of Labour: Situation and Prospects, Report*, Brussels: European Commission, DG Trade.

Grossman, G. and E. Rossi-Hansberg (2006). 'Trading Tasks: A Simple Theory of Offshoring', *NBER Working Paper 12721*.

Hallak, J.C. (2006a). 'Product Quality and the Direction of Trade', *Journal of International Economics*, 68(1), January, 238–265.

Hallak, J.C. (2006b). 'A Product-Quality View of The Linder Hypothesis', *NBER Working Paper 12712*, Cambridge, MA: NBER.

Hallak, J.C. and P.K. Schott (2005). 'Estimating Cross-Country Differences in Product Quality', *mimeo*, Yale University.

Head, K. and T. Mayer (2002). 'Illusory Border Effects: Distance Mismeasurement Inflates Estimates of Home Bias in Trade', *CEPII Working Paper 01*, Paris: CEPII.

Helpman, E. and P. Krugman (1985). *Market Structure and Foreign Trade*, Cambridge: MIT Press.

Hummels, D. and P.J. Klenow (2005). 'The Variety and Quality of a Nation's Exports', *American Economic Review*, 95(3), June, 704–723.

Hummels, D. and A. Skiba (2004). 'Shipping the Good Apples Out: An Empirical Confirmation of the Alchian-Allen Conjecture', *Journal of Political Economy*, 112(6), December, 1384–1402.

International Monetary Fund (2006). 'Czech Republic, Republic of Estonia, Hungary, Republic of Latvia, Republic of Lithuania, Republic of Poland, Slovak Republic, and Republic of Slovenia – Export Structure and Credit Growth', *IMF Country Report* 06/414, Washington, DC: IMF.

Linder, S.B. (1961). *An Essay on Trade and Transformation*, New York: John Wiley & Sons.

Melitz, M.J. (2000). 'Estimating Firm-Level Productivity in Differentiated Product Industries', *mimeo*, Harvard University.

Motta, M., Thisse J.-F. and A. Cabrales (1997). 'On the Persistence of Leadership or Leapfrogging in International Trade', *International Economic Review*, 38(4), November, 809–824.

Rodrik, D. (2007). 'What's So Special About China's Exports?' *NBER Working Paper 11947*, Cambridge, MA: NBER.

Santos Silva, J.M.C. and S. Tenreyro (2006). 'The Log of Gravity', *The Review of Economics and Statistics*, 88(4), November, 641–658.

Schott, P.K. (2004). 'Across-Product versus Within-Product Specialization in International Trade', *Quarterly Journal of Economics*, 119(2), May, 647–678.

Torstensson, J. (1991). 'Quality Differentiation and Factor Proportions in International Trade: An Empirical Test of the Swedish Case', *Weltwirtschaftliches Archiv*, 127, 183–194.

Antidumping

SUMMARY

A recent phenomenon is the rapid spread of antidumping laws amongst developing countries (i.e. China, India, Mexico). Between 1980 and 2003 the number of countries in the world with an antidumping law in place more than doubled, going from 36 to 97 countries. This paper examines a number of potential explanations for this proliferation of antidumping laws. We look for determinants explaining the timing of trade law adoption using a duration analysis. Results suggest that retaliatory motives are at the heart of the proliferation. This raises serious policy issues since antidumping laws should be about combating unfair trade, not about retaliation which runs contrary to the spirit of the WTO. Results also suggest that past trade liberalization raises the probability of a country to adopt an antidumping law. The proliferation of antidumping laws has important policy implications. In the interest of all users, antidumping rules should be renegotiated at the level of the WTO to make their use less 'easy', in order to avoid an escalation of protection worldwide.

— Hylke Vandenbussche and Maurizio Zanardi

Economic Policy January 2008 Printed in Great Britain
© CEPR, CES, MSH, 2008.

What explains the proliferation of antidumping laws?

Hylke Vandenbussche and Maurizio Zanardi

Université Catholique de Louvain, CORE, KULeuven-LICOS and CEPR; Université Libre de Bruxelles (ECARES) and Tilburg University

1. INTRODUCTION

Over the past two decades many countries, especially developing ones, have adopted antidumping (AD) laws. This proliferation mainly took off after 1980. Before, there were only five major users of AD: Australia, Canada, EU, New Zealand and the US. These countries have come to be known as the 'traditional users'. But since 1980 many more countries, the so-called 'new users' (Prusa and Skeath, 2002), have started to adopt and use AD laws, as illustrated in Figure 1. While AD actions are supposedly intended to combat 'unfair trade', by now most economists agree that AD is not so much about stopping unfair trade but has predominantly become a tool of industrial policy used by countries to foster the interests of their national industries (see Box 1 for more information about the way AD laws work).

Contact addresses: Hylke Vandenbussche, Department of Economics, Université Catholique de Louvain, Place Montesquieu 3, 1348 Louvain-la-Neuve, Belgium, E-mail: vandenbussche@core.ucl.ac.be; Maurizio Zanardi, European Center for Advanced Research in Economics and Statistics (ECARES), Université Libre de Bruxelles, Avenue F.D. Roosevelt 50, CP 114, 1050 Brussels, Belgium, E-mail: mzanardi@ulb.ac.be. We thank two anonymous referees, the discussants Christian Schultz and Luigi Guiso and the editor Philippe Martin for editorial guidance during the revision process. Further thanks go to Jan van Ours and to the panel members for constructive comments. Special thanks also go to Ziga Zarnic for research assistance on the data. Any remaining errors are solely our responsibility.

Economic Policy January 2008 pp. 93–138 Printed in Great Britain
© CEPR, CES, MSH, 2008.

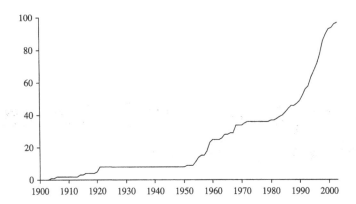

Figure 1. Evolution of the number of countries with antidumping laws

Source: Authors' update of Zanardi (2004a).

Box 1. Antidumping: how it works

While the WTO gives each member the freedom to adopt AD laws (Macrory, 2005; Ognivtsev *et al.*, 2001), it does specify that WTO members can only adopt AD laws consistent with the WTO AD Agreement. In the original GATT agreement, AD was regulated by Article 6. The current WTO AD Agreement defines the rules for implementation of Article 6 of the GATT

Article 6 of the GATT '*recognize[s] that dumping, by which products of one country are introduced into the commerce of another country at less than the normal value of the products, is to be condemned if it causes or threatens material injury to an established industry in the territory of a contracting party or materially retards the establishment of a domestic industry.*' Put differently, Article 6 states that when a firm(s) charges a lower price for its exports than for its domestic sales, it is considered to be *dumping*. When this dumping *injures* the interests of domestic producers of a similar product, unilateral AD duties can be imposed by the importing country. The use of AD is based on the notion that dumping is an unfair business strategy and therefore the 'level-playing field' must be re-established through government intervention.

From an economic point of view several objections can be raised when evaluating the contents of Article 6.

First, GATT rules seem to imply that for the importing country to impose AD protection it suffices to show that it is in the interest of domestic producers to do so.

Second, Article 6 seems to suggest that any form of price discrimination between the market of origin and the export market with a lower price in the export market for the same product is considered 'unfair'. Economists regard this definition as too broad since price discrimination is not necessarily an unfair practice but could just reflect different demand elasticities between the domestic and foreign market (with the foreign demand function being more elastic). The only type of 'unfair' dumping, according to economists, is the case of 'predatory dumping' where exporters aim to drive domestic rivals out of the market and become monopolists (or oligopolists). Two conditions are required for predation to be successful: high entry-barriers in the domestic industry of the importing country and a high concentration of domestic producers (Viner, 1923). These conditions ensure that foreign firms can charge monopoly prices after having driven domestic rivals out of the market without facing the risk of re-entry by other domestic firms. However, a close look at Article 6 shows that the legal definition of dumping is not well equipped to detect predatory dumping. In fact its scope is too wide and includes forms of dumping economists would regard as 'fair' trade (Veugelers and Vandenbussche, 1999).

Article 6 requires there to be a 'causal' relationship between dumping and injury. This aspect uncovers another weakness of the current rules. Current practice shows that it now often suffices for an AD authority to show that an upward trend in the volume of dumped imports coincides with a downward trend in industry performance indicators (e.g. sales, profits, prices, capacity utilization etc.) to infer causality (Grossman and Wauters, 2007; Sapir and Trachtman, 2007). But it is clear that other factors may account for the adverse evolution of a domestic industry. A change in consumer tastes or bad management and inefficient behavior of domestic firms are alternative reasons resulting in the same negative performance in terms of prices, profits, sales, etc.[1]

In sum, economists feel that the rules on dumping, injury to the domestic industry and causality between the two are now rather loose, making the finding of injurious dumping rather easy and resulting in too many affirmative findings and too much protection.

In practical terms, AD procedures begin when a domestic industry files an AD petition with the relevant authority.[2] If dumping and injury are ascertained, trade protection can be granted. Protection can then take different forms. The simplest one is the imposition of AD duties. Alternatively, foreign firms can voluntary decide to increase their prices by agreeing on a price undertaking that eliminates injury to the domestic firms. Importantly, the duties or the agreed prices are firm-specific and are calculated for each dumping exporter.

---

[1] The AD Agreement resulted from the Kennedy Round required dumping to be 'demonstrably the principal cause' of material injury. This stricter requirement was dropped in AD Agreements approved during the Tokyo and Uruguay Rounds.

[2] A petition is valid if it is supported by a majority of the industry (measured in terms of production or employment).

Even before reaching the final decision, provisional AD duties can be imposed if preliminary determinations by the importing country have established the existence of dumping and injury and there are reasons to believe that without such measures injury would continue during the investigation period. Overall, the investigation should not take more than a year to reach completion (except in special circumstances). Following the implementation of the Uruguay AD Code, AD duties and price undertakings should be terminated at most five years from their introduction, except if a review determines that dumping and injury would continue otherwise.

The WTO AD Agreement only provides the general framework that regulates the use of AD but it leaves flexibility to each country in the way it decides to implement it. This leads to a variety of practices. For example, in some countries (e.g. Canada, China, US) two different authorities investigate the existence of dumping and of material injury while in other cases just one agency is in charge of both tests (e.g. EU, India, Mexico). Some countries also seem to prefer negotiated agreements to the formal imposition of AD duties much more than others (e.g. EU and South Korea versus Brazil and US). An important aspect is that some AD laws may include a public interest test to judge the merit of AD protection vis-à-vis the welfare of the country as a whole. Noticeably, the EU has such a provision (the so-called 'Community Interest test') implying that in principle AD protection also has to be in the interest of domestic consumers in the EU community. Sadly, this public interest test is not well enforced and is rarely invoked to dismiss an AD case. Therefore, in practice, AD protection is installed when it is deemed in the interest of domestic producers without considering the interests of other users and consumers.

As this short description illustrates, AD is an exception to the GATT/WTO principle of non-discrimination. AD measures only affect imports from alleged dumpers. Hence, not all countries (and firms within each country) receive the same treatment.

While AD measures by the traditional users have gone down, those by the countries that adopted an AD law after 1980 have gone up. To give just one example: India initiated about 321 AD cases between 1995 and 2002 while during that same period the US initiated 289 and the EU 263, as shown in Table 1. When scaled by the size of imports it turns out that the highest number of AD measures per US$ of imports is now attained by some of these new users, as shown by Finger *et al.* (2002).

Moreover, new users predominantly use AD protection against traditional users, notably the US and the EU. In the words of Dan Ikenson (2002) from the Cato Institute (a think tank in Washington DC) '*the likelihood of continued antidumping proliferation poses a significant threat to US export growth (. . .) the US has become the third largest target of antidumping actions around the world*' and a similar argument applies for the EU

Table 1. Top adopters and sectoral breakdown of AD initiations by adopters

Top adopters	AD initiations in 1995–2002	Top sectors	% of AD initiations in 1995–2002
India	321	Industrial chemical	39.08%
Brazil	99	Iron and steel	30.16%
Peru	86	Machinery	5.71%
Mexico	74	Textile and apparel	5.71%
China	62	Food products	4.01%
Egypt	46	Paper and products	3.21%
Turkey	46	Rubber products	3.11%
Indonesia	40	Other sectors	9.01%
Taiwan	32		
Thailand	31		
. . . as a comparison:			
US	289		
EU	263		

Notes: The statistics about top countries and sectors are calculated only including the countries that introduced an AD law from 1980 onward; some of the top adopters introduced an AD law after 1995 (see Table 2 for details).

Source: Moore and Zanardi (2006).

as well. Therefore, American and European firms are now themselves under threat of facing AD actions by developing countries jeopardizing market access to some of the largest growing markets in the world.

All this shows that the recent proliferation of AD laws raises serious policy issues since the welfare effects of widespread AD protection are negative. Gallaway *et al.* (1999) calculated that the total net welfare costs of affirmative AD and countervailing actions for the United States in 1993 were only second to the MultiFibre Agreement.[3] Moreover, a recent paper by Vandenbussche and Zanardi (2007a) estimated the trade depressing effects of AD proliferation for some new users to be in the range of 8.9% of their annual imports. For example, while India saw its imports rise by 11.3% as a result of trade liberalization over the period 1991–2001, its use of AD measures reduced imports by 10.2%. This suggests that adopting and using AD laws can substantially offset gains from trade liberalization and refutes the notion that AD laws are 'a small price to pay'.

The purpose of this paper is to formulate and test a number of possible explanations for the AD law proliferation. These explanations will be grounded in existing theories of political economy of trade policy and other channels suggested in the literature on the use of AD. In addition to the adoption decision, proliferation also holds another interesting question related to the time gap between adoption of an AD law and the first AD initiation. Our data reveal substantial heterogeneity amongst adopters in terms of the time of their first use, which is worth exploring.

---

[3] Countervailing duties are imposed on imports that receive illegal subsidies in their home country.

Table 2. Countries in the sample (1980–2003)

Countries that did not adopt AD law (1)	WTO membership (2)	Countries that adopted AD law (3)	WTO membership (4)	Date of AD law (5)	Date of first use of AD law (6)
Angola	1994	Albania	2000	1999	n.a.
Bahrain	1993	Armenia	2003	2003	n.a.
Belize	1983	Bangladesh	1972	1995	n.a.
Benin	1963	Belarus	–	1999	n.a.
Botswana	1987	Bolivia	1990	1992	never
Brunei Darussalam	1993	Brazil	1948	1987	1988
Burkina Faso	1963	Bulgaria	1996	1993	2002
Burundi	1965	Cameroon	1963	1998	n.a.
Cambodia	2004	Chile	1949	1986	1994
Chad	1963	China	2001	1997	1997
Congo	1997	Colombia	1981	1990	1991
Côte d'Ivoire	1963	Costa Rica	1990	1996	1996
Djibouti	1977	Croatia	2000	1999	never
Gambia	1965	Cuba	1948	1990	n.a.
Georgia	2000	Czech Republic	1993	1997	1998
Ghana	1957	Dominican Rep.	1950	2001	never
Guinea	1994	Ecuador	1996	1991	1997
Guinea-Bissau	1994	Egypt	1970	1998	1998
Guyana	1966	El Salvador	1991	1995	never
Haiti	1950	Estonia	1999	2002	n.a.
Hong Kong	1986	Fiji	1993	1998	n.a.
Macau	1991	Guatemala	1991	1996	1996
Macedonia, FYR	–	Honduras	1994	1995	never
Madagascar	1963	Hungary	1973	1994	never
Maldives	1983	Iceland	1968	1987	never
Mali	1993	India	1948	1985	1992
Malta	1964	Indonesia	1950	1995	1996
Mauritius	1970	Israel	1962	1991	1993
Mongolia	1997	Jordan	2000	2003	never
Mozambique	1992	Kazakhstan	–	1998	n.a.
Myanmar	1948	Kyrgyz Republic	1998	1998	never
Namibia	1992	Latvia	1999	2000	2001
Nepal	2004	Lithuania	2001	1998	1999
Niger	1963	Mexico	1986	1986	1987
Oman	2000	Moldova	2001	2000	never
Papua New Guinea	1994	Morocco	1987	1997	never
Qatar	1994	Nicaragua	1950	1995	1997
Rwanda	1966	Pakistan	1948	1983	2002
Sierra Leone	1964	Panama	1997	1996	1998
Solomon Islands	1994	Paraguay	1994	1996	1999
Sri Lanka	1948	Peru	1951	1991	1992
Suriname	1978	Philippines	1979	1994	1994
Swaziland	1993	Poland	1967	1997	1997
Switzerland	1966	Romania	1971	1992	never
Tanzania	1961	Russian Federation	–	1998	2000
Togo	1964	Saudi Arabia	2005	2000	n.a.
United Arab Emirates	1994	Senegal	1963	1994	never
		Singapore	1973	1985	1994
		Slovak Republic	1993	1997	never
		Slovenia	1994	1993	1999

Table 2. *Continued*

Countries that did not adopt AD law (1)	WTO membership (2)	Countries that adopted AD law (3)	WTO membership (4)	Date of AD law (5)	Date of first use of AD law (6)
		Spain	1963	1982	1984
		Taiwan	2002	1984	1984
		Thailand	1982	1994	1994
		Trinidad & Tobago	1962	1992	1996
		Tunisia	1990	1994	never
		Turkey	1951	1989	1989
		Ukraine	–	1999	1999
		Uruguay	1953	1980	1998
		Uzbekistan	–	1997	never
		Venezuela	1990	1992	1992
		Vietnam	2006	1998	n.a.

Notes: 'Never' means that the country had not used its AD law by the end of 2003. 'n.a.' means that no information is known about the usage of AD law for this country. '–' means that the country has not yet joined the WTO.

As for the decision to adopt, our empirical analysis is based on a set of 108 countries that did not have an AD law in 1980, which is the starting point of our sample period. Of those 108 countries, 61 adopted an AD law at some point between 1980 and 2003, which is the final year of our sample. The countries that adopted an AD law are listed in Table 2. To analyze the decision of first use we have far fewer observations at our disposal since only 61 countries adopted an AD law.[4] In view of the time dimension in adoption and first use decision, the use of duration (survival) analysis seems warranted. In particular we will use a parametric Weibull model and a semi-parametric Cox model.

An important aspect to note is that while the decision to adopt an AD law is made by a country, the decision to use AD proceedings instead is decided by firms that feel adversely affected by the dumping practices of foreign competitors. This means that AD policy works differently than competition policy where governments can at their own initiative decide to pursue a cartel or investigate an anti-competitive practice when they see fit. In the case of AD laws, governments in principle only administer the laws once they have adopted them, that is they will investigate the complaint made by an import-competing industry[5] and decide whether to grant that industry protection or not but they do not themselves initiate AD cases. Despite the fact that governments in principle only apply the existing rules, it has been shown that AD application is not just a 'technical track' process but leaves room for political influence (see, among others, Finger *et al.*, 1982; Moore, 1992; Tharakan and Waelbroeck,

---

[4] The set of countries that can be used is further reduced because of lack of data.

[5] A petition is valid if supported by a number of firms that is deemed representative (in terms of output or employees) of the allegedly injured industry.

1994). In view of this we will analyze to what extent political reasons also enter the adoption decision.

Although Table 2 makes clear that most countries with an AD law are members of the GATT/WTO, the adoption seems to have moved quite independently from WTO membership. Moreover, it is important to note that there is no formal obligation to adopt an AD law to join the GATT/WTO (Macrory, 2005; Ognivtsev et al., 2001). However, a member country that wishes to introduce an AD law must do it in conformity with the WTO AD Agreement. A casual look at Table 2 already shows a large heterogeneity in the timing of AD law adoption and GATT/WTO membership. But in what follows we will more rigorously verify to what extent GATT/WTO membership is a determining factor in the proliferation of AD laws.

For all the reasons outlined above it is clear that from a policy perspective, it is important to investigate the determinants that lead countries to adopt AD laws. Our main findings can be summarized as follows.

One of our results is that AD law proliferation seems to be driven by 'retaliation motives'. The cumulated number of AD measures a country has received in the past strongly affects the probability of adopting an AD law. This result is in line with modern political economy theories arguing that strategic interaction between governments is important in explaining the emergence of trade protection laws (Bagwell and Staiger, 1999, 2002). However, the adoption of AD laws for strategic purposes suggests an abuse of AD laws, since retaliation is not what these rules are designed to combat (see Box 1) and thus is a violation of WTO rules.

Another robust finding of this paper is that AD law adoption is driven by a 'substitution effect' where more permanent tariffs are traded in for 'ad hoc' AD protection. Empirically we find that substantial trade liberalization in the past raises the probability of a country adopting an AD law. Hence countries seem to substitute tariffs by more contingent type of protection instruments like AD laws.

Traditional political economy models based on the 'conflict of domestic interests' would predict that the proportion of skilled versus unskilled workers is also likely to affect a country's decision to adopt an AD law. Trade policy in these models emerges as the outcome of a democratic majority voting process between winners and losers of protection (Mayer, 1984). However, we do not to find any evidence of that. Several reasons may account for this. Either direct democracy does not work well since workers do not use their right to vote because voting is costly. Or, alternatively, direct democracy is not a good assumption for trade policy issues since individuals do not directly vote on trade protection laws. Even when we look at the extent to which labor power is organized, as measured by union density of a country, we do not find an effect of workers on the decision of a country to adopt an AD law.

The assumption of direct democracy may not be an appropriate one to explain the formation of trade policy. More realistic political economy models instead assume indirect democracy i.e. that trade policy decisions are the result of a two-step political process where first individuals elect policymakers and second policymakers take decisions. 'Protection for sale models' argue that special interest groups affect trade policy by lobbying in the second stage (Grossman and Helpman, 1994). Special interest groups and potential lobbyists in favour of the adoption of AD laws are import-competing industries that intend to use AD protection extensively. Moreover it has been shown that the stronger the financial clout and the more concentrated these industries are, the more likely their lobbying is bound to be successful (Olson, 1965). Our analysis indeed confirms that the size of the two most important beneficiary sectors of AD protection, notably the chemicals and the steel sector (as shown in Table 1) indeed positively affects the likelihood of AD law adoption. In contrast, the size of the textiles sector does not seem to have a determining role in the adoption decision. This is suggestive that financial clout is a more determining factor in trade policy outcomes than voting power. In most countries the textiles sector accounts for a larger share of employment but consists of many small firms which may face coordination problems. Instead, the steel and chemicals sectors are typically dominated by a few large players with substantial market power which makes coordination of lobby efforts and rent-seeking in these sectors easier and puts these industries in a better position to approach policymakers with financial contributions.[6]

We also find that the amount of net inflow of foreign direct investment (FDI) in a country significantly lowers the probability of AD law adoption. This is consistent with lobbying activities from multinational firms against AD laws since they usually source a larger share of their intermediate inputs from abroad.

Short-run macro economic fluctuations like GDP growth and exchange rate volatility do not seem to affect the decision to adopt an AD law. But a more long-run indicator of economic development like the size of the agricultural sector is negatively correlated with the decision to adopt an AD law. This largely explains why most African countries are absent amongst the new adopters and other countries like China, Brazil, India and Mexico to name a few, feature prominently amongst the new adopters. The latter countries have clearly moved away from agriculture into manufacturing. And since AD laws are mainly used to protect intermediate inputs in manufacturing (chemicals, steel, machinery, etc.) and far less to protect agricultural products, we would indeed expect to find that the size of the industrial sector is positively correlated with the decision to adopt an AD law.

As mentioned already, the decision of first use is more difficult to characterize due to a much smaller number of observations. Still, our findings suggest that short-run retaliatory motives and the level of development of a country matter most in explaining the cross-country variation of the first AD initiation.

The policy implications arising from our results are multiple and will be discussed in detail in a separate section. Predominantly they call out for the urgent need to

---

[6] For example, in India the textile sector employs about 35 million people and represents 14% of industrial production, while steel only accounts for 2.1% and chemicals about 7% of industrial production. The numbers are similar for the three other largest 'new users' of AD policy: China employs about 26% of workers in textiles, 4% in chemicals and 3% in steel sector.; Mexico employs about 23% in textiles, 0.3% in chemicals and 5.8% in steel.

renegotiate the AD procedure at the multilateral level, not in the least because the main targets of AD measures by the new adopters are the traditional AD users such as the US and the EU that have thus far blocked any substantial change to the AD rules in the absence of an incentive to do so. With evidence around suggesting that these new adopters are mainly using their AD law against the traditional users (Vandenbussche and Zanardi, 2007a) this is likely to result in a Prisoner's dilemma situation lowering welfare for all.[7] Therefore it is the role of an organization like the WTO to make AD rules less easy to apply to prevent countries from abusing AD laws to improve their terms of trade conditions at the expense of trade partners. Also, the WTO should curb rent-reeking activities by tightening the application of the rules such that special interest groups can less easily affect AD decision-making. Failure to do so is likely to result in substantial trade losses as recently argued by Vandenbussche and Zanardi (2007a).

The structure of the paper is as follows. In the next section we discuss existing political economy models as well as other hypotheses that may explain the proliferation of AD laws. This will provide the guidelines for the variables to be used in the empirical models on the determinants of adoption and first use of AD laws. Section 3 presents a description of the data while Section 4 discusses the methodology we use. The results are presented and discussed in Section 5. Section 6 concludes by discussing the policy implications of our empirical results.

2. WHY DO COUNTRIES ADOPT AN ANTIDUMPING LAW?

Arguably AD laws should only be there to protect a country in the event of unfair (i.e. dumped) imports. According to most economists the only type of unfair dumping that would justify protection is predatory dumping. The extent of predatory dumping is however hard to measure empirically, moreover the legal AD rules are not well equipped to distinguish predation from other types of dumping (see Box 1 for more details).[8]

In this paper we therefore take an indirect approach by arguing that if we find that country level variables that have nothing to do with the fairness of trade seem to affect the decision to adopt an AD law, this casts doubt on the correct motives for adoption and subsequent use of AD. If we find evidence of strategic or political economy motives underlying the adoption decision there is clearly room at the level of the WTO to change the AD rules to bring them more in line with the objective they are supposed to serve.

---

[7] A small literature is emerging arguing that in a dynamic context retaliatory tools like AD laws may prove necessary to uphold a free trade equilibrium (see Martin and Vergote, 2004). This suggests that abolishing AD laws would not be appropriate. Still, the policy conclusions would go in the same direction as argued in this paper (i.e. making the use of AD stricter with less possibility for lobby groups to affect the decision making).

[8] Shin (1998) shows that less than 10% of US AD cases are potentially about predatory dumping, which is the only instance where AD measures are economically justified.

We are unaware of any theoretical or empirical literature that has looked at the underlying motives for AD adoption. Previous literature has mainly focused on explaining the use of AD and its effects (see Box 2 for a short literature review on the use of AD laws). For the purpose of analyzing the proliferation of AD, which is the main research question in this paper, we therefore turn to the political economy literature on the emergence of trade laws and the earlier AD literature on the overall use of AD protection.

Box 2. Short literature review of the effects of antidumping

The economic literature on AD is very long both in its theoretical and empirical dimensions. Here, we will highlight only some of the results that are relevant for the current study and that are not already discussed in the main text of the paper.[9]

At first, a clarification is necessary. Although AD is a response to dumping, the discussion on AD is now independent from the one about dumping, as a result of an increasingly long literature that points out that the occurrence of dumping is not anymore the defining aspect in the application of AD duties and in the industries' motivations in filing such petitions.[10] Indeed, when investigating the determinants of worldwide AD filings, Prusa and Skeath (2005) 'reject the notion that the rise in AD activity is solely explained by an increase in unfair trading' since they find clear evidence that AD actions are motivated by strategic reasons. In a recent survey on AD, Blonigen and Prusa (2003) go as far as to argue that 'all but AD's staunchest supporters agree that AD has nothing to do with keeping trade "fair"'. The only economic rationale to use AD is if the dumping exporters are trying to eliminate the domestic industry in order to become monopolists (i.e. predatory dumping). However, such cases seem to be very rare (e.g. Shin, 1998). Then, it is no surprise that various studies conclude that the use of AD results in net welfare losses for a country. Gallaway et al. (1999) use a computable general equilibrium model to estimate that the annual welfare loss of affirmative AD and countervailing actions for the US were in the range of 4 billion US$ a year in 1993, second only to the costs resulting from the Multifibre Agreement.[11] The US International Trade Commission (1995), DeVault (1996) and Anderson (1993) reach the same qualitative conclusions when analyzing specific US AD cases. Although the existing literature focuses on the US, similar qualitative conclusions should hold for other AD users. These estimates, however, consider only the distortions due to the trade flows directly subject to AD measures. Therefore,

---

[9] See Blonigen and Prusa (2003) and Nelson (2006) for longer surveys of AD.

[10] The legal definition of dumping provided by the WTO AD Agreement is also far from the economic definition.

[11] Countervailing duties are imposed on imports that receive illegal subsidies in their home country.

they should be taken as lower bounds of the actual effects since many strategic effects are at play when firms internalize the existence of AD laws.

Among the strategic effects, it is known that AD procedures can help domestic and international collusion. Theoretically, AD laws can act as price floors (Prusa, 1994), which facilitate collusive outcomes. Moreover, faced with the prospect of AD duties, domestic and foreign firms have an incentive to strike a deal and share the rents that would otherwise be collected by the importing country as tariff revenue (Prusa, 1992; Veugelers and Vandenbussche, 1999; Zanardi, 2004b). Even more alarming, the need for domestic firms to cooperate during the various phases of the investigation can lead to the creation of sustainable cartels (Messerlin, 1990). In the US, this possibility is reinforced by the Noerr-Pennington legal doctrine which provides some antitrust exemption for US firms that cooperate during AD proceedings.

When collusion is achieved or trade protection (e.g. AD duties or price undertakings) is granted, the trade flows of goods under scrutiny obviously decrease. However, Staiger and Wolak (1994) provide econometric evidence that imports are also (negatively) affected by preliminary affirmative decisions. Therefore, firms may actually file AD petitions because of these investigation effects (i.e. harassment) although they do not expect final duties to be imposed.

As for the trade effects resulting from AD duties, it is important to remember that such duties are applied discriminatory to some (exporters within) countries, giving rise to the possibility of trade diversion. This implies that AD protection leads to a shift in the origin of imports, with an increase of imports from countries not named in the AD investigation. Although trade diversion can offset the reduction of trade from named countries (thus reducing the benefit for domestic producers), it involves sourcing from inefficient exporters. Prusa (1997) finds clear evidence of (less than fully offsetting) trade diversion for a sample of US cases. Instead, Konings et al. (2001) and Niels (2003) conclude that for European and Mexican AD duties trade diversion is much lower, suggesting that AD is more effective in keeping imports out.

Because of the various effects that the existence and use of AD laws can generate, it is inherently difficult to quantify the total effects stemming from the overall AD system. Still, Vandenbussche and Zanardi (2007a) use the recent proliferation of AD laws as a unique opportunity in time to evaluate the effect of the adoption and use of AD laws on bilateral trade flows using a gravity equation approach. Their conclusion is that AD can have serious trade depressing effects on imports. In particular, those countries that recently adopted AD laws and intensively use them experience annual trade losses of about 8.9%. Their results illustrate the chilling effects that AD policy can have since for countries like India and Taiwan the dampening effects of AD laws on trade flows are found to largely offset the earlier gains from trade liberalization.

Mainly two complementary theories are currently around to explain the existence of trade policy laws. The first one focuses on the social concerns of voters and public officials (i.e. policymakers take 'optimal decision' from a social welfare point of view). However, in the real world there are ample examples where actual policies seem to be quite different from 'optimal policies'. This brings us to the theory of the self-interested individual and the conflicts of interest where policy decisions are considered to be the outcome of a democratic process where voters vote according to how trade policy affects their interests (Baldwin, 1989; Drazen, 2000; Mayer, 1984).

In the case of indirect democracy the decision to adopt a trade policy can also be affected by financial contributions to policymakers and through lobbying by those that stand to lose or gain a lot from trade policy (Grossman and Helpman, 1994).

Modern versions of political economy models of trade policy also point out that the interests of individuals are not just affected by the policies of the country in which they reside but also and increasingly by the policies and actions of other countries and by decision making at a supra-national level like that of the WTO (Bagwell and Staiger, 1999, 2002).

Drawing from the political economy literature, as well as from other channels suggested in the literature on the use of AD,[12] below we discuss a number of different hypotheses that may explain the decision of a country to adopt (and start using) an AD law.

- **Retaliation hypothesis** (Blonigen and Bown, 2003; Bagwell and Staiger, 1999, 2002; Feinberg and Reynolds, 2006; Prusa and Skeath, 2002)
  Countries may adopt and use AD laws because of a retaliation motive. In particular, some of the new users (e.g. Brazil, China, India, Mexico) of AD today have been heavily targeted by AD measures in the 1980s and 1990s by traditional users like the EU and the US. Therefore the recent proliferation of AD laws could be part of a 'tit-for-tat' strategy where their adoption of AD laws is driven by the fact that they felt 'victimized' by the use of AD by others against their exporters. The new adopters of AD may have understood the flexibility of AD actions as trade policy instruments and decided to arm themselves with the same 'weapons'.
  Such a channel is also consistent with modern political economy models of trade that emphasize that trade policies are the outcome of the actions and policies adopted by *other* governments (Bagwell and Staiger, 1999, 2002). In order to investigate this hypothesis, the numbers of past AD investigations and/or measures a country has received are natural explanatory variables for our empirical models.

- **Substitution effect**

  Many developing countries have embarked on trade liberalization reforms during the recent decade. In many cases, these trade liberalization efforts resulted in

---

[12] However, we are not aware of any other theoretical and empirical study that analyses the determinants of the proliferation of AD laws.

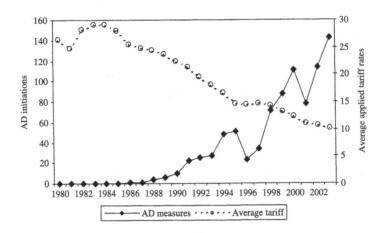

Figure 2. A substitution effect between tariffs and AD

Notes: Annual caseload of AD initiations by countries that adopted an AD law after 1980; average applied tariff rates of countries that do not have an AD law or adopted one after 1980.

many important structural changes in their economies. At the same time, the various GATT rounds of trade negotiations have limited the possibilities for countries to use 'standard' trade policy instruments (e.g. tariffs, quotas). The adoption of an AD law may therefore entail a substitution effect i.e. when countries agree to permanently reduce tariffs, they may want to keep their options open and replace permanent tariffs with another form of trade protection that they can use when the need arises to do so. In that sense an AD law can be regarded as some kind of 'insurance policy'. This possibility is apparent in Figure 2 where the number of AD measures by adopters and their average tariff rates are negatively correlated. The 'substitution hypothesis' can be tested by including measures of past trade liberalization as explanatory regressors. It needs to be pointed out that we may potentially be introducing an endogenous variable since it may be the case that the anticipation of future AD protection may also result in more trade liberalization. To exclude the possibility that our result on the substitution effect is driven by reverse causality, we will use an appropriate instrument for a country's openness that is less endogenous.

● **Institutional reasons**

Even a casual look at the data suggests that there is a large heterogeneity across WTO members in terms of AD laws which most likely can be explained by the observation that the adoption of an AD law is not compulsory under WTO membership (Macrory, 2005; Ognivtsev *et al.*, 2001). Taiwan adopted an AD law 18 years *before* becoming a member of the WTO while Thailand adopted an AD law 12 years *after* joining the GATT. Adoption of AD laws occurs for countries outside the WTO as well as inside the WTO.[13] This can be seen from Table 1 where for each country we list the year of WTO membership and the year of AD law adoption. It also shows that in 2003, 46 WTO members still did not have an AD law. Variables related to the time of WTO membership should be able to show if WTO membership is an institutional factor that can explain a country's decision to set up an AD regime.

● **Contagion effects**
As the number of countries with an AD law increases over time, it may become more attractive for a country without an AD law to implement one. Prusa referred to it as the 'club effect' in his 2001 speech at the CATO Policy Forum. Countries observe other countries using AD and learn by seeing. The more countries that have AD laws, the more other countries learn about them, which leads them to join the club and use AD to their own advantage. Such a club may have a geographical dimension. The number of countries with an AD law (world-wide or in a particular geographical area) are natural choices as variables to include in the empirical analysis to test this hypothesis.

● **Political economy hypothesis** (Baldwin, 1989; Drazen, 2000; Gawande and Krishna, 2003; Grossman and Helpman, 1994; Hillman, 1982; Mayer, 1984)
The standard neo-classical trade theory of Heckscher–Ohlin predicts that protection affects skilled workers differently than unskilled workers. Therefore the proportion of skilled versus unskilled workers at the country level can be a proxy for the number of advocates versus opponents of protection. Hence, if neo-classical trade models are the correct ones to think about then under a majority voting rule, we would expect the proportion of skilled to unskilled workers at the country level to be related to the adoption of an AD law. In addition we also want to verify to what extent the probability of AD law adoption is affected by the presence of strong unions defending the interest of mainly unskilled workers.[14] Labor power may matter in two ways: 1) Unions dislike competition since it threatens their power and are more likely to support laws allowing trade protection; 2) Unions are a source of cost-push shocks which can undermine domestic firms' competitive-ness, hence resulting in a call for the protective use of AD laws (Vandenbussche et al., 2001). For these reasons our analysis should include a measure of union power at the country level.
The 'protection for sale' models (Grossman and Helpman, 1994) assume trade policy to be a two step process: first voters elect political representatives and second policymakers decide on trade policy. Hence trade policy laws are the

---

[13] Countries that are not members of the WTO are free to restrict trade as they like. Still, even in these countries the use of AD from an industry perspective is much easier than having to ask a government to approve special measures.

[14] We thank both referees for pointing out the potential role of unions in an earlier draft of this paper.

result of a process of indirect democracy where lobbying and rent-seeking affect the second stage decision making. Based on this we would expect industries with a reputation as intensive users of AD protection to lobby for adopting AD laws. Table 1 lists the sectors that in the recent past applied most for AD protection. The top users include the chemical sector with 39% of all AD initiations, the steel and metals sector with 30%, and the machinery and the textile sectors as distant third and fourth with just less than 6% each. Clearly, an indication of the size of the domestic steel and chemicals sectors could capture the strength of the lobbying power and the rent-seeking behavior of these industries in terms of favoring the adoption of an AD law.

The extent to which an economy hosts foreign firms may also affect its decision to implement AD laws that subsequently allow domestic industries to trigger protection. Multinational firms (MNEs) usually source more intermediate inputs from abroad than domestic firms. Since it is usually intermediate products and raw materials that are mostly subject to AD protection, MNEs will have a clear incentive to lobby against the introduction of AD laws.[15] In order to verify the relevance of this argument, our empirical specifications will include a measure of FDI flows. *A priori*, we would expect the higher the net inflow of FDI, the lower the probability of AD law adoption.

- **Macro-effects** (Knetter and Prusa, 2003; Leidy, 1997)

  Earlier work has shown that a country's GDP growth and real exchange rate fluctuations have a significant effect on its total AD filings. Smaller and more open economies with flexible exchange rates are more subject to volatile business cycles and may want to use AD laws to smooth out business cycle effects.

  But arguably, the adoption of an AD law is more of a long-run decision where the influence of short-run macro economic conditions may matter less. Thus, it seems desirable to also control for more long-run measures of the level of development of a country. An often heard argument is that while in principle all countries can adopt an AD law, in practice it is only the countries that have the capacity to manage these laws that adopt in the first place. This may explain why very low-income African countries are largely absent in the list of adopters while Latin American countries belonging to more medium level income countries list prominently amongst the new adopters.

  Also, since AD is mostly about the protection of manufacturing products, we would expect countries with a large agricultural sector to be less interested in adopting an AD law, while those countries moving out of agriculture and into manufacturing would be expected to be most keen on having AD laws on the books.

[15] The Congressional Budget Office of the United States reports (CBO, 1998) that 80.9% of US AD measures active on December 31, 1995 were against intermediate goods and raw materials. Similarly, 77.7% of Mexican AD initiations targeted intermediate and capital goods in the period 1987–2002 (Reyes de la Torre and González, 2005).

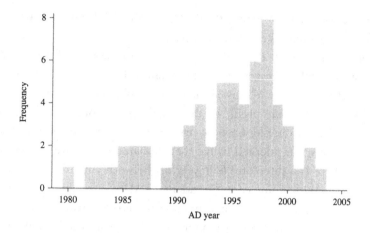

Figure 3. When did countries adopt antidumping laws?

Source: Authors' update of Zanardi (2004a).

The heterogeneity across countries in adoption and first use of AD will allow us to identify which of these channels is better able to explain the time patterns that are observable in the data. We suspect that the decision to adopt is driven more by long-run motives than the decision to start using AD laws. For example it is unlikely that short run macro shocks in the recent past would explain the decision to adopt an AD law. Instead it seems more likely that short run shocks determine when an industry engages in the first use of a newly adopted AD law since once a law is in place a complaint can be filed relatively quickly. However, only the empirical results will provide an answer to these questions.

3. DESCRIPTION OF THE DATA

The sample period for the empirical analysis goes from 1980 until 2003. The starting point of our analysis is mainly motivated by Figure 1 showing that from the 1980s onwards the worldwide proliferation of AD laws really took off. The endpoint of our data is the result of data availability. Between 1980 and 2003, 61 countries introduced an AD law with most adoptions occurring in the second half of the 1990s, as shown in Figure 3. This is the set of 'adopters' for the empirical analysis. In addition, our sample also consists of countries that did not have an AD law by 1980, had not adopted one by the end of 2003 and that had sufficient data availability.[16] In this sense, our sample includes 108 countries in total (although data limitations on some regressors reduce the sample). Table 2 lists all the countries in the dataset together

---

[16] Our control group consists of all countries in the world that satisfy these two criteria.

with the year when they joined the WTO (if they did) and the year when they adopted and first used an AD law (if they did).

A comparison between the year of adoption and the year of *first use* of AD laws uncovers substantial heterogeneity. In fact, almost half (i.e. 27 countries) of all the countries that adopted an AD law during our sample did not begin using AD by the end of 2003 and the time profile of the remaining 34 countries present substantial heterogeneity.[17] For example, Chinese firms initiated their first AD investigation the same year the law was adopted, while their Indian counterparts waited for 7 years. On average there is a three and half year lag between countries' adoption and first use of AD laws. While some countries adopt an AD law but their firms never initiate a demand for AD protection, others countries use it right away. The heterogeneity of first use is an equally interesting dimension of the worldwide proliferation of AD although the available data are far fewer since only 34 countries that adopted also started using AD before 2003.

The variables that we use to test the various hypotheses will be discussed in more detail along with the results while their description and sources are reported in Table A1 in the Appendix.

4. METHODOLOGY

The aim of our empirical model is to investigate the determinants of a country's decision to adopt and subsequently first use AD laws. Therefore, we intend to address two separate, though obviously related, issues: the likelihood that a country adopts an AD law at time t, given that it did not have one in 1980; and the time it takes for import-competing industries to start using such a law after it has been adopted. It is important to emphasize that we do not intend to explain the overall use of AD, as there are already several contributions in the literature on this aspect.

These two policy questions can be considered as 'events'. The time up to an event provides information on what triggered the event (i.e. which explanatory variables are responsible for triggering the event). The appropriate methodology to analyze these decisions is called *survival analysis* (or event analysis or duration analysis).[18] Survival analysis techniques have many applications and are especially well known among labor economists that employ them to study issues such as the duration of unemployment.

There are several types of models that can be used in survival analysis. The most important and well-known models are the proportional hazard models. In these versions, the variable that needs to be explained is the 'hazard rate' $h_i(t)$, which is the probability of an event occurring at a particular moment in time for a particular country i given that it did not occur earlier. The variables that can potentially explain

---

[17] We do not have any information about the use of AD laws in ten countries that adopted after 1980.

[18] Survival analysis deals with the possibility of right censoring (i.e. a subject under investigation does not experience the event by the end of the sample) and the non-normality in the distribution of errors.

the occurrence of an event are represented by a set of (time varying) regressors x_{it} that correspond to the variables that we indicated in order to capture the channels discussed in Section 2. Formally, a hazard model can be presented as follows

$$h_i(t) = h_0(t)\exp(x_{it}\beta) \tag{1}$$

where i stands for the country, t for the year, x_{it} is the matrix of regressors and β is the vector of coefficients to be estimated. $h_0(t)$ in (1) is called the 'baseline hazard rate'. The formulation in (1) clarifies why these models are 'proportional': any change in the explanatory variables results in a new hazard rate, $h_i(t)$ that is proportional to the baseline hazard rate independent of the time variable.

Hazard models differ from each other in terms of the assumptions made about the way the baseline hazard rate is specified. In the case of semi-parametric models (i.e. the Cox model), the baseline hazard rate is left unestimated so that no assumption for the functional form of $h_0(t)$ is required. This flexibility comes at the cost of a loss of efficiency with respect to the case where a baseline hazard rate is appropriately modeled. Parametric models do impose a functional form on the baseline hazard rate. Among the many options, the Weibull model is often used because of its generality since it allows the baseline either to be constant, increasing or decreasing over time. In this sense, it nests three alternatives by assuming the following specification:

$$h_0(t) = pt^{p-1}\exp(\beta_0) \tag{2}$$

where $p > 0$ is an ancillary parameter, t is time and β_0 is the constant. The baseline hazard rate is constant if p is equal to 1 while it is increasing (decreasing) for p above (below) 1.

We will use a Weibull model for the empirical analysis. It remains an empirical issue to see whether calendar time has an effect (i.e. if the parameter p is statistically significant). If it is, it represents a measure of our ignorance in the sense that the regressors do not fully explain the adoption or first use decision. As a sensitivity check we will also present the results for the Cox model, which should not systematically differ if the final parameterization of the baseline hazard rate is correct.

The estimates for the coefficients β in (1) can be interpreted as the contribution of each regressor to the likelihood of the occurrence of adoption and first use. To facilitate the interpretation of the estimates, we will report our results as hazard ratios (i.e. the exponential of individual coefficients β) since they represent the effect of a one-unit change in the independent variable on the likelihood of adopting or first using AD laws.[19] What has to be kept in mind, however, is that in this case what matters is whether the hazard ratios are statistically different from one. A hazard ratio that is statistically higher (lower) than one implies a positive (negative) and significant effect on the likelihood of AD law adoption or first use. For example, a hazard ratio of 1.20 for a dummy variable means that the probability of AD law adoption is 20%

---

[19] Therefore, the scale used in the measurement of each regressor is important. When discussing the economic impact of the variables, we will report the effect of a one standard deviation change on the likelihood to adopt AD laws (Section 5.3).

higher when the dummy is equal to one while a hazard ratio of 0.80 would imply a 20% lower probability. To further simplify comparisons we will also present a table with the effects of a one-standard deviation change in each regressor.

It is important to point out that in a survival analysis framework each country is part of the sample up to the year when the decision (to adopt or first use AD) is taken and it disappears afterwards. When analyzing the decision to adopt, all countries start in 1980[20] and they are included until the year when they adopt, or until 2003 if they have not adopted by the end of the sample (i.e. these countries are censored since we do not observe the event[21]).[22] Obviously, the decision to use an AD law is conditional on having first adopted such a law. Therefore, for the second question of interest countries that adopted at some point during our sample period are included from the year of adoption until the year when an industry first initiated an AD petition, or until the end of the sample if no use of their AD law had been made by the end of 2003.[23]

However, on top of the regressors that we include in the analysis, there may still be unobserved country level heterogeneity. Suppose there are some unobserved factors that are not included in our analysis but that influence the decision to adopt/use AD law, this will bias the estimates of the coefficients. Duration models allow to control for this possibility by including country specific random effects. In this case, the estimated specification becomes

$$h_i(t) = \alpha_i h_0(t) \exp(x_{it}\beta) \tag{3}$$

where the effects α_i are drawn from a distribution with positive support. These kinds of models are called 'frailty models' and they will allow us to verify that our results are robust to all country level heterogeneity not explicitly captured by the regressors. However, it is important to note that the random effects are assumed not to be correlated with the included explanatory variables. They are there to account for the sample selection induced by the sorting of countries over time, which is known to bias the coefficients of the retained explanatory variables to zero (Lancaster, 1990).

5. RESULTS

In this section, we discuss the results for the two questions that form the objective of the paper. To facilitate the analysis, the results of the empirical models are discussed in two separate sub-sections.[24]

---

[20] Our data are left-censored. This is not too much of a problem if we are willing to assume that, conditional on the covariates, countries faced the same risk of adopting an AD law in 1980. In the robustness check, we will also show that the results are unchanged if 1990 is used as the beginning of the analysis.

[21] Right-censoring is not a problem since it is uncorrelated with the covariates.

[22] Countries may enter later if they were born after 1980 (e.g. countries born from the break-up of the Soviet Union).

[23] We have no information about the use or no use of the AD law in ten countries. Therefore, we would be able to use at most 51 countries for a total of 280 observations. As a sensitivity check, we will assume that these ten countries did not use AD.

[24] The results for all the specifications not explicitly reported in the paper are either available in the working paper version (Vandenbussche and Zanardi, 2007b) or from the authors upon request.

5.1. Adoption decision

We start by analyzing the factors that may influence the adoption of an AD law. For this purpose we have 108 countries in our sample of which 61 adopted an AD law at some point during the period of analysis (1980–2003).[25] All the countries are listed in Table 2 and we note that most of those that adopted are developing countries with low to medium-income levels.

The results of various specifications are shown in Table 3. Our empirical models contain variables on the various hypotheses formulated above: retaliation, substitution effect, institutional channel, contagion, industrial composition, level of development, sectoral lobbies, inward FDI and labor power. Our preferred specification is shown in column (1) which is the one with the largest number of observations since all the variables included are available for the majority of countries in our sample. Additional variables are added in subsequent columns but often reduce the number of observations substantially. The subsequent specification in columns (2) to (6) mainly serve the purpose of demonstrating the robustness of the results. Correlations between any two explanatory variables are low as can be verified from the correlation matrix in Table A.2 in the appendix. The last two columns show the results of a frailty model and a Cox model using our main specification in column (1) to verify the robustness of our results when using alternative estimation methods.

Retaliation hypothesis   For the purpose of investigating whether a country's adoption of an AD law is inspired by earlier actions of other trade partners we experimented with *total AD initiations/measures received* in the current year as well as with *total cumulative AD initiations/measures received* in the past (from 1980 onwards). *Initiations* refer to the number of complaints filed by foreign industries while *measures* indicate the number of such complaints that resulted in the imposition of AD duties. Initiations and measures received (cumulated or not) are highly correlated and they all perform relatively well with better results for cumulated measures. When including cumulated AD measures of the past we always find a positive and significant sign suggesting that a country is more likely to adopt an AD law the more it has been targeted in the past by AD measures. This can be seen from all specifications included in Table 3.

In view of the high demand for AD protection in the steel and chemicals industry, it is worth verifying to what extent past AD measures in steel and chemicals received by the countries in the sample may have had an effect on the decision to adopt an AD law. For this purpose, we test for the existence of differential retaliation effects driven by steel and chemical cases by constructing a *cumulative number of past steel measures* and the *cumulative number of past chemical measures*. We find that both of them are significant although past steel measures has a larger and a more significant coefficient. Retaliation driven by sectoral rent-seeking is likely to have negative welfare implications

---

[25] Fewer countries may be included in the various specifications due to data limitations.

Table 3. The adoption of antidumping laws

	Preferred specification (1)	Reverse causality (2)	Sectoral lobbies (3)	Steel imports (4)	Inward FDI (5)	Union density (6)	Frailty model (7)	Cox model (8)
Cumulated AD measures received in the past	1.011*** (0.003)	1.011*** (0.003)	1.007*** (0.002)	1.007*** (0.003)	1.015*** (0.003)	1.008** (0.003)	1.018** (0.008)	1.012*** (0.003)
%Δ Openness index	1.050*** (0.017)		1.035** (0.017)	1.044*** (0.017)	1.046** (0.018)	1.042** (0.017)	1.051*** (0.019)	1.047*** (0.018)
%Δ Continental openness index		1.112*** (0.039)						
WTO entry in past 5 years	1.824* (0.583)	1.522 (1.218)	1.658 (0.636)	1.689 (0.587)	2.028** (0.597)	1.837* (0.597)	2.387** (0.904)	2.150** (0.690)
Number of AD laws in same continent	1.209*** (0.052)	1.218*** (0.050)	1.288*** (0.067)	1.213*** (0.053)	1.270*** (0.053)	1.225*** (0.055)	1.323*** (0.098)	1.377*** (0.084)
Industry VA (% GDP)	1.036** (0.015)	1.037** (0.016)		1.039** (0.016)	1.038*** (0.015)	1.054** (0.023)	1.046** (0.021)	1.047*** (0.016)
Services VA (% GDP)	1.029[a] (0.018)	1.030* (0.018)		1.021 (0.018)	1.032** (0.016)	1.020 (0.020)	1.044** (0.023)	1.044** (0.018)
Chemicals (% VA of manufacturing)			1.075*** (0.027)					
Textiles & clothing (% VA of manufacturing)			0.993 (0.017)					
Ore and metal imports (% of total imports)				1.218[b] (0.147)				
Net inward FDI (% GDP)					0.806*** (0.037)			
Medium union density						0.714 (0.263)		
High union density						0.976 (0.394)		
Medium income	1.806 (0.954)	1.502 (0.839)	1.215 (0.561)	0.874 (0.450)	1.959 (1.068)	0.554 (0.267)	1.351 (0.888)	0.972 (0.511)

Table 3. *Continued*

	Preferred specification (1)	Reverse causality (2)	Sectoral lobbies (3)	Steel imports (4)	Inward FDI (5)	Union density (6)	Frailty model (7)	Cox model (8)
High income non-OECD	0.791	0.685	0.372	0.256	21.394***	0.491	0.530	0.446
	(0.843)	(0.726)	(0.491)	(0.316)	(19.842)	(0.544)	(0.663)	(0.454)
High income OECD	0.788	0.693	13.368***	0.231	0.769	0.297	0.789	0.413
	(1.115)	(0.997)	(9.706)	(0.379)	(1.098)	(0.424)	(1.632)	(0.545)
ρ	1.151	1.09	1.447	1.256	1.337	1.238	1.053	–
	(0.249)	(0.228)	(0.348)	(0.289)	(0.344)	(0.289)	(0.248)	
Observations	1113	1113	628	786	1010	748	1113	1113
Countries included	80	80	60	78	75	60	80	80
Countries adopting AD law	49	49	37	46	49	46	49	49
Log likelihood	37.762	37.853	22.754	24.589	27.887	29.879	36.576	152.51

Notes: The table reports hazard ratios with robust standard errors of the underlying point estimates in brackets. A coefficient above (below) 1 implies that the variable has a positive (negative) effect on the likelihood of adoption. ρ is the ancillary parameter of the Weibull model, which is estimated as $ln(\rho)$ with the reported robust standard errors referring to this point estimate. * denotes significance at the 10% level, ** 5% level, and *** 1% level; (a) this coefficient is marginally significant at 10% with a p-value of 0.101; (b) this coefficient is marginally significant at 10% with a p-value of 0.103. Column (7) shows the results of a frailty model comparable to country level random effects. Column (8) shows the results of a Cox model.

for the AD adopting country. This clearly calls for a tightening of the AD rules at the level of the WTO to reduce the possibilities for rent-seekers. For brevity however we do not report the sectoral split of cumulated AD measures in Table 3.

Substitution effect   Next, we want to verify to what extent the adoption of an AD law is a substitute for more permanent tariffs. Put differently, we want to analyze whether a country is more inclined to adopt an AD law when it has recently liberalized. For this purpose we experiment with different measures of trade openness. In column (1) of Table 3 we capture trade liberalization by including the percentage change (over two years) of an *openness index*. We use the 'Freedom to Trade Internationally' index of the Simon Fraser Institute in Canada. This index is a measure of tariffs and non-tariff barriers as well as other regulatory factors all capturing the general openness of a country.[26] This index has the advantage of being available for a relatively large set of countries and for a long time period.

Including past trade liberalization yields a highly significant hazard ratio larger than one on the trade *openness index*. This is consistent with the substitution effect hypothesis: the more a country has opened up to trade in the past the higher the probability of adoption. However, we may face a problem of endogeneity if reverse causality is at work where past trade liberalization was inspired by the prospect of an AD law. Therefore in column (2) of Table 3 we replace the openness of a country by the *openness index of the continent* to which the country belongs. This should appropriately account for the potential endogeneity of the openness index at the country level. The change in openness at the continental level is highly correlated (i.e. 0.44) with the change at the country level, making it a good 'instrument'.[27] And it is clear that openness at the continental level is more exogenous since it is very unlikely that adoption of ·an AD law by country i could influence the average openness of the continent the country belongs to. The results are reported in column (2) of Table 3. They show that even when including a measure of openness at the continental level we still find a positive and significant sign in the duration model suggesting that more openness has a positive effect on the probability of a country to adopt an AD law.[28]

As a robustness check we also verify our results using an alternative measure for openness where we considered the percentage change (over two years) in the average *applied tariffs* as obtained from the World Bank.[29] The results are qualitatively the same (i.e. a larger reduction in applied tariffs in the past increases the probability of AD

---

[26] The index ranges from zero (closed economy) to ten (open economy) and gives values up to two decimals.

[27] The use of an instrumental variable approach in duration models is not feasible. Therefore we just used 'openness of the continent' as a proxy for 'openness·at the country level'.

[28] The results are also unchanged if we use the lag of the change in the openness index.

[29] The percentage change in applied tariff rates better captures the true extent of trade liberalization than if we were to use bound tariff rates (i.e. the maximum tariffs that a country can impose as a result of its WTO commitments). In fact, most developing countries have large 'overhangs' (i.e. the bound tariff rates are much higher than applied tariffs) so that a change in bound tariff rates may not result in any change in applied protection. Moreover, countries do not disclose their bound tariff rates in a systematic way (i.e. on a sectoral and time dimension).

adoption) but will not be shown to save on space.[30] Since our *openness index* is available for a substantially larger set of countries we use it as our preferred measure. The result on openness is very robust across all specifications shown in Table 3 irrespective of whether we use openness at the country level or openness at the continental level.

Our result on openness at the continental level refutes the possibility of reverse causality. It casts some doubt on the relevance of the 'safety valve argument' which argues that trade liberalization is facilitated by the anticipation of future use of AD. While the safety valve hypothesis has received some attention in previous literature (Finger and Nogués, 2005; Niels and ten Kate, 2006; Feinberg and Reynolds, 2007) the existing empirical evidence in support of it is considered to be weak. In fact, Moore and Zanardi (2006) find that past use of AD is actually hindering further trade liberalization in a sample of developing countries. The results reported in this paper are indicative that the safety valve argument for the decision of a country to adopt an AD law does not receive empirical support.

Institutional hypothesis In order to verify that the adoption of AD laws is not solely driven by WTO membership, we want to include an additional control for whether or not an AD adopting country is a member of the WTO. Also, if our result on openness still holds up after including a control for WTO membership, we know that AD adoption is truly triggered by past trade liberalization efforts rather than by WTO membership. Since WTO membership usually requires countries to engage in trade liberalization, we need to verify to what extent WTO membership is correlated with our measure of trade openness. The correlation between our measures of trade liberalization and the WTO membership dummy is only 0.07. The correlation with the dummy variable included in Table 3 of whether or not a country entered the WTO in the past five years is even lower (i.e. −0.04). Still, this dummy variable yields a positive and significant effect on the probability of AD adoption.[31] However, controlling for WTO membership does not change the significance on the openness index, demonstrating the robustness of substitution effect. The significance of the WTO dummy however depends on the specification used, confirming that the link between AD adoption and WTO membership is weak.

Contagion hypothesis In order to verify the relevance of contagion effects, we include the *cumulative number of countries that have an AD law in the same continent*. Table 3 shows that the correlation with AD adoption is always positive and highly significant.[32] Interestingly,

---

[30] Applied tariffs are available for a considerably smaller set of countries.

[31] We chose a 5 year dummy on the basis of the fact that for those countries that adopted after WTO entry, the average number of years between becoming a WTO member and AD adoption is 13 years while the median value which is less sensitive to outliers is only 5 years.

[32] We note that this variable clearly displays an increasing trend which may interfere with the estimation of the ancillary parameter p. Indeed, this parameter is significant (and greater than one) if such a regressor is excluded. However, a likelihood ratio test clearly favours the model that includes the 'Number of AD laws in the same continent', suggesting that this variable provides more explaining power than a simple trend.

a similar variable calculated at a world level is always insignificant, thus clearly pointing to the relevance of regional effects. Several explanations are possible for this result. Either it suggests that there is some kind of geographical herd behavior taking place, which may not be necessarily based on rational grounds. Or, there is some learning behavior when countries observe neighbors using these measures successfully against developed countries. While the significance of this contagion effect merits further research, it falls outside the direct scope of this paper but it does seem an important control variable to explain adoption.

Political economy motives   In order to verify the political economy motives discussed before, ideally we require detailed information on variables like the industrial, sectoral and skill composition of the economy, union density, total and sectoral import structure, inflow of FDI, etc. However, since most of the countries in our sample are developing countries, data availability on some of these variables is low.

What is most readily available for most countries is the industrial composition over time (i.e. the relative size of the agricultural, industrial and service sectors). Therefore we start by including their *value added as a percentage of GDP*. A good reason to control for industrial composition is that a close look at the list of countries in Table 2 suggests that while most African countries did not adopt an AD law by the end of 2003, many Asian and Latin American countries did. An important difference between these adopters and non-adopters is the size of the agricultural sector. Most African countries display a low change in the size of that sector over time, while adopters like Brazil, China, India, and Mexico all embarked on an 'industrial or service revolution' with shrinking economic activity in agriculture in favor of industry (e.g. China) and services (e.g. India). Table 3 shows that when we include the time varying industrial composition of the economy, the results confirm our prior: the larger the share of value added in industry vis-à-vis the agricultural sector (i.e. the excluded category), the more likely a country is to adopt AD law. For services the result is less strong but mostly significant across specifications.[33] One of the most likely explanations underlying this result is that AD laws after adoption are subsequently most often used to protect intermediate inputs in the manufacturing process. Therefore these laws are of less use to a country with a large agricultural sector.

The availability of the other political economy variables listed above is much more limited. We will discuss and introduce them one by one but mainly for the purpose of verifying the robustness of the variables in our preferred specification in column (1).

Once we look at the role of specific sectors within the industrial sector by including the *value added of the chemical sector* and the *value added of the textiles and clothing sector*, the number of observations drops by about one third. This can be seen from column (3) compared to column (1). The reason for including the size of the chemicals and

---

[33] In column (1) services VA is marginally significant at the 10% level with a p-value of 0.101.

textile sectors is that while the textiles sector is usually a very large sector in terms of employment it only represents about 6% of AD initiations, while the chemical sector is much smaller in terms of employment but accounts for most of the AD initiations (i.e. 39% as shown in Table 1). Ideally we would also like to include the steel industry, the second largest demander of protection but unfortunately data limitations do not permit us to do so.[34] From column (3) we see that indeed the presence of a larger *chemical sector* significantly explains the adoption of AD laws. Instead, the *textiles and clothing sector* is not significant in explaining the adoption of AD law. Several reasons may account for that. First, textile products were already protected by the MultiFibre Agreement during our sample period thus reducing the need for other forms of protection. Secondly, it could be that since the textiles sector is typically less concentrated, it has less financial means to weigh on trade policy than the chemicals sector. In textiles, firms and profit margins are typically smaller although the number of employees is usually much larger. This last interpretation suggests that indirectly our results are more supportive of 'protection for sale' models than of median-voter models.

As a proxy for the clout of the domestic steel sector in column (4) of Table 3 we include the *imports of ores and metals* as an indirect measure of the importance of the domestic steel sector. The inclusion of ores and metal imports forces us to drop many observations and the regressor is only marginally significant at the 10% level (with a p-value of 0.103) implying that a larger import share of ores and metals seems to be positively correlated with a country's adoption of an AD law.

When we add the amount of *net inward FDI* (two year average as a percentage of GDP) in column (5) of Table 3 this results in a drop of about a hundred observations compared to the specification in column (1). We find that net inward FDI is always negatively correlated with the probability of AD adoption and perhaps more importantly its inclusion does not alter the other results.[35] As argued before, multinational firms are more likely to import intermediates and raw materials from abroad which can explain their aversion to trade protection on intermediate inputs (i.e. the typical target of AD actions) and their willingness to lobby against trade protection laws.

As a test for the traditional political economy models, we tried including the country level ratio of *skilled over unskilled workers* instead of the value added variables. Such a variable should control for winners and losers from trade protection as predicted by the neo-classical trade theories. The data used are from the Barro-Lee dataset where skilled people are defined as the number of people above 15 years of age with a secondary school education and above. The problem is that availability of

---

[34] The WDI dataset does not include an indicator of the size of the steel sector. Another database from the World Bank (i.e. the Trade and Production database) does include some sectoral measures but the coverage is really poor resulting in too few observations left for the estimation.

[35] Because of possible endogeneity concerns, we experimented with a continental level of FDI (i.e. similar to our treatment of the openness index). The correlation between the country specific and the continental variable is 0.40 and all the results go through when using this aggregate variable.

these data for our set of countries is low. Including this variable does not yield a significant coefficient and will therefore not be shown.

As an alternative, we also experimented with a measure of labor power. *Union density* data, measured as the percentage of the working population that is unionized, were obtained from various sources (see Appendix for details). The problem with these data is that trade unions play very different roles and have very different bargaining powers in different countries. Also the data are characterized by a lot of missing observations. In view of this shortcoming, we constructed time invariant union density dummies indicating the strength of unions at the country level. Various cut-off points can be chosen but the results are not sensitive to the choice. Column (6) of Table 3 reports the results of a specification with three union dummies: one for density up to 20% (i.e. the excluded category), one for union density between 21 and 40%, and one above 40%. In the estimates reported as well as in other unreported specifications, we fail to find a significant effect of cross-country differences in union density on the decision to adopt an AD law.

Macro effects The last channel that we discussed in Section 2 relates to macro effects. We can control for macro effects in various ways. We tried including short-run macro controls that substantially vary over time such as *GDP growth* and the change in *the real exchange* rate vis-à-vis the US$ (both over a two year period). These short-run macro controls do not appear relevant in explaining adoption. Also a measure of *GDP variability* as a control for the chances that a recession emerges did not seem to be relevant for the adoption decision. Replacing the change in the real exchange rate by a similar measure of *exchange rate variability* which may capture a country's change in competitiveness did not seem to have a significant effect on the adoption decision either.[36] One reason why short run macro evolutions may matter less for the adoption of an AD law is that this is more of a long run decision that is likely to be driven by long-run factors rather than short-run macroeconomic evolutions.

We also tried including dummy variables (as reported in Table 3) capturing the *income level* of a country: medium income, high income non-OECD, and high-income OECD countries (as defined by the World Bank) with low-income countries as the excluded dummy. The definition of these dummies does not change very much over time. By including these dummies we control for cross-sectional income level differences across countries. Note that the correlation with the industrial composition variables is low (see Table A2 in the Appendix) since income dummies are not time varying. Although including these *income dummies* as macro controls does not change the qualitative results (although some estimates have a lower level of significance), the dummies themselves are not significant in the adoption decision.

---

[36] For this purpose we calculated the ratio of standard deviation of GDP (or real exchange rate) to its mean value over the past five years.

Before concluding, we note that the ancillary parameter p of the Weibull model is not significant in any of the models shown in Table 3. As we discussed in the section on methodology, we should expect this coefficient not to be significant if the regressors are able to explain the decision to adopt. We can conclude that the baseline hazard is constant so that the Weibull model that we have been using is equivalent to an exponential model. In other words, the probability of adopting is not affected by the simple passing of time.

5.1.1. Robustness   While not shown here for brevity, we also checked the sensitivity of our results to the inclusion of some other regressors. We give a brief account of the results of some of these experiments. We tried adding geographical controls in the form of *dummies for continents*. None of the *continental dummies* were significant and, importantly, none of our results change. We also split the sample into two subperiods since a close look at the adoption dates shows that most of the countries in our sample adopted an AD law in the course of the nineties. The results are unchanged when only considering the 1990s; when only using the 1980s the significance on the change in the openness index and the industry value added is lost. As a final check, we also dropped the low-income countries from our sample. It can be argued that low-income countries have different (political and economic) priorities which are not captured by our list of regressors and may bias the results. Even if this is the case, the results illustrate that the low-income countries do not bias or drive our results since all the conclusions reached before go through.

What we do show in the last two columns of Table 3 is the results of alternative methodologies to check the robustness of our results. In column (7) we estimate a Weibull model with frailty and in column (8) we use a Cox model. A frailty model is comparable to an analysis with random effects in a panel data setting.[37] The results show that when applying a frailty model to our specification in column (1) the conclusions on our two main variables of interest (i.e. retaliation and substitution effect) as well as the other channels are unchanged by the inclusion of random effects. And finally in the last column of Table 3 we use a Cox semi-parametric model instead of the Weibull parametric model. The Cox model is semi-parametric in the sense that it does not estimate the baseline hazard rate and hence no value for the ancillary parameter p is shown at the bottom of column (3). Using the same regressors as in column (1) we obtain exactly the same qualitative results. This reassures us that the variables we include do a good job in explaining the adoption decision independently of the type of hazard model we use.

---

[37] The frailty can be modelled differently depending on the distribution from which the α_i in (3) are drawn. The specification in column (7) was estimated assuming an inverse Gaussian distribution. The gamma distribution is another popular choice. Although there is no clear rule to choose among distributions, we note that the effects of covariates differences completely vanish in gamma frailty models as time goes by while they do not when using an inverse Gaussian distribution (Cleves *et al.*, 2004). Independently of the chosen distribution, frailty models assume that the unobserved heterogeneity is uncorrelated with the other explanatory variables.

5.2. First use decision

The decision to use an AD law is conceptually distinct from the decision to adopt an AD law. In particular, a country decides to adopt an AD law but it is an import competing industry that files a petition to request AD protection.[38] There is substantial heterogeneity across countries as for the time gap between adoption and first use of AD laws. This observation seems worth exploring since it is a research question that can also be addressed with the same type of methodology we have been using to explain AD adoption, although AD adoption is a country's responsibility while its use is an industry decision.

While other papers have already tried to explain the overall AD use by new users (i.e. Prusa and Skeath, 2002; Bown, 2006), we use a hazard model to explain the time of the first AD initiation given that a country has adopted an AD law during our sample period (1980–2003). We should point out that the number of observations at our disposal to explain the time from adoption to first use is substantially lower than in the adoption case since we now only include the 34 countries that adopted an AD law whereas previously we had adopters and non-adopters in the sample. Partly due to this low number of observations (i.e. between 240 and 280) the results are less robust than in the analysis of the adoption decision and conclusions are more fragile.

As argued above, the same reasons that explain the decision to adopt could affect an industry's first use of AD. We experimented with various specifications of the full model. Here we will only briefly give an account of the results that came out of these experiments.[39] The results that arose for the first use decision are somewhat different than for the adoption decision. The main robust finding is that the first time that AD is used in a country seems strongly correlated with short-run retaliation motives. Including the lagged value of *AD measures received* by all trade partners positively and significantly affects the first use decision. While *cumulative measures* in some specifications also holds up, last year's *AD measures received* always performed stronger independently of the specification. Note that in the adoption model, it was the other way round. There, *cumulated AD measures* seemed more important than last year's AD measures received. This can be understood in view of the fact that the adoption of an AD law is more of a long-run decision which may depend less on short-run fluctuations in terms of measures received, whereas the first use of AD is likely to be triggered by more recent events like the AD measures domestic exporting firms faced abroad in the past year.

This retaliatory use of AD is worrisome since it suggests again that strategic considerations play a role in the use of the AD instrument, which arguably are in contrast with the non-discriminatory spirit of the WTO.

---

[38] A petition is valid if supported by a number of firms that is deemed representative (in terms of output or employees) of the allegedly injured industry.

[39] Results available in the working paper version (Vandenbussche and Zanardi, 2007b).

The only other significant effect is that amongst the countries that adopt AD laws, industries in the richer ones begin using it sooner. In terms of the macro-economic variables, we find that *medium* and *high income non-OECD countries* within the group of adopters have a higher probability of first use than low income countries. This could be consistent with the argument that *medium* and *high income countries* have more capacity to manage and implement the AD laws than low income countries that may often lack the expertise to apply all the AD rules into practice.

None of the other variables of the adoption model proved to be significant in explaining the first use decision.

5.3. Economic significance

Ideally we would like to know how each channel affects the probability of adoption. Up to this point in the analysis this was not really possible since the hazard ratios reported in the various tables while showing the direction in which an individual regressor affects adoption of AD, can not be easily compared across regressors. The reason is that hazard ratios represent the effect of a one-unit change of the variable of interest and they are sensitive to the measurement unit.

To overcome this problem and to facilitate the comparison of which channel is more economically relevant, in Table 4 we calculate the effects of a one-standard deviation change of each regressor on the probability of adoption of an AD law.

Table 4. Economic significance (decision to adopt an AD law)

	% Impact on hazard	Mean (st. dev.)
Cumulated AD measures received in the past	14.42***	2.19
	(3.67)	(11.80)
%Δ Openness index	49.60**	2.78
	(2.45)	(8.26)
WTO entry in past 5 years	*82.43*	*0.09*
	(1.88)	*(0.29)*
Number of AD laws in the same continent	73.32***	2.23
	(3.39)	(2.90)
Industry VA (% GDP)	53.89*	28.83
	(1.96)	(12.11)
Services VA (% GDP)	39.76	48.30
	(1.39)	(11.65)
Average hazard rate (1,113 observations)		0.04
		(0.090)
Average hazard rate for the countries adopting an AD law in the year when they adopt the AD law (49 observations)		0.19
		(0.247)

Notes: The table reports the percentage impact of a one-standard deviation change in each regressor on the hazard rate, except for dummy variables (in italics in the table) where the effect of the dummy switching from 0 to 1 is reported. The other column reports the mean and standard deviation of each regressor. The last two rows report average hazard rates. Robust z-statistics in brackets. * denotes significance at the 10% level, ** 5% level, and *** 1% level.

Whenever the regressor is a dummy variable, the percentage change reflects the effect of the dummy switching from 0 to 1. These computations are performed on our preferred specification (i.e. column (1) of Table 3). This exercise does not completely solve the problem because some variables exhibit much more volatility around their means than others, as can be seen in Table 4 where the last column reports means and standard deviations of each regressor.

In terms of retaliation, we can say that 12 additional AD measures received in the past (i.e. one standard deviation) raise the probability of AD law adoption in the current year by 14.4%. Similarly we can say that an increase in past trade openness by 8 points raises the probability of AD law adoption by almost 50%. However, it is difficult to say how likely it is that such a one-standard deviation change will materialize. The institutional WTO variable always enters with a large coefficient but its significance varies a great deal across specifications. One reason is that this variable is very sensitive to the set of countries included in the sample, since there is a large hetero-geneity across countries and the number of countries included in the analysis varies between specifications. Based on our results in column (1) we can say that if a country became a WTO member in the past five years, the probability of adopting AD laws is increased by 82.4%. Finally, an increase of the value added of the industrial sector as a percentage of GDP of 12% raises the probability of adopting AD laws by more than 50%.

In order to provide an overall assessment of the model, in the last two rows of Table 4 average hazard rates are reported. The first one is based on all observations included in the regression while the second one is calculated for the year and the countries when an AD law was included. The second hazard rate is almost fivefold larger, confirming the ability of the model to explain the determinants of AD law adoption.

6. POLICY RELEVANCE

The fact that many countries have adopted AD laws in recent years provides us with a unique opportunity in time to study the reasons for this AD proliferation. The new adopters of AD laws appear to be mainly developing countries. The main purpose of AD laws within the WTO context is supposedly to combat 'unfair imports'. However, economists by now agree that the current WTO AD Agreement is not well equipped to detect true cases of unfair trade (Shin, 1998). This suggests that other considerations may underlie a country's decision to engage in AD policy. These considerations are likely to be more 'political' in nature and may have little to do with combating unfair trade.

One of the important conclusions arising from this paper is that retaliation motives are at the heart of the proliferation of AD laws and the decision to start using them. This raises serious policy issues since retaliation motives run clearly contrary to the general anti-discriminatory principle that guides the WTO and is suggestive that countries 'abuse' their AD laws. Interestingly, new adopters direct their AD measures mainly against the traditional users of AD that targeted them with AD measures in the past, notably the US and the EU (Vandenbussche and Zanardi, 2007a). With these retaliation motives at work, there is a serious risk of Prisoner's dilemma outcomes where countries engage in too many unwarranted AD cases. On this ground, it seems that there is an urgent need for a substantial tightening of the dumping and injury criteria that the AD authorities are required to use in determining whether to impose AD duties.

Paradoxically, the proliferation of AD laws and the capacity of developing countries to retaliate may also open up opportunities for change. Until now the political will to change AD laws was largely absent among the developed countries. For many years developing countries have been insisting on a change of the AD rules which they felt were inadequate and were in many cases unjustly hurting the interests of their exporters. However, the traditional users, notably the US and the EU, have always opposed major changes of the AD law. The recent proliferation of AD may change the attitude of the US and EU and make them more willing to agree on changes in order to avoid a building up/running up of AD protection from developing countries which now adversely hurts the traditional exporters. It seems that there are some signs in this direction. The EU Trade Commissioner, Peter Mandelson, has recently released the Green Paper on the EU trade defense instruments where the EU displays its willingness to change. One prominent reason for this has been the recent 2005 'leather shoe' case against China and Vietnam. This case revealed that AD duties were hurting instead of benefiting a large share of the EU producers.[40] This resulted in large opinion differences between member states in terms of whether or not to impose AD duties. A compromise was reached by substantially shortening the period for which AD duties apply.

Hopefully, it will become clear that it is in the interest of all AD users to renegotiate the AD rules to make their use less 'easy'. For a start, AD rules should be guided more by economics principles than purely legal definitions which would tighten its application and reduce the number of type I errors (classify dumping as unfair where it is not). Along this line, changes in the AD law may benefit from the longer experience of competition laws and practices. In fact, economists have long been arguing that AD laws, if not scrapped, should resemble competition laws more (see, among others, Hoekman and Mavroidis, 1996; Messerlin, 1994). In that case we would observe fewer AD cases passing the hurdle and resulting in trade protection.[41]

The fact that we find that past trade liberalization positively affects a country's adoption of an AD law suggests that AD laws are used as a substitution tool when

---

[40] The largest and most efficient EU shoe producers had for some time been outsourcing the more labor intensive parts of the shoe production process to China and Vietnam. By introducing AD duties on the imports of shoes in the EU, these firms were adversely affected while AD protection mainly benefited the smaller and more inefficient producers.

[41] One option would be to eliminate AD laws and install a world competition law (and authority) to 'level the playing field' and make sure that all firms play by the same rules. Given the current problem of finding an agreement among the WTO members, it seems unrealistic that such an option would be seriously taken into consideration in the near future.

an economy becomes more open to trade. This seems to confirm earlier allegations that an AD law is a substitute for more permanent tariffs but of a more ad-hoc and selective type. The danger of this phenomenon is that gains from trade liberalization could be in part offset by welfare losses resulting from the adoption of AD laws. Recently, Vandenbussche and Zanardi (2007a) have shown that for the new users of AD, the trade losses resulting from the systematic implementation of an AD policy substantially offset the increase in trade that was obtained under past trade liberalization efforts. However, it is also important to point out that the WTO provides instruments (i.e. safeguards) other than AD to accommodate industries that are substantially and negatively affected by trade liberalization without the need to show unfair imports. The reason why AD actions are more popular measures and far more frequently used than safeguards is that it is more difficult for a country to impose protection under the current safeguard rules due to stricter rules. If safeguards are too difficult to be used, the rules governing their use should be changed instead of using AD as a second best instrument to wield protection to specific sectors (or firms) in distress.

Our analysis also showed that political economy motives underlie AD decisions. We find some evidence that countries with a substantial chemicals and steel sector adopt AD more often and start using it faster than others. This seems to suggest that the chemicals and steel sectors are relatively more successful in lobbying for the protection of their domestic interests. A possible remedy at the level of the WTO would be to tighten the AD rules to make them less subject to rent-seeking from particular sectoral interest groups. One way to accomplish this may be to introduce a *Public Interest Clause* into the WTO AD Agreement and make it compulsory in any AD law. At present, the WTO AD agreement does not require a public interest test for imposing AD duties. However, an effective public interest clause ensures that AD protection can only be imposed when it is in the interest of *all* domestic parties, including (intermediate and final) consumers. At present only a few countries, including the EU, have such a clause while the large majority of countries do not even pay lip service to consumers' interests.[42] And even in those countries that officially have a public interest clause (e.g. Argentina, Australia, Canada and EU), its enforcement is, at best, sporadic so that consumers' interests are often equated to domestic producers' interests. A reform at the level of the WTO agreement on AD entailing a clear operational definition of Public Interest would ensure two things. First that all countries include such a test in their national AD law and second that countries clearly have to demonstrate the elements involved in the Public interest test (Sapir, 2006).

Despite the fact that they do not seem to have much explanatory power for the proliferation of AD laws, short-run macro shocks appear to be important in explaining the overall use of AD measures as convincingly argued by Knetter and Prusa (2003)

---

[42] Interestingly, consumers are mentioned only once in the WTO AD Agreement and only to allow representative consumer organizations to provide relevant information.

and Leidy (1997). This is suggestive that AD is used to shelter domestic firms from negative shocks instead of countering dumping practices. This would imply that the causality investigation in AD procedures needs to be tightened. The causality clause requires the protecting country to demonstrate a causal link between dumped foreign imports and injury to the domestic industry. This causality is now checked rather loosely. It suffices to show that a downward trend of domestic sales coincides with an increasing trend of imports. Ideally, causality should be established by turning to more sophisticated methodological approaches. A multivariate regression analysis that related injury to dumping and controls for the macroeconomic environment would establish more precisely which elements significantly contributed to the domestic injury and which did not. As an alternative, a simulation approach could be used although this would demand more data with regard to the assumptions on various demand and supply elasticity parameters (Grossman and Wauters, 2007; Sapir and Trachtman, 2007). Also in this case, modification could be made to the WTO AD Agreement in order to force AD authorities to conduct more sound economic analyses.

Adoption and first use are crucial aspects of the proliferation of AD laws. An understanding of countries' decisions on these matters is essential in view of the multilateral trade negotiations taking place at the level of the WTO. Both the EU and the US should welcome the opportunity in the Doha Round, or beyond, to renegotiate the rules of AD in order to prevent further proliferation and worldwide trade depression of which they seem to become the main target. This is even more relevant since the results presented in this paper show that retaliation motives play a crucial role both in explaining adoption and in triggering the first use of AD. Today it seems that the US is only prepared to discuss the technical aspects of AD (see Moore, 2007) which is regrettable since adoption and use of AD laws by new users is resulting in global trade chilling effects as shown recently by Vandenbussche and Zanardi (2007a). We should not let AD erode the trade gains that have been achieved through painful trade reforms. Now that we understand better the phenomenon behind the proliferation of AD, efforts can be made to limit it before more welfare gains from past trade liberalization are lost.

Discussion

Luigi Guiso
Ente Luigi Einaudi

This paper documents an impressive worldwide upward trend in the adoption and use of antidumping laws (AD) after the mid-1980s and tries to identify factors that may explain why countries adopt AD laws and why they use them. The bottom line is that the adoption of AD laws is correlated with proxies of institutional variables and retaliation motives as well as with measures of the desire to build a safety net when countries liberalize trade. The explanation of the timing of the first use of AD measures, not surprisingly, is more difficult to predict, but a response to antidumping measures received by other countries has a strong explanatory power.

I found the issue raised interesting points and is certainly of policy relevance for the current debate within the WTO about what to do with AD laws. As far as I understand, the difficulty arises because although antidumping can (as the authors recognize) be considered a good pressure valve for countries undergoing rapid trade liberalization, they can also create political and economic tension. Political tension stems from debate over the recent rise in antidumping suits, sparking concerns that while negotiations dismantle transparent and stable tariff barriers, members are substituting discriminatory, unpredictable antidumping suits. Thus providing evidence about the motives for adopting AD laws and for using them bears directly on this relevant controversy that often sees developing and developed countries on opposite sides. Developing countries object to the proliferation of antidumping laws and safeguards because they are particularly vulnerable to unpredictable shifts in market access. While industrialized countries insist that conditional domestic protection is key to gradually liberalizing international trade.

The paper does a good job at putting together a number of indicators of potential motives for adopting/using AD laws and then running a horse race to see which ones are relevant. It also attaches interpretations to the correlations obtained, often stressing causality as running from the left hand variables to the right hand variables.

One interesting finding is that WTO participation is correlated with AD adoption; this suggests that countries adopt AD laws in view of WTO membership. But why? The favored interpretation is that this reflects a country protective reaction to exposure to international competition and simultaneous removal of trade barriers that participation in the WTO entails. An alternative interpretation, in my view, is that participation in WTO and adoption of AD laws are both driven by a third, unobserved factor that leads a process of trade liberalization – a change in 'philosophy' or policy style, in favor of more market-friendly policies and economic freedom. A similar argument applies to the results on the safety net hypothesis where measures of trade liberalizations (index of openness) are found to be positively correlated with the adoption of AD laws, while changes in tariffs are correlated negatively with AD laws. The point that I am making is that many of the variables that are chosen as potential drivers of AD adoption – including trade liberalizations and participation is WTO – are endogenous and can be seen as part of an underling process that leads a country to change its attitude towards international trade. To address this difficult issue of causality properly one should find an instrument for trade liberalization–exogenous forces that move a country towards trade liberalization, a difficult task.

Another instance where the same problem shows up is the main specification when total trade is used to test the substitution effect hypothesis (AD replaces tariffs). Here the problem is reverse causality: the substitution hypothesis implies that more openness causes more demand for AD laws; on the other hand, more AD laws, *ceteris paribus*, may cause less openness. In this case the problem is addressed by replacing a country openness with a measure of openness in the area. How good an instrument this is, however is not clear.

In my view the most robust evidence in support of the idea that AD laws are used (abused) to protect national industries in the wake of a process of trade liberalization is the effect that past initiations/measures received have on AD laws (the retaliation hypothesis). It is hard to imagine in this case causality running the other way round. Thus, while a reading of the various effects one by one may be consistent with different interpretations, a joint reading of the correlations presented in the paper looks supportive of the author's argument.

Christian Schultz

University of Copenhagen

This paper addresses an important policy question. Antidumping laws are the subject of a lively policy debate among economists, lawyers and politicians all over the world. A particular concern in this debate is the proliferation of antidumping measures and the possibility of curbing misuse by amending the WTO system. Before policy measures are taken it is important to understand how the present system works. Vandenbussche and Zanardi have written an interesting paper, which analyzes why countries adopt antidumping (AD) laws and what causes them to start using the law actively. While AD laws may be beneficial, as they perhaps make it easier for countries to open up and liberalize trade more generally, they can be misused and hinder prosperous trade. A central message from the paper is that the determinants the paper identifies for adoption and first use of AD, point to misuse as an important phenomenon.

The paper sets up various possible hypotheses for why antidumping laws are adopted. There is no firm theory behind the hypotheses, rather they reflect common sense. The hypotheses are: retaliation, a substitution effect hypothesis (trade liberalization reduces the option to use traditional trade policy tools, and an AD law may to some extent substitute for this), institutional reasons (WTO membership, time passed since WTO membership), contagion effects (neighboring countries have adopted an AD law), political economy factors (strong industries) and macro effects. Through a survival analysis the authors try to estimate the influence of these factors in determining a country's decision to adopt an antidumping law and subsequently make use of it.

A section on methodology carefully explains the empirical strategy. For the reader, who is uninitiated in the mysteries of survival analysis, this is a welcome service.

The results are broadly that cumulated AD measures received in the past (long-term retaliation), recent membership of WTO, number of AD laws on the same continent (a measure of contagion), an openness index, and industry's share of GDP all make the adoption of an antidumping law more likely. Measures relating to macroeconomic factors like GDP growth, real exchange rate movements, or the income level of the country do not matter.

As for the first use of AD measures, the number of AD measures received in the past year is highly significant, indicating that retaliation is important. Similarly, the income level of the country influences the adoption positively. There are weaker effects from the number of active AD laws in same continent and ore and metal's share of total imports. The latter effect is interpreted as relating to political economy effects, since it is well-known that the steel and chemical industries are often protected by AD measures.

The paper is intriguing, but as noted above there is no firm theory behind the hypotheses, they rather reflect the common wisdom, partly stemming from the relevant literature, and a good portion of common sense. While the authors' common sense is much like mine, a disadvantage stemming from this strategy is that some of the hypotheses seem to be interrelated. For example, the distinction between the substitution hypothesis and the so-called institutional reasons seems blurred. Similarly, under the political economy hypothesis it seems that there are elements of the substitution effect as well as the retaliation hypothesis. Furthermore the relation between the hypothesis and the variable supposed to reflect the influence of this particular channel may sometimes be questioned.

An open question which remains is whether there are common determinants of some of the variables employed. For instance, the decision to become a WTO member is not an exogenous variable. This decision may be driven by a number of factors, which could easily also affect the decision to adopt an AD law and use an AD law. This raises the question of what the significance of the 'WTO entry in last 5 years' on the right hand side means? If there are common factors determining WTO membership and adoption of an AD law, the two variables will be related in the regression even though there is no causal relation between the two. More generally, one may worry whether the causality is always from the right hand side to the left hand side in the regressions. Similarly, the contagion hypothesis is a bit controversial in that there are no economic theories behind it. One wonders whether the significance of the variable 'number of AD laws in same continent' just picks up some other correlated effects. In all fairness, the authors are aware of the problems, but I think they still deserve to be mentioned.

It is my judgement that the authors have come a good way in uncovering determinants for adoption and first use of AD laws. However, I would find it very interesting to go further and try to relate the adoption of AD laws and their first use to more fundamental variables. In line with the recent progress in the theory of competition policy and political economy, one has a strong feeling that it would pay to dig deeper and try to relate to more fundamental and structural variables.

From the political economy perspective, it seems obvious to see whether the political structures of the countries affect the issues at hand. Are democracies more prone to adopt and use AD laws than dictatorships? Are right or left wing governments more prone to introduce and use AD? Is there a difference between parliamentary and presidential systems? A large literature in political economy has studied the effects and determinants of corruption. A natural question to ask is whether more corrupt countries are more prone to adopt and use AD? Similarly, it is a natural question whether the legal system of a country has an impact on AD. Is there a difference according to whether a country has common law or not? While the size of industry and the size of industries that are well known to receive AD-protection, steel and chemicals, enter the regressions, Olson's analysis would suggest that industries would more easily overcome the collective action problem if they were more concentrated. This leads to the hypothesis that more concentrated industries lobby harder for protection and thus to more AD. The list could be made much longer; my point here is just that it seems a natural next candidate to try to uncover such more fundamental determinants.

A potential problem, which the paper does not address, and which may also be important in further research on these issues, is that a government typically has several protective measures at hand. Technical trade barriers come to mind. Economic and political economy theories typically aim at predicting when protective trade measures are taken, not at predicting when the particular measure is AD. It appears that a more detailed analysis is called for in order to address this issue.

The paper has a nice section explaining the WTO AD system, according to which the use of AD is sometimes justified. The methods employed in the paper do not allow a distinction between justified and non-justified use of AD, the presumption being, I guess, that most use is non-justified anyway. In this perspective, the retaliation result is very interesting; it seems hard to believe that retaliatory use of AD can be justified according to the WTO rules.

Panel discussion

Fontagné thought that the relation between WTO accession, tariffs and AD law was not fully clear in the paper as entry in the WTO necessarily implied partial phasing out of tariffs and that possible introduction of antidumping regulation was conditional on WTO entry. Seabright suggested that the presence of AD laws can be partly explained by political economy issues as they represent a failure of domestic competition laws. The authors replied that AD laws represent a second best measure when competition laws do not operate well.

O'Rourke thought that the choice to use AD laws rather than other policies certainly depended on industrial structure: some industries may be more vulnerable to the kind of temporary shocks AD can be useful against. This also implies that the growth process of various countries may explain the proliferation of AD laws. Drazen believed that this type of research required more theoretical structure on the political economy mechanisms at work. It is certainly important to better understand who the gainers/losers in each country are to analyze the determinants of AD laws and draw some policy implications.

DATA APPENDIX

Table A1. Description and sources of variables

Variables	Description	Sources
Adoption AD law	Year of adoption of AD law. Number of countries with AD laws.	Zanardi (2004a) and authors' updates.
AD variables	Variables related to the number of initiations and measures targeted to each country (in a given year or cumulated) at a sectoral level.	Zanardi (2004a) and Moore and Zanardi (2006).
Openness index	Index of 'Freedom to trade internationally' (interpolated).	Economic Freedom Index published by the Fraser Institute.
Applied tariffs	Average (unweighted) applied tariff rates (interpolated).	World Bank: http://siteresources.worldbank.org/INTRES/Resources/tar2005.xls
Union density	Dummy variables based on trade union density.	AIAS, Blanchflower (2006), ILO (1998), Ishikawa and Lawrence (2005), Kuruvilla et al. (2002), OECD – Labour Market Statistics, Roberts and Wibbels (1999), US Department of Labor, Visser (2003).
Skilled/unskilled population	Ratio of skilled to unskilled people aged 15 or older (interpolated).	Barro–Lee dataset.
Macro-economic variables	Variables related to a country economic structure and performance (e.g. GDP, exchange rate, FDI).	World Development Indicators. CHELEM for Taiwan.
WTO membership	Membership of the GATT/WTO and year of accession.	WTO website.

Table A2. Correlation matrix

Variables	Cumulated AD	Openness	WTO entry	Number of AD laws	Industry VA	Services VA	Medium income	High income non-OECD	High income OECD
Cumulated AD	1								
Openness	0.051	1							
WTO entry	-0.038	-0.042	1						
Number of AD laws	0.107	0.054	0.078	1					
Industry VA	0.179	-0.088	0.124	0.014	1				
Services VA	-0.050	-0.085	0.028	0.116	-0.137	1			
Medium income	0.137	0.003	0.136	0.127	0.358	0.238	1		
High income non-OECD	0.017	-0.101	0.046	-0.047	0.278	0.226	-0.290	1	
High income OECD	-0.002	-0.021	-0.048	0.185	0.044	0.172	-0.150	-0.043	1
Openness continent	0.072	0.440	0.084	0.123	-0.087	0.020	0.028	-0.105	-0.052
Chemicals	0.062	-0.049	0.032	-0.086	0.102	-0.101	0.245	-0.329	-0.099
Textiles and clothing	-0.024	-0.035	0.015	0.013	-0.199	0.162	-0.164	0.279	-0.078
FDI	0.114	-0.028	0.068	0.341	0.081	0.116	0.068	0.303	0.009
Medium union	-0.074	0.048	-0.044	0.174	0.080	-0.031	0.180	-0.089	0.054
High union	0.275	0.067	-0.125	0.018	0.167	-0.077	-0.130	0.094	0.086

Notes: The upper part of the table reports correlations for 1113 observations. The rows for the regressors used in columns (2) to (6) of Table 3 report correlations for each of these variables with the variables in each column for the observations included in each respective specification.

REFERENCES

Anderson, K. (1993). 'Antidumping Laws in the US; Use and Welfare Consequences', *Journal of World Trade*, 27, 99–117.

Bagwell, K. and Staiger, R.W. (1999). 'An Economic Theory of GATT', *American Economic Review*, 89, 215–248.

Bagwell, K. and Staiger, R.W. (2002). *The Economics of the World Trading System*, Cambridge, MA: MIT Press.

Baldwin, R.E. (1989). 'The Political Economy of Trade Policy', *Journal of Economic Perspectives*, 3, 119–135.

Blanchflower, D.G. (2006). 'A Cross-Country Study of Union Membership', *IZA Discussion Paper No. 2016*, Bonn: IZA.

Blonigen, B. and Bown, C. (2003). 'Antidumping and Retaliation Threats', *Journal of International Economics*, 60, 249–273.

Blonigen, B. and Prusa, T.J. (2003). 'Antidumping', in Choi, E.K. and Harrigan, J. (eds.), *Handbook of International Trade*, Oxford, UK and Cambridge, MA: Blackwell Publishers.

Bown, C. (2006). 'The WTO and Antidumping in Developing Countries', *mimeo*, Waltham, MA: Brandeis University.

Cleves, M.A., Gould, W.W. and Gutierrez, R.G. (2004). *An Introduction to Survival Analysis Using Stata (Revised Edition)*, College Station, TX: Stata Press.

Congressional Budget Office (1998). 'Antidumping Action in the United States and Around the World: An Analysis of International Data', *CBO Paper*, Washington, DC.

DeVault, J. (1996). 'The Welfare Effects of US Antidumping Duties', *Open Economies Review*, 7, 19–33.

Drazen, A. (2000). *Political Economy in Macroeconomics*, Princeton, NJ: Princeton University Press.

Feinberg, R. and Reynolds, K. (2006). 'The Spread of Antidumping Regimes and the Role of Retaliation in Filings', *Southern Economic Journal*, 72, 877–890.

Feinberg, R. and Reynolds, K. (2007). 'Tariff Liberalisation and Increased Administrative Protection: Is There a *Quid Pro Quo*?' *World Economy*, 30, 948–961.

Finger, J.M., Hall, H.K. and Nelson, D. (1982). 'The Political Economy of Administered Protection', *American Economic Review*, 72, 452–466.

Finger, J.M., Ng, F. and Wangchuk, S. (2002). 'Antidumping as a Safeguard Policy', in Stern, R. (ed.), *Issues and Options for US–Japan Trade Policies*, Ann Arbor: University of Michigan Press.

Finger, J.M. and Nogués, J.J. (eds.) (2005). *Safeguards and Antidumping in Latin American Trade Liberalization: Fighting Fire with Fire*, New York, NY: New York.

Gallaway, M.C., Blonigen, B.A. and Flynn, J.E. (1999). 'Welfare Costs of the US Antidumping and Countervailing Duty Laws', *Journal of International Economics*, 49, 211–244.

Gawande, K. and Krishna, P. (2003). 'The Political Economy of Trade Policy: Empirical Approaches', in Choi, K.C. and Harrigan, J. (eds.), *Handbook of International Trade*, Oxford: Blackwell.

Grossman, G. and Helpman, E. (1994). 'Protection for Sale', *American Economic Review*, 84, 833–850.

Grossman, G. and Wauters, J. (2007). 'United States Sunset Reviews of Anti-dumping Measures on Oil Country Tubular Goods from Argentina', paper presented at a conference organized by the American Law Institute at WTO, Geneva.

Hillman, A. (1982). 'Declining Industries and Political Support Protectionist Motives', *American Economic Review*, 72, 1180–1187.

Hoekman, B. and Mavroidis, P.C. (1996). 'Dumping, Antidumping and Antitrust', *Journal of World Trade*, 30, 27–52.

Ikenson, D.J. (2002). 'Dump Antidumping Regs', National Review Online, http://www.freetrade.org.

ILO (1998). *World Labour Report: Industrial Relations, Democracy, and Social Stability 1997–98*, Geneva: ILO.

Ishikawa, J. and Lawrence, S. (2005).'Trade Union Membership and Collective Bargaining Coverage: Statistical Concepts, Methods and Findings', *DIALOGUE Paper No. 10*, Geneva: ILO.

Knetter, M. and Prusa, T.J. (2003). 'Macroeconomic Factors and Antidumping Filings: Evidence from Four Countries', *Journal of International Economics*, 61, 1–17.

Konings, J., Vandenbussche, H. and Springael, L. (2001). 'Import Diversion under European Antidumping Policy', *Journal of Industry, Competition and Trade*, 1, 283–299.

Kuruvilla, S., Das, S., Kwon, H. and Kwon, S. (2002). 'Trade Union Growth and Decline in Asia', *British Journal of Industrial Relations*, 40, 431–461.

Lancaster, T. (1990). *The Econometric Analysis of Transition Data*. Cambridge: Cambridge University Press.

Leidy, M.P. (1997). 'Macroeconomic Conditions and Pressures for Protection under Antidumping and Countervailing Duty Laws: Empirical Evidence from the United States', IMF Staff Papers 44, 132–144.

Macrory, P.F.J. (2005). 'The Anti-Dumping Agreement', in Macrory, P.F.J., Appleton, A.E. and Plummer, M.G. (eds.), *The World Trade Organization: Legal, Economic and Political Analysis*, vol. I, New York: Springer.

Martin, A. and Vergote, W. (2004). 'Antidumping: Welfare Enhancing Retaliation?' *MPRA Paper No. 5416*.

Mayer, W. (1984). 'Endogenous Tariff Formation', *American Economic Review*, 74, 970–985.

Messerlin, P. (1990). 'Anti-Dumping Regulations or Pro-Cartel Law? The EC Chemical Cases', *The World Economy*, 13, 465–492.

Messerlin, P. (1994). 'Should Antidumping Rules be Replaced by National or International Competition Rules?' *Aussenwirtschaft*, 49, 351–374.

Moore, M.O. (1992). 'Rules or Politics? An Empirical Analysis of ITC Anti-Dumping Decisions', *Economic Inquiry*, 30, 449–466.

Moore, M.O. (2007). 'Antidumping Reform in the Doha Round: A Pessimistic Appraisal', *Pacific Economic Review*, 12, 335–379.

Moore, M.O. and Zanardi, M. (2006). 'Does Antidumping Use Contribute to Trade Liberalization? An Empirical Analysis', *CentER working paper 61*, Tilburg University, The Netherlands.

Nelson, D. (2006). 'The Political Economy of Antidumping: A Survey', *European Journal of Political Economy*, 22, 554–590.

Niels, G. (2003). 'Trade Diversion and Trade Destruction Effects of Antidumping Policy: Empirical Evidence from Mexico', paper presented at the ETSG conference, Madrid.

Niels, G. and ten Kate, A. (2006). 'Antidumping Policy in Developing Countries: Safety Valve or Obstacle to Free Trade?' *European Journal of Political Economy*, 22, 618–638.

Ognivtsev, V., Jounela, E. and Tang, X. (2001). 'Accession to the WTO: The Process and Selected Issues', in *WTO Accession and Development Policies*, Geneva: UNCTAD.

Olson, M. (1965). *The Logic of Collective Action*, Cambridge, MA: Harvard University Press.

Prusa, T.J. (1992). 'Why are so Many Antidumping Petitions Withdrawn?' *Journal of International Integration*, 33, 1–20.

Prusa, T.J. (1994). 'Pricing Behavior in the Presence of Antidumping Law', *Journal of Economic Integration*, 9, 260–289.

Prusa, T.J. (1997). 'The Trade Effects of U.S. Antidumping Actions', in Feenstra, R. (ed.), *The Effects of US Trade Protection and Promotion Policies*, Chicago: University of Chicago Press.

Prusa, T.J. and Skeath, S. (2002). 'The Economic and Strategic Motives for Antidumping Filings', *Weltwirtschaftliches Archiv*, 138, 389–413.

Prusa, T.J. and Skeath, S. (2005). 'Modern Commercial Policy: Managed Trade or Retaliation?' in Choi, E.K. and Hartigan, J. (eds.), *Handbook of International Trade*, vol. 2, Oxford, UK and Cambridge, MA: Blackwell Publishers.

Reyes de la Torre, L.E. and González, J.G. (2005). 'Antidumping and Safeguard Measures in the Political Economy of Liberalization: The Mexican Case', in Finger, J.M. and Nogues, J.J. (eds.), *Safeguards and Antidumping in Latin American Trade Liberalization: Fighting Fire with Fire*, Washington DC: World Bank.

Roberts, K.M. and Wibbels, E. (1999). 'Party Systems and Electoral Volatility in Latin America: A Test of Economic, Institutional, and Structural Explanations', *American Political Science Review*, 93, 575–590.

Sapir, A. (2006). 'Some Ideas for Reforming the Community Anti-Dumping Instrument', paper prepared for EU Trade Commissioner Mr Mandelson for Seminar on Trade Defense Instruments, 11 July 2006 (http://www.bruegel.org).

Sapir, A. and Trachtman, J.P. (2007). 'Subsidization, Price Depression and Expertise: Causation and Precision in Upland Cotton', paper presented at a conference organized by the American Law Institute at WTO, Geneva.

Shin, H.J. (1998). 'Possible Instances of Predatory Pricing in Recent US Antidumping Cases', in Lawrence, R. (ed.), *Brookings Trade Forum 1998*, Washington DC: Brookings Institute Press.

Staiger, W.R. and Wolak, F.A. (1994). 'Measuring Industry-specific Protection: Antidumping in the United States', *Brookings Papers on Economic Activity, Microeconomics*, 51–118.

Tharakan, P.K.M. and Waelbroeck, J. (1994). 'Antidumping and Countervailing Duty Decisions in the EC and in the US: An Experiment in Comparative Political Economy', *European Economic Review*, 38, 171–193.

US Department of Labor, *Foreign Labor Trends* (various issues).

US International Trade Commission (1995). 'The Economic Effects of Antidumping and Countervailing Duty Orders and Suspension Agreements', *Investigation No. 332–344. Publication 2900*, Washington DC.

Vandenbussche, H., Veugelers, R. and Konings, J. (2001). 'Union Wage Bargaining and European Antidumping Policy', *Oxford Economic Papers*, 53, 297–317.

Vandenbussche, H. and Zanardi, M. (2007a). 'The Global Chilling Effects of Antidumping Proliferation', revised version of *CEPR discussion paper 5597* (2006).

Vandenbussche, H. and Zanardi, M. (2007b). 'What Explains the Proliferation of Antidumping Laws?', *UCL working paper 2007/66*, UCL, Louvain la Neuve, Belgium.

Veugelers, R. and Vandenbussche, H. (1999). 'European Anti-Dumping Policy and the Profitability of National and International Collusion', *European Economic Review*, 43, 1–28.

Viner, J. (1923). *Dumping: A Problem in International Trade*, Chicago, IL: The University of Chicago Press.

Visser, J. (2003). 'Unions and Unionism Around the World', in Addison, J.T. and Schnabel, C. (eds.), *International Handbook of Trade Unions*, Cheltenham, UK: Edward Elgar Publishing Ltd.

Zanardi, M. (2004a). 'Antidumping: What are the Numbers to Discuss at Doha?' *The World Economy*, 27, 403–433.

Zanardi, M. (2004b). 'Antidumping Law as a Collusive Device', *Canadian Journal of Economics*, 37, 95–122.

Market services productivity

SUMMARY

Since the mid-1990s, market services have positively influenced labor productivity growth in the US, but not in most European countries. We analyze these cross-country differences in growth dynamics using industry-level measures of output, inputs, and multifactor productivity (MFP) from the new EU KLEMS database. We find that using detailed data has important implications for empirical analysis of policy influences on growth. Increased investment in information and communication technology (ICT) capital and growth in human capital contributed substantially to labor productivity growth in market services across all European countries and the US. However, countries differ most strongly in the rates of efficiency improvement in the use of inputs. We find no evidence of an externality-driven relationship between such efficiency changes and the growth of ICT use or of employment of university-educated workers. We also find that entry liberalization has been beneficial for productivity growth in telecommunications, but not in other service industries.

— *Robert Inklaar, Marcel P. Timmer and Bart van Ark*

Market services productivity across Europe and the US

Robert Inklaar, Marcel P. Timmer and Bart van Ark

Groningen Growth and Development Centre, University of Groningen, The Netherlands

1. INTRODUCTION

Labor productivity growth in the European Union has been substantially slower than in the United States since the mid-1990s. The prospects for Europe to become the most dynamic region of the world in the near future, as established in the Lisbon Agenda, therefore seem to be dim. Table 1 summarizes labor productivity growth across Europe and the US. Even though productivity growth slowed down for the European Union-15 as a whole, this table shows that European performance has not been universally poor.[1] Countries like Austria, Finland and the UK showed much

The authors would like to thank Wendy Carlin and Jonathan Temple and other participants at the 45th Panel Meeting of Economic Policy in Frankfurt for valuable comments. This research was supported by the European Commission, Research Directorate General as part of the 6th Framework Programme, Priority 8, 'Policy Support and Anticipating Scientific and Technological Needs' and is part of the 'EU KLEMS project on Growth and Productivity in the European Union'. We are grateful to all participants in the EU KLEMS consortium for their contribution to the project. The authors would also like to thank participants at seminars at the Productivity Commission (Australia), University of Queensland, the EMG Workshop at the University of New South Wales and the AEA 2007 meetings in Chicago, and four anonymous referees.

The Managing Editor in charge of this paper was Giuseppe Bertola.

[1] The EU-15 refers to all member states before the May 2004 Accession Round. In this paper we do not address the performance of the ten new member states, even though those are part of the EU KLEMS database. Also, in the remainder of the paper we exclude five EU-15 countries from our analysis, i.e. Greece, Ireland, Luxembourg, Portugal and Sweden. The latter countries had to be excluded from the measures of capital and MFP in this paper, because series adequate for growth accounting at the industry level are still missing for the whole of the period 1980–2004. In 2005, these 10 European countries made up 92% of GDP in the EU-15 and 83% of GDP in the EU-25.

Economic Policy January 2008 pp. 139–194 Printed in Great Britain
© CEPR, CES, MSH, 2008.

Table 1. Growth rates of GDP per hour worked in European countries and the US, 1980–2006 (average annual growth in %)

	1980–1995	1995–2006
EU-15	2.3	1.4
United States	1.3	2.2
Austria	2.4	2.3
Belgium	2.0	1.4
Denmark	2.5	1.2
Finland	3.0	2.5
France	2.5	1.8
Germany	2.4	1.7
Greece	0.9	2.5
Ireland	3.6	4.2
Italy	2.1	0.4
Luxembourg	2.6	1.9
Netherlands	1.7	1.5
Portugal	2.1	1.7
Spain	3.0	−0.2
Sweden	1.3	2.5
United Kingdom	2.6	2.0
Average of 15 EU countries	2.3	1.8
Standard deviation	0.7	1.0

Notes: Countries that were members of EU-15 before 1 May 2004.

Source: GGDC/TCB Total Economy Database, January 2007, www.ggdc.net

better performance than laggard countries such as Italy and Spain. This raises the broader question of what is driving cross-country differences in productivity growth. By now, it is well known that market services have been the major driver of strong US labor productivity growth since the 1990s (Triplett and Bosworth, 2004) and these industries are at the heart of the labor productivity growth differences between the EU-15 and the US (van Ark *et al.*, 2003, 2008; Blanchard, 2004). A largely unanswered question is still *why* labor productivity growth in market services has differed across Europe and the US.

The main sources of labor productivity growth are investment in physical and human capital and gains in efficiency, also referred to as multifactor productivity (MFP) growth. In this paper, we will provide a detailed accounting of the importance of these sources of labor productivity growth in service industries. For this purpose we make use of the recent release of the EU KLEMS database, which provides a comprehensive overview of output, inputs and productivity at the industry level for a large set of European countries and the US.[2] Our focus on market services should prove particularly useful, not only because the US experience shows that it can be a

---

[2] The EU KLEMS database is the product of a joint research project, funded by the European Commission, Research Directorate General, in which the Groningen Growth and Development Centre at the University of Groningen is one of the key collaborators. The empirical work in this paper is mostly based on the database released in March 2007, which is freely available at www.euklems.net, described in Timmer *et al.* (2007a).

substantial source of growth, but also because services are amongst the most intensive users of new technologies (in particular ICT) and skilled labor. This puts the developments in market services at the heart of the Lisbon Agenda aimed at creating a dynamic knowledge-based economy, and deserving of further study. If it is true that the growth effects of investment in skills and ICT differ strongly across countries, this should show up most clearly in a study of market services.

After analyzing the sources of labor productivity growth, we undertake an analysis of factors driving technological change and efficiency gains. Aghion and Howitt (2006) suggest that the post-World War II catch-up of European economies to the US has slowed down recently as the technology gap with the US has narrowed. Policies and institutions which facilitated imitation of technologies in the past are not well suited for growth close to the technology frontier. The latter should be based on innovation in a competitive market environment, rooted in a country's own resources such as skilled labor and research and development. The growth-policy recommendations in the Sapir report (Sapir *et al.*, 2004) are in large part based on this line of argument, supported by two key empirical studies. First, Vandenbussche, Aghion and Méghir (2006) show that economies with more university-educated workers show faster MFP growth, in particular when they are close to the technology frontier. Second, Nicoletti and Scarpetta (2003) show that lowering entry barriers stimulates MFP growth. However, their findings are mostly limited to manufacturing industries, which begs the question whether such effects can also be found in market services. This is all the more important since many of the most highly regulated industries today are in market services (Conway and Nicoletti, 2006) and because many of the policy initiatives for regulatory reform focus on opening up of services markets, in particular the EU Services Directive.

The main contribution of this paper is that we address these issues using the new EU KLEMS database. This database contains novel measures of the skill distribution of the workforce and the composition of investment. It makes it possible to accurately measure and analyze the role of high-skilled labor and investment in ICT-capital for labor productivity growth at a detailed industry level. In Section 2, we show that growth differences in market services closely mirror aggregate growth differences across countries. We find that the use of ICT and university-educated workers contributes substantially to labor productivity growth in market services in all European countries and in the US. However, most of the cross-country growth differences are not due to differences in the pace of investment in ICT and human capital. Instead, differences in efficiency gains are the key factor in cross-country differences in labor productivity growth in market services (Section 3). We cannot find any evidence of externalities to the use of ICT and university-educated workers which might explain differences in efficiency gains across countries. As such, our results regarding the effect of human capital stand in contrast to the findings of Vandenbussche *et al.* (2006). We show that this can be traced to the use of more sophisticated productivity data and our industry-level focus. Furthermore, we find that lower regulatory barriers to entry in post and telecommunications have stimulated MFP growth which extends the findings by Nicoletti and Scarpetta (2003) to the services sector. This illustrates the importance of a detailed industry focus. It also provides support for further liberalization, not only within countries, but also across borders as envisaged in the EU Services Directive. However, although our evidence is suggestive of a role for product market liberalization to improve market services productivity growth, it must be treated with caution as we do not find similar supportive evidence for other services industries. Section 5 concludes.

2. MARKET SERVICES AND AGGREGATE GROWTH

Ever since the work by Baumol and Bowen (1966) on the cost disease hypothesis in cultural arts, economic growth in advanced countries is presumed to suffer from slow productivity growth in services. In essence, Baumol's cost disease states that productivity improvements in services are less likely than in the goods-producing industries because many services are inherently labor-intensive, which makes it difficult to substitute labor for capital (Baumol, 1967). As services make up an increasing share of the economy as countries grow richer, a decline in aggregate productivity growth would be inevitable. It turns out, however, that the cost disease hypothesis no longer has much validity at least for the market services sector in the United States, which broadly includes trade, transportation, communication, financial, business and personal services. While the share of market services in the US increased from 37 to 44% between 1980 and 2004, labor productivity growth accelerated from 1.4% from 1980–1995 to 3.3% from 1995–2004 (see Table 2).[3] In a seminal study looking in detail at the productivity performance of individual service industries in the US, Triplett and Bosworth (2006) show that since 1995, 15 out of 22 two-digit services industries experienced an acceleration in labor productivity that at least equalled the economy-wide average. Hence the authors titled their study 'Baumol's Disease has been cured.' Most European countries, however, still seem to suffer from Baumol's disease. While the share of market services in nominal GDP in Europe has been steadily increasing from on average 34% of GDP in 1980 to 41% in 2004, labor productivity growth rates in European market services have been slow and declining in most cases.[4] Only the Netherlands and the UK recorded accelerating productivity growth in market services after 1995 (see Table 2).

Before proceeding we need to provide a more precise measure of the importance of market services in accounting for the trend in aggregate labor productivity growth.

[3] Market services as defined in this study include nine industries, see Appendix Table 1 for precise definitions. The increase in the GDP share of market services is the result of a number of interacting forces (Schettkat and Yokarini, 2006). First, a high income elasticity for services and an increase in per capita income lead to higher demand for services in general. In addition, there is an increasing marketization of traditional household production activities (Freeman and Schettkat, 2005). Finally, there is a tendency for outsourcing of business, trade and transport activities by firms boosting business demand for market services.

[4] As indicated in footnote 1, the EU-average in the remainder of this paper relates to 10 of the 15 EU countries, excluding Greece, Ireland, Luxembourg, Portugal and Sweden.

Table 2. Share in GDP and average annual labor productivity growth in European countries and the US, market services, 1980–2004 (%)

	Share of market services in GDP (%)			Growth of value added per hour worked	
	1980	1995	2004	1980–1995	1995–2004
Austria	37	40	43	2.1	0.7
Belgium	32	40	44	1.4	1.2
Denmark	34	38	40	3.0	0.9
Finland	30	34	36	2.5	1.7
France	36	38	41	1.9	1.3
Germany	32	38	40	2.3	0.8
Italy	36	40	42	0.6	0.3
Netherlands	34	42	46	0.3	2.4
Spain	31	38	41	1.0	0.4
UK	33	41	49	1.9	2.5
US	37	41	44	1.4	3.3
Average	34	39	42	1.7	1.4
Standard deviation	2.4	2.2	3.3	0.8	1.0

Source: EU KLEMS database, March 2007 (http://www.euklems.net), described in Timmer *et al.* (2007).

The contributions of market services to aggregate labor productivity can be calculated using a shift-share approach. Following this approach the contribution of an industry to aggregate productivity growth is measured by weighting its labor productivity growth rate by its share in aggregate value added. Figure 1 summarizes the relative contributions of market services and the other industries (including manufacturing, mining, utilities and agriculture) to labor productivity growth in the market economy for each country in the period 1995–2004.[5] The countries are ranked according to total market economy productivity growth ranging from the highest growth rate in Finland to the lowest growth rate in Spain.[6] It appears that the divergence in market economy productivity growth is mainly due to differences in the contribution of market services, which is highest in fast-growing economies such as Finland, the US, the Netherlands and the UK, and close to zero in Germany, Italy and Spain. This confirms the results from recent studies for the US by Jorgenson, Ho and Stiroh (2005) and Bosworth and Triplett (2007) which indicate that market services are the most important driver of the American growth resurgence. The differentiating role of market services also confirms our previous studies on the growth differential

---

[5] Market economy excludes health (ISIC industry N), education (ISIC M), private households with employed persons (ISIC P) and government sectors (ISIC L). We also exclude real estate (ISIC 70), because output in this industry mostly reflects imputed housing rents rather than sales of firms. The measurement problems in the public services are more substantial than in market services, and in several cases (in particular for government) the output growth is measured using input growth. Still, labor productivity growth measures for non-market services tend to be somewhat higher for the EU than for the US, so that the market economy productivity measures show an even larger gap between the EU and the US since 1995 and in particular since 2000, than the measures for the aggregate economy.

[6] Strong productivity growth in other industries in Finland is driven primarily by growth in IT-goods production (Daveri and Silva, 2004). Other countries covered in this study have a much smaller IT-producing sector.

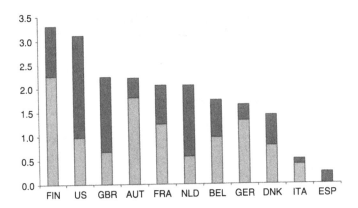

Figure 1. Contribution of market services (dark) and other industries (light) to market economy labor productivity growth in Europe and US, 1995–2004

Notes: Following Stiroh (2002) aggregate labor productivity growth can be written as:

$$\ln \frac{VA_t/H_t}{VA_{t-1}/H_{t-1}} = \sum_i \bar{v}_i^{VA} \ln \frac{VA_{i,t}/H_{i,t}}{VA_{i,t-1}/H_{i,t-1}} + \left(\sum_i \bar{v}_i^{VA} \ln \frac{H_{i,t}}{H_{i,t-1}} - \ln \frac{H_t}{H_{t-1}} \right)$$ where VA and H denote gross value added

and hours worked respectively, and $\bar{v}_i^{VA}$ is the two-period average share of industry i in aggregate value added. The contribution of an industry to aggregate productivity growth is measured by weighting its labor productivity growth rate by its share in aggregate value added. The term in brackets is the reallocation of hours. It reflects differences in the share of an industry in aggregate value added and its share in aggregate hours worked. The reallocation term is positive if employment shifts from low productivity industries towards high productivity industries. 'other industries' also includes the reallocation-term.

Source: EU KLEMS database, March 2007 (http://www.euklems.net), described in Timmer *et al.* (2007a).

between Europe and the United States (O'Mahony and van Ark, 2003; Losch, 2006; Inklaar, Timmer and van Ark, 2007).

A more in-depth focus on the market services sector reveals that growth differences are particularly large in retail and wholesale trade and financial services. This raises the question to what extent the differences in performance across Europe are a statistical artefact due to differences in measurement methods by national statistical institutes, as for example suggested in a report of the European Commission (2004). Based on a survey of the current state of services output measurement practices we conclude that for many market service industries, output measures in the National Accounts should give a fairly accurate – albeit not perfect – internationally comparable picture of developments (see discussion in Appendix 1).

3. THE GROWING ROLE OF SKILLS AND ICT-CAPITAL IN GROWTH

It has often been stated that growth in today's knowledge economy is strongly driven by an increasing use of skills and ICT-capital in the so-called knowledge economy. In this section we use a growth accounting methodology to measure the relative contributions of various capital assets and labor types to growth in market services. Section 3.1 introduces the basic data source for this paper, the EU KLEMS database. In Section 3.2 we discuss recent trends in investment in ICT and non-ICT assets in market services across Europe and the US. This is followed by an analysis of the developments in the use of skilled labor over the past decades (Section 3.3). Based on these input measures, a decomposition of labor productivity growth in market services is provided in Section 3.4. We show that investment in ICT and the use of skilled labor are important drivers of labor productivity growth in all countries. On average, they account for a large part of the growth in all European countries. However, *differences* in investment rates and the use of skilled labor cannot fully explain the *differences* across countries in labor productivity growth. This suggests that the fastest growers are particularly characterised by their more efficient use of inputs as measured by multifactor productivity (MFP). The determinants of MFP growth are analysed in more detail in Section 4.

3.1. EU KLEMS database and growth accounting methodology

In this study we exploit a new growth accounts database, called EU KLEMS.[7] This database has been constructed with the explicit aim of providing internationally comparable series on output, inputs and productivity by industry within a consistent framework for a large set of European countries and the United States. In this database, various sets of inputs are distinguished: capital (K), labor (L), Energy (E), Materials (M) and Services (S). Accurate measures of labor and capital input contributions to growth are based on a breakdown of aggregate hours worked and aggregate capital stock into various components. Hours worked are cross-classified by educational attainment, gender and age (to proxy for work experience) into 18 labor categories to account for differences in the productivity of various labor types, such as high- versus low-skilled labor. Thus labor input measures in EU KLEMS take account of changes in the skill-level of the labor force. Similarly, capital stock measures are broken down into different asset types to study the impact of the increasing use of ICT assets. We make a distinction between three ICT assets (office and computing equipment, communication equipment and software) and three non-ICT assets (transport equipment, other machinery and equipment and non-residential structures).[8]

The EU KLEMS database provides a long time-series going back to 1970 through linking of National Accounts data series from different release vintages. National Accounts series are further subdivided into the industry, labor and capital detail on the basis of additional secondary data sources. For example, industry detail for output and labor input (employment and hours) series is obtained from industry surveys. For a breakdown of various labor categories, additional sources are used, such as Labour Force Surveys, which are available on an annual basis for most countries. Separate

---

[7] This database is publicly available at www.euklems.net and described in Timmer *et al.* (2007a).

[8] Residential capital is excluded from the analysis here to focus on assets in the market economy. Investment in residential buildings is almost exclusively concentrated in the real estate industry, which is excluded in this study.

series on investment particularly in computers and communication equipment are normally not provided in the National Accounts, so that a breakdown of investment into various asset types was done using additional information from input–output tables and investment surveys. Further details on the sources and methods used for each country can be found in Appendix 2 and Timmer *et al.* (2007a).

To assess the contribution of the various inputs to aggregate growth, we apply the growth accounting framework as developed by Jorgenson and associates (see, for example, Jorgenson, Ho and Stiroh, 2005). For the purpose of this paper we will decompose the growth of labor productivity (value added per hour worked) into the contribution of ICT capital services, non-ICT capital services, labor services and multifactor productivity (see Box 1). The growth contribution of each input is calculated as the growth rate of the input per hour worked multiplied by the share of the input in value added (see Appendix 2 for a more formal description).

Box 1. What does multifactor productivity growth measure?

Multifactor productivity (MFP) growth is measured as the difference between the volume growth of outputs and the volume growth of inputs. As such, it captures increases in the amount of output that can be produced by a given quantity of inputs. Put alternatively, it captures the reduction in input costs to produce a given amount of output. Many factors may cause changes in MFP growth. Under strict neo-classical assumptions, MFP growth measures disembodied technological change. In practice, measured MFP includes a range of other effects. First, in addition to technical innovation it also includes the effects from organizational and institutional change. For example, the successful reorganization of a business to streamline the production process will lead to higher MFP growth. Second, MFP also captures changes in returns to scale. For example, there is some evidence that scale is important for realising productivity growth in retail trade, possibly because of the large outlays required for modern inventory management systems. Foster, Haltiwanger and Krizan (2006) show that much of US productivity growth in retail trade is due to the spread of national chains. If a firm originally operates below its minimum efficient scale, increasing production will lead to an increase in measured MFP. Third, MFP measures pick up any deviations from the neo-classical assumption that marginal costs reflect marginal revenues. If, on the one hand, there are externalities related to investments in ICT in network industries this will increase MFP. On the other hand, when ICT investments have been driven more by herd-behavior than by economic fundamentals, MFP is underestimated and the contributions of ICT investment to growth are overestimated. Fourth, being a residual measure, MFP growth also includes the effects from unmeasured inputs, such as research and development and other intangible investments. Finally, MFP includes measurement errors, such as mismeasurement of the quality change of new services products, or of high-tech inputs. We partly address this problem by using deflators for IT-investment that correct for quality change. In Appendix 1 we discuss the – in our view – limited degree of mismeasurement of services output.

In this paper we use MFP measured at the industry-level, not at the firm-level. Importantly, industry-level MFP reflects not only the average change in MFP of each firm within the industry, but also includes the effects of reallocation of market shares across firms. For example, MFP growth in a particular industry might increase through a shake out of the least productive firms, for example, because of increased competitive pressure after liberalizing domestic markets. Similarly the privatization of public firms might lead to a reduction in input use. It should be stressed that all effects on measured MFP discussed here can be broadly summarized as 'improvements in efficiency', as they improve the productivity with which inputs are being used within the industry. See Hulten (2001) for a more extensive discussion of the MFP concept.

3.2. The role of investment in ICT and non-ICT capital

The availability of investment series by asset type and by industry is one of the unique characteristics of the EU KLEMS database, allowing for a detailed analysis of investment in specific types of assets by individual industry. In Table 3 we provide the

Table 3. Investment-to-value-added ratios for ICT- and non-ICT capital, market services in Europe and the US, averages over 1980–1995 and 1995–2004

	1980–1995		1995–2004	
	ICT	Non-ICT	ICT	Non-ICT
Austria	3.6	16.8	4.2	15.9
Belgium	n.a.	n.a.	n.a.	n.a.
Denmark	5.8	15.1	6.2	16.2
Finland	4.2	19.6	5.2	11.8
France	2.9	12.8	4.1	12.0
Germany	2.8	11.6	3.9	14.0
Italy	3.3	19.4	3.4	18.4
Netherlands	3.8	13.4	4.8	11.6
Spain	4.4	11.5	4.5	15.3
UK	4.0	14.9	6.6	13.0
US	4.2	9.9	5.9	8.6
Average	3.9	14.5	4.9	13.7
Standard deviation	0.9	3.3	1.1	2.8

Notes: Ratios of nominal gross fixed capital formation over nominal value added in market services. The figures for Germany 1980–1995 refer to West Germany 1980–1991. Figures for Italy exclude business services (ISIC 71–74).

Source: EU KLEMS database, March 2007 (http://www.euklems.net), described in Timmer *et al.* (2007).

shares of investment expenditure in gross value added in market services for each country. The trend of increasing investment in ICT capital in market services stands out clearly. On average, over all countries, the ICT investment to value added ratio increased from 3.9% during 1980–1995 to 4.9% during 1995–2004. The latter period includes the ICT investment boom in the run-up to the millennium as well as the post-2000 bust. Strikingly, ICT investment rates in 2004 are back to the levels of the beginning of the 1990s, suggesting that expenditures on ICT assets have become a routine and stable part of firms' strategies. It should be stressed though that expenditures on non-ICT assets are still at least double or triple the outlays for ICT assets. Even in market services, which are the most intensive users of ICT, investment in non-ICT related equipment and non-residential structures are still dominant. Table 3 also shows that there is a substantial variation in investment rates across countries. For example, ICT investment rates are the highest in Denmark, Netherlands, UK and the US in the period 1995–2004 but much lower in large continental European countries such as France, Germany, Italy and Spain. Investment in traditional (non-ICT) assets is highest in Austria, Denmark and Spain. This raises the question to what extent differences in investment rates can explain differences in labor productivity growth rates.

To answer this question one has to transform the investment flows into a measure of capital services. Capital services measure the flow of services of the capital stock which is being used during a particular period of time. To measure capital services on the basis of investment series, a number of procedural steps have to be taken. First, nominal investment series are deflated and accumulated into stock estimates using the Perpetual Inventory Method (see Appendix 2 for details). The deflators for IT-hardware reflect the rapid changes in quality (see Box 2 on ICT investment deflators). The capital stocks for the different assets are then aggregated on the basis of the user cost of each asset to form capital service flows.

The user cost approach is crucial for the analysis of the contribution of capital to output growth. It was introduced by Jorgenson and Griliches (1967) and is based on the assumption that marginal costs reflect marginal productivity. A simple example may illustrate this approach. Suppose that a firm uses a computer and a building for one year. If the annual costs of using one euro of computers is higher than the cost of using one euro of buildings, computers have a higher marginal productivity, and this should be accounted for. There are various reasons why the cost of computers is higher than for buildings. While computers may typically be scrapped after five or six years, buildings may provide services for several decades. Besides, prices of new computers are rapidly declining while those of buildings do not in normal circumstances. This decline in value of computers entails a cost. Typically, the user cost of computers is 50 to 60% of the investment price, while that of buildings is less than 10%. Therefore the growth in the computer capital stock gets a heavier weight in calculating capital services than the growth in the building stock. Appendix 2 explains the derivation of the capital services estimates in more detail.

Box 2. ICT investment deflators

To transform the nominal investment series into volumes, price deflators for each asset type are needed. Price measurement for ICT assets has been an important research topic in recent years, as the quality of those capital goods has been rapidly increasing. Until recently, large differences existed in the methodology to obtain deflators for ICT equipment between countries, and the use of a single harmonized deflator across countries was widely advocated and used (Schreyer, 2002; Colecchia and Schreyer, 2002; Timmer and van Ark, 2005). This deflator was based on the US deflators for computer hardware, which were commonly seen as the most advanced in terms of accounting for quality changes using hedonic pricing techniques (Triplett, 2006). However, in recent years, many European countries, such as France, Germany, Netherlands and the UK have made significant progress in either developing and implementing their own quality-adjusted deflators for IT equipment, using high-frequency matched models or hedonic-type deflators, or by using deflators based on adapted price indices from the US Bureau of Economic Analysis. These new deflators typically show price declines of about 10% annually. For those countries (Austria, Belgium, Finland, Spain and Italy) which have not implemented a quality-adjusted investment deflator for computers yet, we continued to use the harmonization procedure suggested by Schreyer (2002).

In Table 4 the contributions of the increase in capital services from ICT and non-ICT assets per hour worked to labor productivity growth are given for the periods 1980–1995 and 1995–2004. Two general trends stand out. First, in the most recent period ICT capital is dominating non-ICT capital as a driver of productivity growth. On average, ICT capital contributes 0.8 percentage points to productivity growth across all countries during 1995–2004, while non-ICT capital contributes only 0.2 percentage points. This might be surprising given the higher investment-to-value added ratios in non-ICT as shown in Table 3, but due to the user-cost approach, the rapid growth in short-lived ICT assets gets a relatively large weight. Still the dominance of ICT is not only due to an increase in the contribution of ICT over time, but to a general decline in the contribution of non-ICT per hour worked in many European countries. This dominance of ICT as a contributor to growth is true for most countries, with the major exception of Spain.[9]

Major differences in the importance of ICT for growth can be found across countries, reflecting the long-run differences in ICT investments. While ICT capital contributes 1.2 percentage points or more to labor productivity growth in Denmark,

---

[9] Arguably, market services growth in Spain is still heavily reliant on catching-up in non-ICT based technologies.

Table 4. Contribution of ICT and non-ICT capital deepening to labor productivity growth in market services, average annual growth (in percentage points)

	1980–1995		1995–2004	
	ICT-capital	Non-ICT capital	ICT-capital	Non-ICT capital
Austria	0.5	0.4	0.8	0.0
Belgium	0.9	0.3	0.9	0.2
Denmark	1.4	0.2	1.4	−0.5
Finland	0.5	0.4	0.6	−0.7
France	0.4	0.4	0.5	0.3
Germany	0.3	0.6	0.7	0.6
Italy	0.3	0.4	0.2	0.4
Netherlands	0.5	0.1	0.8	0.2
Spain	0.6	0.8	0.5	0.7
UK	0.7	0.6	1.2	0.5
US	0.9	0.4	1.4	0.3
Average	0.7	0.4	0.8	0.2
Standard deviation	0.3	0.2	0.4	0.4

Notes: The figures are a weighted average of ICT and non-ICT capital deepening rates across nine market services industries, where the weight is given by the share of the industry in ICT or non-ICT capital compensation.

Source: EU KLEMS database, March 2007 (http://www.euklems.net), described in Timmer *et al.* (2007).

the UK and the US, contributions are 0.5 percentage points or less in major continental countries such as France, Italy and Spain and there are no signs of catching up. The reason for these seemingly large structural differences are still not very well understood. Conway *et al.* (2006) and Gust and Marquez (2004) suggest that part of these cross-country differences in ICT investment are due to the impact of different regulatory environments, in particular regulations affecting product and labor markets.[10] But much of the cross-country differences remain unexplained.

3.3. The role of changes in labor composition

Another important input in market services which has attracted attention is the use of skilled labor. Technological change has been frequently characterized as skill-biased, especially in knowledge-intensive sectors such as telecommunications, finance and parts of business services.[11] In Table 5 the shares of high-skilled workers in market services employment are given for 1980, 1995 and 2004 for our group of countries (summed over the two other dimensions, gender and age). The table shows that there has been a steady increase in the importance of high-skilled workers over time. Typically, the share of high-skilled workers has doubled or even tripled in the

---

[10] See also the model by Alesina *et al.* (2005).

[11] See for a skill-taxonomy of industries, Chapter 2 of O'Mahony and van Ark (2003).

Table 5. The share of high-skilled workers in market services employment (%)

	1980	1995	2004
Austria	3.3	7.6	10.9
Belgium	6.7	12.0	15.5
Denmark	2.7	5.8	8.5
Finland	14.6	29.8	30.7
France	6.3	11.9	16.1
Germany	3.7	6.6	8.0
Italy	4.7	7.4	14.1
Netherlands	3.8	8.6	11.2
Spain	5.3	12.1	19.4
UK	8.0	12.8	18.0
US	19.4	26.9	30.6
Average	7.1	12.9	16.6
Standard deviation	5.2	8.1	7.8

Notes: High-skilled workers are defined as those with college education or above (see also footnote 16).
Source: EU KLEMS database, March 2007 (http://www.euklems.net), described in Timmer *et al.* (2007).

past two decades, suggesting an important role for growth in market services. Despite the resurgence of employment growth in continental Europe, the upward trend in the share of high-skilled labor has continued since the mid-1990s (Garibaldi and Mauro, 2002). This finding does not lend support to the popular notion that increases in employment have led to an increase in the share of low-skilled workers in market services. For example, Blanchard (2004) suggested that labor productivity growth declines during periods of increased employment as it is based on employing low-skilled workers, which were previously unemployed. However, the upward trend in the skill-content of the employees reflects the long-run impact of investments made in the educational systems as newcomers on the labor market have had on average more schooling than the existing labor force. This pattern appears true for all service industries, with the largest changes in knowledge-intensive industries like post and telecommunications and finance, and the smallest (but still positive) changes in personal and social services.[12]

As for the case of capital, the productivity of various types of labor, such as low- versus high-skilled labor, will differ and standard aggregate measures of labor input, such as number of persons employed or hours worked, will not account for such differences. In the growth accounting approach, it is assumed that the flow of labor services for each labor type is proportional to hours worked, and workers are paid

---

[12] The large cross-country differences in the share of high-skilled labor in Table 5 may appear surprising. For example, this share is much lower in Germany than in Spain, the UK or the US. This is due to the problem of lack of precise comparability of skill categories across countries. In the EU KLEMS database high-skilled workers are defined as those with college education or above. However, educational systems within Europe and the US are very different. In particular the different role of vocational schooling systems causes problems of comparability across countries. For example, in Germany vocational training is important to enter many occupations, but this is unknown in the US (see also Koeniger and Leonardi, 2007, p. 89). For time series of MFP in a country, it is most important, however, to use a consistent skill definition over time within each country. This has been the primary aim in the EU KLEMS database. See Mason, O'Leary and Vecchi (2007) for a detailed comparison of skill levels in major European countries.

their marginal productivities. The growth of labor services is then given by the growth rate of hours worked by each labor type, weighted by its share in labor compensation. Typically, a shift in the share of hours worked by low-skilled workers to medium- or high-skilled workers will then lead to a growth of labor services which is bigger than the growth in total hours worked. We refer to this difference as the labor composition effect.[13]

3.4. Sources of labor productivity growth

Based on the developments in labor and capital input measures described above, a decomposition of labor productivity growth in market services industries into the contribution of factor inputs and MFP growth can be made (Table 6). The contributions are given for each country for the periods before and after 1995. The table shows that, for example, in France during the period 1980–1995 annual average labor productivity growth was 1.9%. The increased use of ICT capital per hour worked contributed 0.4 percentage points to this growth. Similarly, non-ICT capital deepening and the changes in the labor composition contributed 0.4 and 0.5 percentage points respectively. The remaining 0.6 percentage points of labor productivity growth were due to improvements in MFP.

Table 6 shows that during 1980–1995, changes in labor composition contributed 0.4 percentage points to labor productivity growth when averaged over all countries. This contribution is mainly caused by an increase in the average skill levels of the employees. The contribution declined, but still remained positive after 1995 (0.2 percentage points on average). In both periods, changes in labor composition were as important for growth as increases in non-ICT capital per hour worked. The foremost conclusion to be drawn from this table is the importance of investments in fixed capital and human capital in driving labor productivity growth during both periods. Averaged over all countries, investment in factor inputs almost fully accounted for labor productivity growth in both periods and changes in MFP were, on average, only minor.

However, when it comes to explaining differences in labor productivity growth between countries, investments in human and physical capital are not of much help. As indicated by the standard deviations in Table 6, cross-country differences in labor composition are generally too small to account for the divergence in labor productivity growth and the same is true for non-ICT capital deepening. While the differences in contributions from ICT are bigger, these can only explain part of the observed growth differences. For example, the difference in the contribution of ICT between

---

[13] This difference is also known as 'labor quality' in the growth accounting literature (see e.g. Jorgenson, Ho and Stiroh, 2005). However, this terminology has a normative connotation which easily leads to confusion. For example, lower female wages would suggest that hours worked by females have a lower 'quality' than hours worked by males. Instead we prefer to use the more positive concept of 'change in labor composition'.

Table 6. Sources of labor productivity growth in market services in Europe and the US, 1980–1995 and 1995–2004, average annual growth (in percentage points)

	Labor productivity growth	Contribution from:			
		ICT capital deepening	Non-ICT capital deepening	Labor composition change	Multifactor productivity growth
1980–1995					
Austria	2.1	0.5	0.4	0.4	0.7
Belgium	1.4	0.9	0.3	0.5	−0.4
Denmark	3.0	1.4	0.2	0.4	1.0
Finland	2.5	0.5	0.4	0.9	0.7
France	1.9	0.4	0.4	0.5	0.6
Germany	2.3	0.3	0.6	0.2	1.2
Italy	0.6	0.3	0.4	0.2	−0.3
Netherlands	0.3	0.5	0.1	0.2	−0.6
Spain	1.0	0.6	0.8	0.5	−1.0
UK	1.9	0.7	0.6	0.2	0.4
US	1.4	0.9	0.4	0.2	0.0
Average	1.7	0.7	0.4	0.4	0.2
Standard deviation	0.8	0.3	0.2	0.2	0.7
1995–2004					
Austria	0.7	0.8	0.0	0.2	−0.4
Belgium	1.2	0.9	0.2	0.4	−0.3
Denmark	0.9	1.4	−0.1	0.3	−0.7
Finland	1.7	0.6	−0.7	0.0	1.9
France	1.3	0.5	0.3	0.4	0.1
Germany	0.8	0.7	0.6	0.0	−0.6
Italy	0.3	0.2	0.4	0.2	−0.6
Netherlands	2.4	0.8	0.2	0.1	1.3
Spain	0.4	0.5	0.7	0.4	−1.2
UK	2.5	1.2	0.5	0.4	0.4
US	3.3	1.4	0.3	0.3	1.3
Average	1.4	0.8	0.2	0.2	0.1
Standard deviation	1.0	0.4	0.4	0.2	1.0

Notes: The figures are weighted averages of growth rates of inputs and outputs across nine market services industries, where the weight is given by the share of the industry in output or the costs of the relevant input. Labor productivity is defined as value added per hour worked. Input measures are on a per hour worked basis. Figures might not add up due to rounding.

Source: EU KLEMS database, March 2007 (http://www.euklems.net), described in Timmer *et al.* (2007).

the highest investor (the US) and a lowest investor (Italy) explains 1.2 percentage points out of a labor productivity difference of 3.0% during 1995–2004. The remaining 1.8 percentage point difference is almost entirely due to the differences in MFP growth between Italy and the US. Indeed cross-country differences in MFP growth seem to drive divergence in labor productivity growth. Although MFP growth is *on average* not an important contributor to growth, it has by far the largest variation in growth contributions, ranging from −1.2 percentage points in Spain, up to 1.3 percentage points in the US during the most recent period. In France, Germany and Italy, MFP growth is negligible or even negative. US growth rates of MFP are matched only in the Netherlands and Finland. Across all countries, the correlation between labor productivity and MFP growth rates is higher than 80% for both periods. This suggests that we need to focus on the determinants of MFP growth in trying to explain the recent variation in European labor productivity growth rates.

4. DETERMINANTS OF PRODUCTIVITY GROWTH

In the previous section we showed how investment in physical capital and human capital accounts for a substantial portion of labor productivity growth in market services in many countries. At the same time we found that cross-country differences in labor productivity growth are mainly due to differences in the efficiency with which the inputs are being used, as measured by MFP growth. To get further insight into the causes of MFP growth differences, we need to move beyond the growth accounting framework and explain differences in MFP growth. In this section we will use regression analysis to statistically gauge the importance of a number of potential determinants of MFP growth. For this purpose, we use a dynamic catching-up model that is commonly used in the literature.[14] Of the many determinants, we will focus here in particular on whether ICT use and the use of skilled labor generates externalities and whether regulatory barriers to entry hamper productivity growth.

4.1. The basic model of productivity growth

Following the dynamic catching-up model, MFP growth in an industry is determined by the strength of the domestic innovation process and the speed of imitation of best-practice technologies developed elsewhere.[15] The potential for technology transfer is captured by the technology gap relative to the global productivity leader. But the social and technological capabilities of an economy determine to what extent an industry innovates and exploits imitation opportunities. Aghion and Howitt (2006) argue that traditional European institutions were mostly suited for catching-up to the technology frontier and not so much for fostering innovation. For example, educational systems are more geared towards vocational schooling rather than higher education, capital markets are biased towards large incumbent firms rather than start-ups, labor market regulation promotes on-the-job training but hinders reallocations across firms and innovation systems, including patent protection laws and public R&D-institutes stimulate incremental innovation rather than major breakthroughs. To capture this idea, additional variables reflecting these institutional differences across countries are added to the model. Such variables might influence MFP growth

---

[14] See e.g. Cameron *et al.* (2005), Griffith *et al.* (2004), Nicoletti and Scarpetta (2003) and Vandenbussche *et al.* (2006).

[15] Innovation is defined as the development of technologies which are not only new to the country, but also new to the world.

by affecting the pace of innovation and the speed of technology imitation. For example, Griffith *et al.* (2004) find that spending on research and development (R&D) in manufacturing industries increases the pace of innovation but also speeds up technology imitation.

The basic model to be estimated is then:

$$\Delta \ln \text{MFP} = \beta(\text{Technology gap}) + \gamma X + \delta(X * \text{Technology gap}) \qquad (1)$$

where X denotes one of several possible determinants of MFP of policy interest. The key parameters are β, which quantifies the importance of technology imitation that depends on the size of the technology gap, γ which shows the direct effect of X on productivity growth, and δ which gauges whether X has a larger effect on productivity growth for industries that are farther away from the frontier (positive sign) or closer to the frontier (negative sign). The regressions will also include dummies to control for fixed country-specific, industry-specific and time-specific factors.

In this section, we look at three possible determinants of MFP growth, namely the use of ICT capital, the use of university-educated workers and regulatory barriers to entry as all three have been suggested as important drivers of productivity growth.[16] The latter two play a prominent role in the recommendations of the Sapir Report (2004). Our focus on market services precludes us from examining some other explanatory variables which have been suggested, such as R&D and international trade, as their role is much more limited in services than in manufacturing industries.[17]

4.2. Technology gaps

To implement our empirical model, measures of technology gaps are a crucial ingredient. In this paper, we follow standard practice and measure technology gaps as MFP gaps even though MFP measures also reflect other factors besides technology (see Box 1). In the case of MFP gaps we need to measure the differences in output levels between countries that cannot be accounted for by differences in the use of inputs. The basic challenge of measuring MFP gaps is similar to that for measuring MFP growth. While the basic concept is fairly straightforward, the empirical implementation in the literature varies substantially, with most studies using crude productivity measures. In Table 7 we illustrate the difference between crude and sophisticated MFP level measures and show how better measurement can change the conclusions on technology leadership substantially. This will also have a major impact on the analysis of the determinants of MFP growth in the remainder of this section.

There are four main areas of concern when calculating MFP gaps, namely the measurement of output, relative prices, employment and capital, mirroring the

---

[16] See e.g. Brynjolfsson and Hitt (2003) on ICT, Vandenbussche *et al.* (2006) on university-educated workers and Nicoletti and Scarpetta (2003) on barriers to entry. For more details, see, respectively, Sections 4.3, 4.4 and 4.5.

[17] See e.g. Cameron *et al.* (2005) and Griffith *et al.* (2004) for the importance of those variables in manufacturing industries.

Table 7. Relative MFP measures, averaged across market services industries, 1997, US = 1

	(1)	(2)	(3)	(4)	(5)	(6)
Output measure	'Crude MFP' Value added	Value added	Value added	Value added	Value added	'Sophisticated MFP' Gross output
PPP measure	GDP PPP	GDP PPP	GDP PPP	GO PPP	GO PPP	IO PPP
Employment measure	Persons	Hours	Hours by type	Hours by type	Hours by type	Hours by type
Capital measure	Stock	Stock	Stock	Stock	Services	Services
Austria	0.82	0.80	0.89	0.80	0.82	0.87
Belgium	0.82	0.95	1.01	1.01	1.05	1.09
Denmark	0.76	0.84	0.98	1.07	1.07	1.10
Finland	0.81	0.81	0.81	0.78	0.78	0.87
France	0.91	0.96	1.09	1.02	1.04	1.09
Germany	0.75	0.83	1.01	1.04	1.05	1.09
Italy	0.84	0.75	0.85	0.73	0.76	0.86
Netherlands	0.77	0.88	1.02	1.05	1.09	1.09
Spain	0.81	0.77	0.85	0.80	0.86	0.88
UK	0.79	0.80	0.98	0.93	0.94	0.97
US	1.00	1.00	1.00	1.00	1.00	1.00

Notes: Each column shows the MFP level relative to the United States in 1997, averaged over the nine market services. MFP levels in column (1) are calculated by subtracting the (cost-share weighted) relative levels of persons engaged and capital stocks, from the relative level of value added. All inputs and outputs are converted to a common currency using OECD GDP PPPs for 1997. For column (2), total hours worked by all persons is used as the measure for employment. For column (3), hours worked by university-educated and non-university-educated are distinguished and weighted using shares in labor composition. In column (4), industry-specific PPPs for industry gross output are used for converting value added and capital stocks to a common currency. In column (5), six different capital assets are converted to a common currency using capital services PPPs and weighted using shares in capital composition. In column (6), differences in relative prices for intermediate inputs are also taken into account and MFP levels are calculated by subtracting the (cost-share weighted) relative levels of hours worked by university- and non-university educated workers, capital services by six different capital assets and 45 types of intermediate inputs from the level of output. All conversions to a common currency are made using industry- and input-specific PPPs. See Inklaar and Timmer (2007b) for a more detailed description of the last measure.

discussion of productivity growth measurement.[18] First of all, most studies compare levels of value added, implicitly ignoring the role of intermediate inputs in the production process. Second, the output in different countries can only be compared once differences in relative prices are accounted for. This requires the use of purchasing power parities (PPPs). Many studies use GDP PPPs, since those are readily available, but these reflect relative prices of all goods and services in the economy. Here it is more appropriate to use PPPs that reflect the relative prices of output of that particular industry. Moreover, in this study we also take into account relative prices of the various inputs.

When it comes to measuring labor input, some studies only measure the relative number of persons engaged while others also account for differences in average hours worked across countries. It is preferable to measure differences in total hours worked by different types of workers as well, so as to account for differences in the composition of the workforce in different countries. Finally, most studies use a measure of the relative capital stock, but this does not adequately account for differences in the composition of capital input. Our detailed measure is based on a comparison of capital service levels, accounting for asset heterogeneity.

Table 7 shows the relative MFP level of each country, averaged across market services industries in 1997. The first column, which we label 'Crude MFP', uses the least sophisticated output, relative price and input measures. According to this productivity measure, the US is the most productive country in market services. However, once the necessary adjustments are made, five European countries show substantially higher levels than the US. This is because input levels in US market services are higher than indicated by the crude measures. Average hours worked in the US are generally much higher than in Europe, as indicated by the differences between columns 1 and 2. Similarly, skill levels in market services are higher in the US than in most European countries, biasing the crude MFP level (column 3). Another downward adjustment to US levels is made when moving from capital stocks to a measure including capital services, which adjusts for the higher share of ICT in the US as found in Table 3 (column 5). Looking at the final column, labelled 'Sophisticated MFP', the US no longer has the highest productivity level as about half of the European countries show higher MFP levels in 1997. The example of Germany is the most extreme: 'Crude MFP' shows Germany with the lowest productivity level and a gap of, on average, 25% compared to the US, while 'Sophisticated MFP' indicates that Germany is almost 10% more productive than the US on average. The rankings of MFP levels among European countries also shift considerably once more sophisticated output and input measures are introduced. The UK appeared to be leading Germany on the basis of the crude measure, but especially once corrections are made for longer hours worked and the relative high services output prices in the UK, Germany is leading the UK on MFP in market services by a wide margin in 1997. The adjustments can be even larger at a detailed industry level.[19]

---

[18] Inklaar and Timmer (2007b) provides a more detailed and rigorous discussion of these issues.

[19] Not shown, but available upon request from the authors.

As stressed before, Table 7 shows average levels across nine market services industries and technology levels differ substantially across industries. Table A3 (at the end of the Appendix) shows the technology leader in each of the nine market services industries, as well as the numbers two and three, in 1980, 1995 and 2004. Looking across all years, industries and countries, the average MFP level relative to the frontier is 69%, suggesting that there is substantial potential for imitation of frontier technologies. Given the problems in the measurement of services output volumes in some industries (see Appendix 1) these numbers need to be interpreted with care. Level comparisons are more sensitive to cross-country differences in measurement practices than growth rate comparisons.

4.3. The impact of ICT use on MFP growth

Once the technology gaps have been measured, we can begin testing the importance of our potential explanatory variables for cross-country differences in MFP growth. The first variable to be tested is ICT use. Since US labor productivity growth accelerated after 1995, much effort has gone into determining the importance of ICT use and the lack of acceleration in most other developed countries.[20] ICT, like other types of fixed capital, contributes to labor productivity growth by increasing the amount of capital input per hour worked. In Section 3 we showed that ICT use accounted for a major part of labor productivity growth, under the assumption that the benefits of ICT capital are reflected by the price paid for its use. A more contentious hypothesis is that ICT generates positive externalities, i.e. benefits that are higher than the costs being paid by the investor. Such externalities could be caused by, for example, network effects or complementary investments, such as organizational change, that go unmeasured.[21] The evidence on externalities from ICT use is mixed. There is some firm-level and industry-level research for the US that suggests super-normal returns to ICT, but a recent survey and meta-analysis concludes that the hypothesis of normal returns seems to hold (Stiroh, 2004).[22] The evidence for countries other than the US is more scattered and these national studies are generally not directly comparable.[23] Using the EU KLEMS database, we can focus on MFP and test for externalities of ICT use across a larger group of countries and industries. The externalities should show up as a positive correlation between ICT use and MFP growth as indicated in the model from Section 4.1.

---

[20] See e.g. Jorgenson and Stiroh (2000) and Timmer and van Ark (2005).

[21] See e.g. Stiroh (2002) and Basu, Fernald, Oulton and Srinivasan (2004).

[22] See e.g. Brynjolfsson and Hitt (2003) for a firm-level study and Stiroh (2002) and Basu, Fernald, Oulton and Srinivasan (2004) for industry-level studies.

[23] See OECD (2004) for a collection of national studies. Basu *et al.* (2004) and O'Mahony and Vecchi (2005) are among the very few cross-country studies of the productive impact of ICT and find super-normal returns to ICT-use in the US, but not in the UK. Some of our own comparative analysis focused on labor productivity growth, making it hard to identify externalities, or was of a more descriptive nature. See van Ark, Inklaar and McGuckin (2003) and Inklaar, O'Mahony and Timmer (2005).

Table 8 shows the results of this exercise. We first show a regression in which only the technology gap is used to explain MFP growth. The technology gap is defined as minus the log of the relative MFP level, so that a larger gap equals a lower relative level. Regardless of whether we use crude or sophisticated MFP growth and level measures, industries that are farther away from the technological frontier show faster MFP growth. In the light of the theoretical models discussed above, this might be interpreted as the result of international technology transfers, which benefit laggard countries more than countries close to the frontier. This finding of convergence of MFP levels within service industries confirms earlier analysis by, for example, Bernard and Jones (1996) and Nicoletti and Scarpetta (2003).

The results in Table 8 show that the evidence of the effects of ICT on MFP growth is mixed and depends on which measure of ICT adoption is used. The growth of ICT capital services is often used in the literature, but shows relatively little variation across industries since global price declines of ICT assets account for much of this growth.[24] Moreover, the right-hand side of Table 8 shows that using sophisticated MFP measures actually shows a negative relationship between ICT use and MFP growth. This would imply that the returns to ICT investments are lower than their costs. However, this evidence is relatively weak. When we use our preferred measure of ICT adoption, which is the share of ICT capital compensation in output, no such effect is found as shown in columns 9 and 10.[25] Similarly, there is also little evidence to suggest that ICT has a differential impact depending on the size of the technology gap as indicated by the insignificant interaction effects in Table 8. As a result, our cross-country analysis broadly confirms Stiroh's (2004) finding for the US that ICT assets are like other assets and earn their marginal product. This means that the contribution of ICT to labor productivity growth is well approximated by the growth accounting method applied in Section 3. ICT externalities do not explain the cross-country differences in MFP growth.

4.4. The impact of human capital on MFP growth

Skilled labor has also been suggested as another driver of technological change and an important source of productivity growth. Recently, Vandenbussche et al. (2006) presented a model where economies with a larger share of university-educated workers exhibit a faster rate of innovation, because skilled labor has a comparative advantage for innovation compared to imitation. Hence the growth-enhancing effect of skilled labor will be stronger for economies closer to the frontier as the opportunities for growth through imitation decrease. Vandenbussche et al. (2006) present cross-country

---

[24] See Inklaar and Timmer (2007a).

[25] In Appendix 4, we provide further robustness exercises. There we show that allowing for a longer time-horizon as in Brynjolfsson and Hitt (2003) and also advocated by O'Mahony and Vecchi (2005) does not change the results. We also show that the evidence for a negative relationship is found in only some industries and countries and that these negative coefficients are never found for both ICT use measures at the same time.

Table 8. The relationship between technology gaps, ICT use and productivity growth

Dependent variable: MFP growth	Crude MFP					Sophisticated MFP				
	1	2	3	4	5	6	7	8	9	10
Technology gap	0.027*** (0.005)	0.027*** (0.005)	0.019*** (0.006)	0.027*** (0.005)	0.021*** (0.006)	0.019*** (0.004)	0.019*** (0.004)	0.014** (0.005)	0.020*** (0.004)	0.021*** (0.005)
ICT use (growth of ICT)		−0.020 (0.015)	−0.050** (0.023)				−0.024*** (0.009)	−0.038*** (0.012)		
ICT use (cost-share in ICT)				−0.042 (0.049)	−0.102 (0.083)				−0.053 (0.035)	−0.034 (0.056)
Technology gap*ICT use			0.057** (0.029)		0.120 (0.111)			0.038 (0.024)		−0.033 (0.089)
Number of observations	2376	2376	2376	2376	2376	2376	2376	2376	2376	2376

Notes: The table shows OLS regression estimates, explaining annual MFP growth by the technology gap relative to the frontier, measures of ICT use and the interaction between the technology gap and ICT use. *, ** and *** denote a coefficient significantly different from zero at, respectively, the 10%, 5% and 1% levels. Standard errors, consistent for heteroscedasticity and autocorrelation are in parentheses. For definitions of crude and sophisticated MFP, see Table 7. The industry-level data are a balanced panel for 9 market services industries in each of the 11 countries for the period 1980–2004 and all regressions include country, industry and year dummies. See Appendix 4 for robustness analysis.

evidence supporting this model and their study has subsequently been used in the Sapir Report (2004) to support the policy argument that higher education stimulates innovation. Their finding of skill externalities is all the more important because in an earlier study, Krueger and Lindahl (2001) conclude that while there is a high private return to education, the evidence for externalities at the level of industries or aggregate economies is far from conclusive.

However, the study by Vandenbussche et al. (2006) has two important drawbacks. First, growth differences between countries are only analyzed at the aggregate level, instead of across industries within countries, which leaves open the possibility that the positive correlation between human capital and MFP growth is due to a country-specific factor that is correlated with both human capital and growth.[26] The second drawback is that they rely on crude MFP measures that do not take into account differences in hours worked or in the educational attainment of the labor force. This means that their analysis cannot make a distinction between private and social returns to education. Only findings of social returns (or externalities) would provide a solid basis for policy initiatives.

In Table 9, we show that while the use of crude MFP measures provides a weak confirmation of the Vandenbussche et al. (2006) results, when using sophisticated MFP measures, the positive correlation between human capital and MFP growth is absent. In the left panel, we replicate the set-up by Vandenbussche et al. (2006), using aggregate economy data, no country fixed effects and crude MFP measures. Columns 1 and 2 show a significant positive effect of high-skilled workers on MFP growth. The interaction term also has a negative sign as predicted by the model of Vandenbussche et al. (2006), but is not significant. However, the positive effect of the share of high-skilled workers disappears once sophisticated MFP measures are used as shown in columns 3 and 4. In Appendix 4, we show that correcting the crude MFP measures for differences in hours worked and differences in the composition of the workforce causes the significant positive effect to vanish. In other words, Vandenbussche et al. (2006) are only estimating the private return to education, which is in part transferred to MFP growth due to measurement issues. In the right-hand panel, we redo the analysis for our set of nine market services industries. The industry-level estimates are consistent throughout and do not provide evidence that a larger share of high-skilled workers has an impact on MFP growth.[27] Our results for the use of skilled labor are therefore similar to those for ICT use: there is no evidence of productivity externalities from employing university-educated workers. As for ICT, this means that the contribution of a higher-educated workforce to labor productivity growth is well-captured in the growth accounting exercise from the previous section.

---

[26] See Temple (2000) for a more extensive discussion of the problem with cross-country growth regressions. This possibility is not entirely dispelled by the fact that the positive correlation between human capital and MFP growth disappears once taking into account country fixed effects.

[27] In Appendix 4 we show further robustness results, namely the results for all six MFP measures, results using different measures of the high-skilled share, including those from the same source as Vandenbussche et al. (2006), and different sets of dummies. None of this changes the main results reported in Table 9.

Table 9. The relationship between high-skilled workers and productivity growth at the aggregate and services industry level

Dependent variable: MFP growth	Total economy				Industry-level			
	Crude MFP		Sophisticated MFP		Crude MFP		Sophisticated MFP	
	1	2	3	4	5	6	7	8
Technology gap	0.027**	0.044**	0.015*	0.007	0.027***	0.021***	0.019***	0.020***
	(0.011)	(0.020)	(0.008)	(0.014)	(0.005)	(0.007)	(0.004)	(0.005)
High-skilled share	0.043**	0.065**	0.004	-0.009	-0.017	-0.034	-0.019	-0.017
	(0.020)	(0.027)	(0.016)	(0.034)	(0.035)	(0.038)	(0.023)	(0.023)
Technology gap*High-skilled share		-0.106		0.056		0.050		-0.006
		(0.126)		(0.121)		(0.038)		(0.034)
Number of observations	264	264	264	264	2376	2376	2376	2376

Notes: The table shows OLS regression estimates, explaining MFP growth by the technology gap relative to the frontier, the share of high-skilled (university-educated) workers in total hours worked and the interaction between the technology gap and the high-skilled share. *, ** and *** denote a coefficient significantly different from zero at, respectively, the 10%, 5% and 1% level. Standard errors, consistent for heteroscedasticity and autocorrelation are in parentheses. For definitions of crude and sophisticated MFP, see Table 7. The industry-level data are a balanced panel for 11 countries, while the industry-level data are a balanced panel for 9 market services industries in each of the 11 countries, all of these for the period 1980–2004. The total economy results include year dummies and the industry-level results include country, industry and year dummies. See Appendix 4 for robustness analysis.

4.5. The impact of regulatory barriers to entry on MFP growth

Analyzing the effect of competition on productivity growth has taken great flight in recent years (see e.g. Aghion and Griffith, 2005 and Crafts, 2006 for overviews). The outcome of recent theoretical work is that more competition in product markets stimulates productivity growth because it stimulates innovation. Moreover, this effect might be stronger when an industry is closer to the technology frontier as those industries need to rely more on innovation compared to imitation.[28] Testing this prediction is not straightforward as competition in product markets cannot be observed directly. In some cases, changes in the regulatory regime can be used as a proxy for changes in competition. For example, Griffith, Harrison and Simpson (2006) use information on the implementation of the European Single Market Programme in different years and different countries and assuming a stronger effect in some manufacturing industries than others to establish that deregulation improved productivity growth in manufacturing by stimulating spending on R&D. Eventually, the liberalization of market services that is mandated in the EU Services Directive may provide a similar testing ground for the effects of regulation on productivity growth in market services.

In the meantime, the product market regulation measures compiled by the OECD are the most useful for the purpose of measuring the impact of regulation on productivity. Nicoletti and Scarpetta (2003) described the OECD Product Market Regulation Database measures in detail and provide the first systematic empirical analysis of the impact of regulation on productivity in a cross-country setting.[29] Their study has been highly influential and has been another source of inspiration for the Sapir Report (2004). Nicoletti and Scarpetta (2003) find some evidence that entry liberalization in services increases productivity growth, which supports the theoretical notion that entry barriers decrease the intensity of competition. Paradoxically, they find an impact of deregulation in services on productivity growth in manufacturing industries, but not in services industries.[30] In this section, we will further explore the link between deregulation and productivity growth by focusing on market services industries only, and zooming in on individual services industries for which long-run data on entry liberalization exist. One might expect that due to the heterogeneity in regulatory changes, evidence of an impact might only be found at a detailed industry level. With the EU KLEMS database such a detailed industry study is feasible.

We provide two analyses: one based on a regulation index averaged across all services industries, in the spirit of Nicoletti and Scarpetta (2003), and one based on industry-specific regulation indices. Table 10 shows that there is no effect of the average level of barriers to entry in services on MFP growth in market services

---

[28] See e.g. Acemoglu, Aghion and Zilibotti (2006) for such a model.

[29] Conway and Nicoletti (2006) present updates of their indicators for non-manufacturing industries.

[30] In Table 8, Nicoletti and Scarpetta (2003) report a significant impact of entry liberalization in services on productivity growth across all industries. However, in Table 7 they showed that this entry liberalization trend in services did not significantly affect productivity growth in services.

Table 10. The effect of barriers to entry on productivity growth in market services

Dependent variable: MFP growth	Crude MFP				Sophisticated MFP			
	1	2	3	4	5	6	7	8
Technology gap	0.027***	0.020**	0.016	0.050**	0.019***	0.009	0.009	0.010
	(0.005)	(0.009)	(0.010)	(0.021)	(0.004)	(0.007)	(0.006)	(0.012)
Barriers (average)	0.011	0.006			0.000	−0.004		
	(0.011)	(0.012)			(0.007)	(0.007)		
Barriers (industry-level)			−0.024**	−0.002			−0.010	−0.009
			(0.011)	(0.014)			(0.007)	(0.010)
Barriers*Technology gap		0.010		−0.052**		0.015		−0.002
		(0.012)		(0.022)		(0.009)		(0.017)
Number of observations	2376	2376	715	715	2376	2376	715	715

Notes: Dependent variable in the regressions is annual MFP growth in market services industries, independent variables are the technology gap of the industry relative to the productivity frontier and measures of barriers to entry from the OECD and their interaction. ** and *** denote a coefficient significantly different from zero at, respectively, the 5% and 1% level. Standard errors, consistent for heteroscedasticity and autocorrelation, are in parentheses. For definitions of crude and sophisticated MFP, see Table 7. Average barriers to entry uses an average index of barriers to entry, calculated by averaging across the entry barriers indices of all non-manufacturing industries for which the index is available for the 1980–2003 period, see Conway and Nicoletti (2006). Industry barriers to entry uses industry-specific entry barriers indices for retail (1996–2003), transport and storage (1980–2003, output-weighted average of road, rail and air transport), post and telecommunications (1980–2003 output-weighted average of post and telecommunications) and professional services (1996–2003).

industries. Moreover, this finding does not depend on the MFP measure that is used (columns 2 and 6).[31] There are also no significant interaction effects. This confirms the results of Nicoletti and Scarpetta (2003). One reason for this finding might be that entry liberalization occurred in different industries at different times, so using the trend averaged over industries may miss the relevant variation in the data. In the remaining columns of Table 10, we look at the effect of industry-specific barriers to entry on MFP growth. Unfortunately industry-specific data are more limited and only available for four industries, but the results seem more in line with theoretical predictions: all coefficients are negative, although only significant if crude MFP measures are used (column 3). The mixed nature of the results may be due to the fact that there is insufficient change over time in the barriers to entry in some industries. For example, in most countries, barriers to entry in retail trade hardly changed in the period for which data are available. To identify the effects of barriers to entry, an even more detailed focus on an industry with more variation in the regulatory measures might be needed.

Table 11 attempts this by looking at barriers to entry in two individual industries: transport and storage services and post and telecommunications services. For both industries, the OECD constructed a time series of barriers to entry covering our entire sample period from 1980 onwards and both industries experienced substantial entry liberalization in most countries.[32] This is most strongly so in post and telecommunications, which changed during the 1990s from a very restrictive to an almost fully liberalized industry environment in nearly all countries.[33] Table 11 shows that there is little effect of changes in barriers to entry in the transport industry, but in post and telecommunications, lower barriers are strongly related to higher MFP growth, even when sophisticated measures are being used (columns 7 and 8).[34] This finding provides support for the notion that lower barriers to entry promote productivity growth by increasing competition.

These results also raise the question of why we do not find such strong results for transport and storage. One possibility is that the change in barriers to entry for the post and telecommunications services was so strong that its effects became identifiable through the general noise in the data, while this was not the case in transport. An alternative explanation might be that the barriers to entry measure in transport is an average of a quite heterogeneous set of regulations, since it covers barriers to entry in rail, road and air transport. The summary OECD measures of regulation may not capture all the complexities of product market regulation and their interaction with

---

[31] Nor does it depend on the period covered, results are available on request. See also Appendix 4 for further tests using average trends as well as indirect measures of regulation as used by Conway *et al.* (2006).

[32] The OECD publishes indicators for road, rail and air transport and for postal services and telecommunications. We use output weights to construct weighted averages of these individual series.

[33] See Conway and Nicoletti (2006) on the trends and also Boylaud and Nicoletti (2000) on regulation and performance in telecommunications.

[34] Appendix 4 probes the robustness of this result by looking at different sets of dummies, different periods and alternative regulation indicators. These broadly confirm the main result in Table 11.

Table 11. The effect of barriers to entry on productivity growth in transport and communications

Dependent variable: MFP growth	Transport and storage				Post and telecommunications			
	Crude MFP		Sophisticated MFP		Crude MFP		Sophisticated MFP	
	1	2	3	4	5	6	7	8
Technology gap	0.203***	0.427***	0.115***	0.128***	0.075***	0.041	0.077***	0.068***
	(0.072)	(0.131)	(0.035)	(0.041)	(0.025)	(0.034)	(0.023)	(0.023)
Barriers	−0.022	0.056*	−0.012	−0.007	−0.056***	−0.130***	−0.041***	−0.060***
	(0.021)	(0.034)	(0.008)	(0.008)	(0.015)	(0.039)	(0.012)	(0.021)
Barriers*Technology gap		−0.334***		−0.011		0.091**		0.037
		(0.118)		(0.014)		(0.044)		(0.029)
Number of observations	264	264	264	264	264	264	264	264

Notes: Dependent variable is MFP growth in the transport industry or the telecommunications industry. All regressions include country and year dummies. For further notes, see Table 10.

labor market regulation and fine-grained industry-specific regulations such as, for example, land-zoning in retailing, accounting standards in business services or sanitation requirements in the hotel business.[35] Finally, it might be the case that regulatory barriers to entry in post and telecommunications represent a larger part of the overall entry barriers, which will also include fixed start-up costs, than in transport.[36] These possible explanations are not mutually exclusive, but in general point to the importance of detailed regulatory and productivity measures to analyse the impact of regulation on productivity.

5. CONCLUDING REMARKS

Over the past decade, much of Europe has missed out on productivity growth opportunities in market services. While growth surged in the US and some European countries, like Finland and the UK, most countries in Europe show slow and declining productivity growth in market services. Compared to the manufacturing sector, relatively little is known of the sources of labor productivity growth in market services. In this paper, we provide the most comprehensive evidence to date on the sources of growth by using the new EU KLEMS database. This database provides detailed information on outputs, inputs and productivity at the industry level for European countries and the US.

The first part of our analysis showed that investment in new technologies (ICT) and human capital have contributed substantially to growth across Europe and the US. Some European countries, like Denmark and the UK, show contributions from ICT use that are comparable to those in the US, while others, such as Italy and Spain, show much lower contributions. However, differences in investment rates of ICT and human capital cannot account for the cross-country differences in labor productivity growth in market services. Instead, the differences in the rate of efficiency gains, also referred to as multifactor productivity (MFP) growth, are as pronounced as the differences in labor productivity growth.

To arrive at these conclusions, we relied on a growth accounting methodology. This method assumes, amongst other things, that there are no productive externalities to the use of inputs. However, investors in ICT may for example benefit from network effects, while a large pool of skilled laborers might have a positive impact on the overall innovation process. We systematically analyze these possibilities but find no evidence in support of such externalities. This contradicts one of the key conclusions from the Sapir Report (2004). We show that the reason for this is that an analysis based on crude productivity data cannot distinguish between the private and social

---

[35] See Baily and Kirkegaard (2004) and Crafts (2006) on some of these considerations. Also see Kox and Lejour (2005) on the impact of differences in regulation across countries.

[36] See also the discussion in the Sapir Report (2004, p. 37), in particular on the distinction between fixed-line and mobile telephony.

returns to education. When this distinction is made, it appears that externalities cannot explain the differences in MFP growth. Since we do not find externalities to the use of ICT and university-educated workers, the case for government intervention in stimulating the diffusion of ICT or a preferential treatment of higher education vis-à-vis primary and secondary schooling is not supported by our analysis.

We also look at the impact of regulatory barriers to entry in services, since high barriers are likely to dampen the intensity of competition in the product market and hence, reduce the incentives for innovation. We find limited evidence in support of this hypothesis: MFP growth in post and telecommunications benefited substantially from entry liberalization during the 1990s. This supports the view that deregulation fosters productivity, but since we could not find similar evidence for other industries, the evidence suggests caution in the formulation of policy recommendations. For further insights, we need more detailed data on services regulation measures and a better understanding of how regulation affects competition in services. However, our analysis does not reject the notion that a decline in entry barriers in services may unlock the productivity growth potential of other market service industries provided that substantive action in this area is undertaken. Since various service industries have recently been liberalized within individual countries, cross-border liberalization, as envisaged in the EU Services Directive, is a natural way forward to gain productivity advantages in services across Europe.

A few cautionary notes are in order. First, while we find that, by and large, output measures of services tracks the 'true' performance of the sector reasonably well, there is substantial scope for improvement, especially for output measures for the financial and business services industry. Convergence towards best measurement practices and a higher degree of transparency by national statistical offices should help to inspire more confidence in the official statistics. Second, there is a large heterogeneity in productivity performance across market services and pooling these industries together in econometric analysis might not be warranted. Some of the market industries are as large as the total manufacturing sector and differ greatly in the degree of openness to international trade, foreign direct investment and intensity of formal R&D. Our findings of significant results from deregulations on MFP growth in post and telecommunications confirm that industry heterogeneity should be explicitly recognized in growth analysis.

Finally, when discussing multifactor productivity trends in services, it is important to take a broad view of 'technology'. While one might equate 'technology upgrading' with the introduction of new vintages of machinery, formal R&D and other hard science, in particular in manufacturing, the concept of technology as used in economic theory is actually much broader and therefore also applicable to services. 'Technology' describes the available knowledge about the various ways in which inputs, such as capital and labor, can be combined in the production of goods and services (Hulten, 2001). For service industries in particular, this may be more strongly related to changes in organizational structure, management and work practices than 'hard' technological changes. These types of technology might less easily spillover from one firm to another than manufacturing technologies, as they are embodied in company and management cultures. In fact, for a study of services a re-examination of the mechanisms through which technologies transfer from laggard to frontier countries seems needed. With the exception of recent work by, for example, Bloom and van Reenen (2006), measurement of the importance and transfer of intangible assets across countries, is still an underdeveloped field.[37] Integrating new measures and insights from both industry-level and micro-level research can be another important line of research that should provide further explanations for why productivity growth rates in market services have diverged across Europe and the US, as well as provide indications of the conditions under which Europe can exploit the growth potential of market services.

Discussion

Wendy Carlin
University College London and CEPR

In this paper the authors provide the first detailed analysis of market services productivity across European countries and the US using the newly assembled EU KLEMS database. The database is now available for other researchers and the current paper will stimulate a rich vein of research. The paper is motivated by the difference in the aggregate performance of the US and European countries in labor productivity growth since 1995. It investigates the role that MFP growth – as opposed to factor accumulation – played in that difference and the possibility that externalities to ICT or human capital investment or differences in product market regulation can account for it. In my comment I will put into sharper focus a number of aspects of the data that emerge from their analysis. I begin by summarizing the case presented by the authors, point to some gaps in the case and highlight some of the issues associated with the new level estimates of MFP.

A way of bringing out the role of MFP performance in accounting for the differences in labor productivity growth between European countries and the US since 1995 is presented in Figure 2. This shows the decomposition in the productivity growth shortfall to the US in the 1995–2004 period into the four components of ICT and non-ICT capital deepening, the change in labor composition and MFP growth. I have ordered the countries in the figure according to the percentage contribution of MFP growth to explaining the *shortfall* to US labor productivity growth. Three countries illustrate the variation in experience. At the far right of the MFP columns, is the UK where more than the entire labor productivity growth deficit relative to the US in this

[37] See Black and Lynch (2005) for an overview of measuring organizational capital.

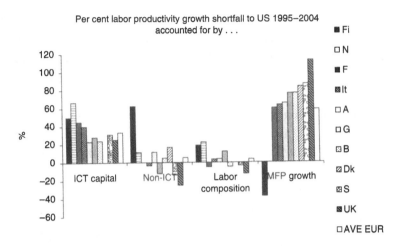

Figure 2. Decomposing the labor productivity growth shortfall to the US, 1995–2004

Source: Table 6 in this paper.

period is accounted for by weaker MFP growth: ICT investment was also weaker whilst non-ICT investment and labor composition changes were stronger than in the US. Interestingly as Table 6 in the paper shows, MFP growth in the UK slowed down slightly between 1980–1995 and 1995–2004 in contrast to its rapid acceleration in the US. At the opposite end of the spectrum is Finland where MFP growth in the post-1995 period was faster than in the US (shown by the negative bar) – whereas factor accumulation was weaker. The Netherlands is also interesting because its productivity growth shortfall is mainly accounted for by weaker ICT investment: MFP growth was at the same rate as in the US.

The core of the analysis in the paper is centred on the estimation of a dynamic catching up model where MFP growth is a function of a catch-up term (the β coefficient), the candidate growth factors, which are ICT, human capital and regulation, (the γ coefficients) and the interaction between the growth factors and the technology gap (the δ coefficients). The model is motivated by the hypothesis that there are potentially differential effects on productivity growth in industries that are close to the technology frontier as compared with their effects on industries far from it. For example, higher education is predicted to have a positive direct (frontier) effect but be less important for catching up, which would be captured by a negative interaction effect. Regulatory barriers are predicted to depress MFP growth at the frontier (negative γ) and to have a more detrimental effect for industries closer to the frontier (positive δ).

The predictions are tested using the disaggregated industry data for market services over the period from 1980 to 2004. Across a wide range of specifications, there is clear evidence of MFP convergence to the technology leader. However, there is no evidence that ICT investment or an increase in the proportion of university educated

Table 12. MFP leaders by market services industry: 1980 and 2004

	1980			2004		
	1st	2nd	3rd	1st	2nd	3rd
Motor trade	Belgium	Denmark	UK	Belgium	Netherlands	Finland
Wholesale	Belgium	Germany	UK	Germany	Netherlands	Finland
Retail	Denmark	Belgium	Germany	Denmark	Germany	France
Hotels & Rest.	France	Germany	Denmark	Austria	Germany	US
Transport	Netherlands	UK	US	Netherlands	US	France
Post & Telecomm.	UK	US	Belgium	France	Germany	UK
Fin. Intermediation	Italy	UK	US	Italy	Belgium	Denmark
Bus. Services	UK	US	Spain	US	Belgium	Denmark
Social & personal	Netherlands	Austria	Denmark	France	Netherlands	Germany

Source: Table A3, at the end of the Appendix.

workers has a direct effect on the rate of technological progress (the frontier effect) or that its effects depend on the technology gap. The results on human capital stand in contrast to those for the aggregate economy reported by Vandenbussche *et al.* (2006). Inklaar *et al.* demonstrate that the source of the difference between their results and those of Vandenbussche *et al.* lies with their corrections to the MFP measures – in particular their corrections in the measured labor inputs for changes in hours worked and in skill composition. Their claim is that once inputs are measured correctly, there is no additional impact of either ICT or higher education on MFP growth. This finding is of considerable policy relevance since if it is valid, the heavy emphasis in recent European debates on the likely innovation benefits from government policies to promote higher levels of investment in ICT and higher education would be misplaced – at least in so far as it applies to market services.

The authors find a little more support for the argument that regulatory barriers affect MFP – but only in one industry, post and telecommunications. However, they do not find any support for the presence of an interaction effect whereby lowering barriers has a greater effect in boosting productivity growth in industries closer to the frontier.

In view of the considerable investment in data collection and in the creation of sophisticated measures of MFP and given that the initial results using these measures do not provide clear support for policies that are being promoted in Europe, it is important to think carefully about the construction of the MFP measures and to look at what the measures reveal. The most striking finding is that contrary to the impression given by the paper's motivation, the author's calculations show that the US is not the technology leader as measured by 'sophisticated' MFP in market services. In 1980, the US was the MFP leader in none of the nine market services industries and ranked second in two. By 2004, the US led in one industry and was second in one. Table 12 lists the first three countries in each of the market services industries according to the

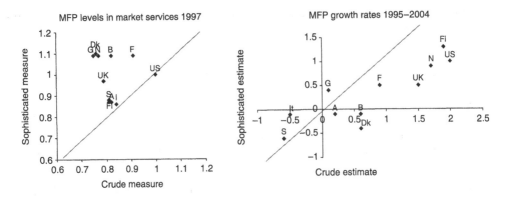

Figure 3. The effect of more sophisticated measurement of MFP on country rankings in levels and growth rates.

Source: Table 7 in the paper and Table A2 in the Appendix.

authors' preferred measure of MFP. There are several surprising aspects of the data: first is the limited presence of the US as technology leader either at the beginning or the end of the period, second is the apparently remarkably good performance of the UK in 1980 just as the Thatcher reforms were being launched, and third is the premier position of Italy as productivity leader in financial services.[38]

The analysis in the paper reveals that the world looks quite different when viewed through the lens of the more sophisticated measures of productivity. The corrections make a substantial difference both to the cross-country levels and to growth rates. Figure 3 shows that although the US is the leader in a bench-mark year (1997) when the crude measure of MFP is used, five European countries have higher MFP after the various adjustments have been made. This difference is due mainly to correcting for the quality of labor input (US inputs are higher than are captured by 'persons') and to implementing double deflation using industry level PPPs. In the right hand panel of Figure 2, which shows the data for the post-1995 period, it is clear that in moving from the crude to the sophisticated measure of MFP, relative growth rates are also affected. There are big downwards adjustments for the US, UK and Denmark and upward adjustments for Germany and Italy. The substantial productivity growth advantage of the UK over Germany virtually disappears when the more sophisticated measure is used.

To sum up, the paper by Inklaar *et al.* produces results about the determinants of productivity growth in market services that are somewhat at odds with prevailing views in the European debate – in particular, they do not find that ICT or higher education are important for MFP growth either directly or differentially for industries close to or further from the technology frontier. They find some support for the role

[38] The most recent OECD Economic Survey of Italy (2007) provides a summary of evidence of inefficiency relative to other OECD countries in the Italian financial services industry (pp. 74–75).

of regulatory barriers in the post and telecommunications industry but not more generally. As I have illustrated, the sophisticated measures of MFP levels and growth rates that they derive are also somewhat puzzling: in contrast to the motivation of the paper and much of the debate in Europe, the data reveal that it is not European countries but the US that is lagging in productivity levels in most industries throughout the period. Although the authors point out that the problems with cross country comparability in measurement are greater for levels than for growth rates, nevertheless the levels play a key role in the econometric analysis (via the catch-up term). Taken at face value, these productivity indicators suggest that if Europe is already ahead in MFP in most market services industries, its problem needs to be reformulated.

Alternatively, the results may indicate that further thought is needed in checking that the sophisticated MFP measure accounts for all relevant factors. Two possible confounding factors come to mind. The first relates to the assumption of competitive factor and product markets – the example of the top ranking of the Italian financial intermediation industry is suggestive that rents may be being captured in the MFP measure. Second, the measure of human capital that is used may be too narrow, with the result that some of it is included by default in measured MFP. Inklaar *et al.* use the share of university graduates in labor input as the high skill measure. If this omits a substantial proportion of vocationally qualified high-skill workers in some countries, it may lead to an overestimate of MFP levels in such countries. The authors are aware of this potential problem but point out that the data to deal with it are not generally available. To indicate that the problem exists we focus on four countries for which much more detailed comparable human capital data are available (US, UK, France and Germany). We can then compare the ranking of the level of high-skill human capital that Inklaar *et al.* use with the ranking based on the richer classification (Mason *et al.* 2007; cited by Inklaar *et al.*). Whereas Germany ranks fourth and France third of these four countries in Inklaar *et al.*'s measure of the human capital content of market services, Germany ranks first in each market services industry and France second in more than half of them in Mason *et al.*

Jonathan Temple
University of Bristol

This paper uses a new dataset, created as part of the EU KLEMS project, to analyze productivity in Europe, and especially the productivity of market services. The main aims of the empirical analysis are (1) to describe and compare productivity levels and growth rates in market services in the US and 11 European economies; (2) to examine the role of information and communication technologies in service sector productivity growth; and (3) to explain the differences between the EU, where growth in the service sector has often been slow, and the US, where it has often been fast.

The construction of the dataset is a major and valuable contribution in itself, and one that will enable some important research questions to be addressed. The current paper already shows how to make constructive and informative use of the new data. In discussing the paper's empirical analysis, there are two sets of points I would like to make: one set narrowly statistical, and the other more general.

The statistical points relate to the use of convergence ideas in the empirical models. Some of the models estimated in the paper, such as those in Table 8, relate growth in multifactor productivity (MFP) to the extent of international technology gaps. In the paper's models, these gaps are defined as minus the log of the relative MFP level, so that a larger gap corresponds to a lower relative MFP level. The paper estimates the relationship between growth and technology gaps using pooled regressions, based on data on 11 countries and 9 market services sectors. The empirical findings are modified slightly when the authors use their new series for relative MFP, rather than cruder ones.

In estimating a relationship between growth and initial conditions, this exercise bears a family resemblance to the conditional convergence regressions used in the literature on aggregate economic growth. As elsewhere in the sector-level work on productivity, there is probably more to be learnt from the cross-country growth literature than first meets the eye. First, given that the implied rates of convergence are relatively low, one issue is whether tests of this kind can distinguish genuine convergence from cases where relative MFP is not mean-reverting. Second, it would be interesting to consider the possible implications of measurement error for the estimates. This is especially so, given that a major contribution of this paper is the construction of new and more sophisticated MFP series, which should be more accurate than those previously available.

To see why this is relevant, it is worth considering the relationship between measurement error and convergence. Investigations of convergence are essentially asking whether today's outcomes are strongly or weakly related to past outcomes. A weak association corresponds to a faster rate of convergence. Put differently, if units like countries or sectors are converging to steady-states quickly, this means that the influence of the initial conditions must be dissipating quickly. It is then easy to see what can happen under measurement error. Since the errors in the data will weaken the association between today's outcomes and past outcomes, they will tend to bias the results towards faster convergence. This effect has been discussed in De Long (1988) and Temple (1998).

If we look at the results in Table 8, the move from the basic MFP series to the more sophisticated series lowers the estimated rates of convergence. This pattern is appealing, because it is the one we should expect, if the MFP data constructed by the authors genuinely contain less (classical) measurement error than the more basic data. There would be several ways of exploring this further. In principle, it would be possible to use instrumental variables, method-of-moments corrections, or carry out reverse regressions, as in Temple (1998). Until the literature on sector-level productivity acknowledges the possibility of measurement error in more detail, some of its findings on convergence should be treated with caution.

The second point I want to make is about the underlying economics. The empirical analysis in the paper points towards an interesting research question, which is why differences in services MFP across countries might persist. Perhaps part of the explanation lies in productivity differences across firms within a given country. Many services involve significant scope for quality differences, and output that is non-standardized: think of architects, for example. These characteristics have implications not only for measurement, but also for market structure, because they could allow firms of widely-varying productivity to co-exist even in equilibrium. It could be argued that the service sector has exactly the combination of sunk costs (through reputation-building) and *ex ante* uncertainty about productivity that leads to equilibrium productivity differentials in Hopenhayn (1992) and Melitz (2003).

This suggests, for future research, an interesting explanation for international differences in service sector productivity. Differences across countries may be strongly influenced by the extent to which productivity varies within each country: for example, those countries with a long tail of weak performers will have lower average productivity. In turn, this perspective could shed new light on product market regulation and competition policy. There might be scope for investigating these questions with KLEMS data, or perhaps more obviously, with data at a more disaggregated level.

These ideas hint at the way that better data can invite deeper research questions and provide a firmer basis for policy analysis. Whether or not these specific ideas can be easily pursued, the authors deserve great credit for putting together such a useful dataset, and for analyzing it to such good effect.

Panel discussion

Philippe Aghion remarked that the paper's results are hard to reconcile with recent contributions finding that ICT or human capital or institutional structures account for cross-country differences in productivity. While the literature hotly debates which of these factors may be more relevant, this paper finds that none of the standard factors accounts for productivity differences, and this is puzzling. Peter Schott pointed out that comparisons of labor input quality across countries are very imprecise, and wondered whether firm-level data may be more informative in the relevant respects. Stephen Redding suggested that firm-level data might indeed be useful for the purpose of assessing the relationship between export activity and productivity, and that data on multinational firms could help disentangle firm and country effects. Anne Sibert pointed out that since the role of ICT is more important when reorganization is easier, interactions between ICT and possibly different measures of regulation (such as land-use restrictions in the case of retail trade) should play a key role.

Francesco Caselli found it very striking that, according to the paper's results, so many countries appear to have experienced many years of negative productivity growth. He wondered whether composition effects may spuriously produce such evidence as countries reallocate factors between different value-added sectors within services industries, or perhaps negative measured productivity growth could be due to adjustment or adoption costs. Christian Schultz noted that the tightness of labor markets might influence such aspects. Werner Sinn added that public employment could also be relevant: in the public sector, production is essentially measured on the basis of wages, which may not be appropriate for the purpose of assessing welfare-relevant productivity developments. Daria Taglioni thought that the output of services sectors is indeed generally difficult to measure, even in the private sector, and that the implications of measurement difficulties for the paper's results could be assessed considering their different relevance for different manufacturing sectors, many of which have a large services component.

APPENDIX 1. OUTPUT MEASUREMENT IN MARKET SERVICES

Market services productivity trends are much less studied than trends in manufacturing. A major reason for this is the concern about the availability of adequate measures of services output and productivity, often referred to the overviews of measurement issues by Griliches (1992, 1994). It is well-known that the problem of measuring output is in general much more challenging in services than in goods-producing industries. Indeed, Griliches (1994) classified a large part of the services sector as 'unmeasurable'.[39] Most measurement problems boil down to the fact that service activities are intangible, more heterogeneous than goods and often dependent on the actions of the consumer as well as the producer. While the measurement of nominal output in market services is generally less problematic, being mostly a matter of accurately registering total revenue, the main bottleneck is the measurement of output volumes, which requires accurate price measurement adjusted for changes in the quality of services output.[40]

There is no doubt that problems in measuring services output still exist, but many statistical offices have made great strides forward in the measurement of the nominal value and prices of services output.[41] Still, progress has been uneven, both across industries and countries.[42]

To provide an assessment of statistical practices in European countries, we have made use of a series of recent surveys of volume measurement practices by national

---

[39] See also Sichel (1997) for the likely impact of these 'unmeasurable' industries and Wölfl (2003) for an extensive general overview of measurement issues in services.

[40] A prominent exception to measurement problems for nominal output is for banking, see Wang, Basu and Fernald (2004).

[41] See, for example developments in the US Bureau of Labor Statistics (BLS) (Horrigan, Bathgate and Swick, 2006). Triplett and Bosworth (2004) discuss the long-term improvements made in the US statistical system on measuring services. The Voorburg Group on Service Statistics, which was set up in 1986, has brought together statisticians from national statistical institutes around the world, including Europe, to review and improve methods concerning the measurement of services (see http://www4.statcan.ca/english/voorburg/2004-background.htm).

[42] In a study of measurement practices in the UK, Crespi et al. (2006) argue that measurement problems in the UK are most severe in finance and business services.

statistical institutes (NSI's) in the European Union. These inventories were mandated by Eurostat. Using the Eurostat (2001) *Handbook on Price and Volume Measures in National Accounts*, NSI's have graded their volume measurement techniques in each industry as an A, B or C-method. An A-method is considered as most appropriate, a B-method as an acceptable alternative to an A-method, and a C-method as a method that is too biased to be acceptable, or one that is conceptually wrong. For example, for business and management consultancy services, an A-method would be the collection of actual or model contract prices and such prices need to account for changes in the characteristics of the contracts over time. A typical B-method could be the use of charge-out rates or hourly fees for business services or the price index of a closely-related activity, such as accounting or legal services. A C-method would be any other deflation method, such as using the overall CPI or PPI (Eurostat, 2001, pp. 107–108).

The inventories by the NSI's referred to above describe the state of measurement practices in each country around the year 2000. Most countries gave explicit grades for each industry and where possible, we cross-checked this grading with the description in the Handbook.[43] Table A1 shows the share of output in each industry that is deflated using A, B and C-methods, averaged across those European countries in our dataset for which these inventories were available. The table shows that measurement practices in market services are far from perfect since A-methods, with the exception of hotels and restaurants, account for only a small share of output in most industries. It also shows that measurement is most problematic in finance and business services,

Table A1. Average share of value added in market services in European countries deflated using A, B or C-methods around the year 2000 (%)

ISIC rev3 code	Industry	A	B	C
50	Motor trade	0	78	22
51	Wholesale trade	0	78	22
52	Retail trade	0	78	22
55	Hotels and restaurants	73	20	8
60–63	Transport and storage	9	70	21
64	Post and telecommunications	1	86	13
65–67	Financial intermediation	0	54	46
71–74	Business services	6	47	46
90–93	Social and personal services	16	47	37
	Average	12	62	26

Notes: Classification into A, B and C-methods are by national statistical offices, based on Eurostat (2001). A-method is defined as most appropriate, B-method as acceptable and C-method as unacceptable. Average share is calculated based on information for Austria, Belgium, Denmark, Finland, France, Germany, Italy, Netherlands and the UK. For each country and each industry we use information on the share of value added deflated using A, B or C-methods, and for each industry (as well as the total average) these shares are averaged across countries.

---

[43] In a number of cases, the grades were adjusted to better conform to the Handbook. For some countries, coding was missing and had to be done based on the given description of measurement practice.

where nearly half of output is deflated with C-methods. As might be expected, there is also substantial variation in measurement across countries, but generally hotels and restaurants are best measured and finance and business services are worst measured. However, it also becomes clear that the scope of measurement problems should not be overstated: on average about a quarter of output is deflated using inappropriate (and thus potentially misleading) deflators while for the remainder, at least acceptable methods are used. For example, Inklaar and Timmer (2007c) provide an analysis of how B-method deflation in retail trade compares to a conceptually superior alternative (A-method). They conclude that while more appropriate deflation leads to somewhat different growth rates of output and productivity, the broad pattern of growth differences across countries (which is what matters for this study) is not strongly affected.

A few notes of caution are in order here. First, the inventories of measurement practices reflected the situation around the year 2000 and it is not known to what extent new practices are carried through in revisions of historical time series published by the statistical offices. Second, while the best measured and worst measured service industries are the same across countries, there is still substantial variation. For example, in one (small) European country the share of C-methods is 77%, while in another country, this share is only 5% compared to an average share of C-methods of 26%. This suggests that convergence to best measurement practice within Europe would already allow for a more accurate assessment of productivity growth in market services. This would not so much require additional conceptual work, but more effective adoption of best practices among NSI's (see also Crespi *et al.*, 2006). In general, researchers and other users would benefit substantially from more openness and transparency by NSI's about measurement practices. The unpublished, confidential and infrequent measurement inventories in Europe stand in sharp contrast to easily accessible publications as published in the *Survey of Current Business* of the US Bureau of Economic Analysis, which regularly reports on updates in the methodologies used in constructing the US National Accounts.

APPENDIX 2. DATA SOURCES AND METHODOLOGY

Growth accounting set-up

To assess the contribution of the various inputs to aggregate economic growth, we apply the growth accounting framework as developed by Jorgenson and associates (see, for example, Jorgenson, Ho and Stiroh, 2005). It is based on production possibility frontiers where industry gross output is a function of capital, labor, intermediate inputs and technology, which is indexed by time, T. Each industry, indexed by j, can produce a set of products and purchases a number of distinct intermediate inputs, capital service inputs, and labor inputs to produce its output. The production functions are assumed to be separable in these inputs, so that:

$$Y_j = f_j(K_j, \, L_j, \, X_j, \, T) \tag{A1}$$

where Y is output, K is an index of capital service flow, L is an index of labor service flows and X is an index of intermediate inputs, either purchased from domestic industries or imported. Under the assumptions of competitive factor markets, full input utilization and constant returns to scale, the growth of output can be expressed as the (cost share) weighted growth of inputs and multifactor productivity (denoted by A^Y):

$$\Delta \ln Y_{jt} = \bar{v}_{jt}^X \, \Delta \ln X_{jt} + \bar{v}_{jt}^K \, \Delta \ln K_{jt} + \bar{v}_{jt}^L \, \Delta \ln L_{jt} + \Delta \ln A_{jt}^Y \tag{A2}$$

where $\bar{v}^i$ denotes the two-period average share of input i in nominal output and $\bar{v}^L + \bar{v}^K + \bar{v}^X = 1$. Each element on the right-hand side indicates the proportion of output growth accounted for by growth in intermediate inputs, capital services, labor services and MFP, respectively. By dividing through total hours worked and rearranging, the breakdown of value added per hour growth can be made as follows:

$$\Delta \ln \frac{VA_{jt}}{H_{jt}} = \bar{w}_{jt}^K \, \Delta \ln \frac{K_{jt}}{H_{jt}} + \bar{w}_{jt}^L \, \Delta \ln \frac{L_{jt}}{H_{jt}} + \Delta \ln A_{jt}^{VA} \tag{A3}$$

where $\bar{w}^i$ denotes the two-period average share of input i in nominal value added. This formulation allows us to assess the contribution of capital deepening (capital services per hour worked) and labor composition change (labor services per hour worked) to labor productivity growth.

Growth accounting decompositions are made on the basis of certain restrictive assumptions such as cost-minimizing producers and competitive factor and product markets. These are unlikely to be fully satisfied in practice, but growth accounting provides a straightforward, non-parametric and consistent method which can be used as a starting point to identify the contributions of inputs and productivity to growth. It can also serve as a benchmark as most economy policy frameworks are nowadays focused on creating an economic environment that more or less satisfies the free-market conditions. In Section 4 we found no evidence that the growth accounting assumptions on the returns to skills and ICT capital had to be rejected.

Data sources

The data for this paper are taken from the first version of the EU KLEMS database (March 2007). This database is publicly available at www.euklems.net. This is a new database which provides measures of economic growth, productivity, employment creation, capital formation and technological change at a detailed industry level for European Union member states, Japan and the US from 1970 onwards. It has been put together by a consortium of sixteen research institutes across Europe in close cooperation with National Statistical Offices and is financed by the European Commission. The database is specifically designed to provide all data necessary for growth and level accounting exercises as described in the main text.

The EU KLEMS database provides long time-series going back to 1970 through linking of national account data series from different vintages in a harmonized and consistent way. National Account series are further subdivided into the necessary industry, labor and capital detail on the basis of additional secondary data sources. For example, industry detail in output and employment series is increased by additional information from industry surveys. To have a breakdown of various labor categories, use is made of additional surveys, such as Labor Force Surveys, which are available on an annual basis for most countries. For a breakdown of investment into various asset types, additional information from input–output tables and investment surveys was used. Especially series on investment in computers and communication equipment are normally not provided in the National Accounts. Further detail on the sources and methods used for each country can be found in Timmer et al. (2007a).

The database has a number of unique characteristics compared to other existing multi-country industry-level databases such as the OECD STAN database. Specifically, the EU KLEMS database contains measures of gross output, intermediate inputs, labor service input and capital services input at the level of 30 industries (of which 9 are market service industries). Hours worked are cross classified by age (3 types), gender (2 types) and educational attainment (3 types). Labor services input is measured by weighting hours worked by each of the eighteen types of labor in a Törnqvist aggregation procedure, where weights are given by the share of each type in total labor compensation. Thus, the changes in the composition of the labor force are taken into account which is important as in most countries, the share of more productive higher-skilled workers is increasing, albeit at different speeds. Similarly, changes in the composition of the capital stock are taken into account by distinguishing six asset types at the industry level (see below for the measurement of capital stocks and services). This is the first time that labor and capital services measures are available at an industry-level for a wide range of countries.

Importantly, output and input measures in EU KLEMS are harmonized across countries in various ways. This includes harmonization of industrial classifications and harmonization of classifications for labor types and capital assets. But also the measurement of capital stocks was harmonized by using similar assumptions concerning the depreciation model (which is a perpetual inventory model with geometric depreciation rates) and depreciation rates (which vary by asset type and industry but not by country).[44] As investment prices of IT-hardware are not quality-adjusted in all countries, we use the harmonization procedure introduced by Schreyer (2002) to adjust for differences in deflation measures (see Box 2 in main text).

---

[44] Although depreciation rates most likely vary across countries due to differences in the pace of structural change, there is no empirical evidence available which can be used to model this. Assuming identical rates across countries is a second-best solution. The rates are based on the rates used by the BEA in the US national accounts (Fraumeni, 1997).

Growth of capital services

According to the perpetual inventory model (PIM), the capital stock (S) is defined as a weighted sum of past investments with weights given by the relative efficiencies of capital goods at different ages:

$$S_{i,T} = \sum_{t=0}^{\infty} \partial_{i,t} I_{i,T-t} \tag{A4}$$

with $S_{i,T}$ the capital stock (for a particular asset type i) at time T, $\partial_{i,t}$ the efficiency of a capital good i of age t relative to the efficiency of a new capital good, and $I_{i,T-t}$ the investments in period $T - t$.[45] As in the work of Jorgenson et al., a geometric depreciation pattern is applied (Fraumeni, 1997). With a given constant rate of depreciation δ_i different for each asset type, we get $\partial_{i,t} = (1 - \delta_i)^{t-1}$, so that:

$$S_{i,T} = \sum_{t=0}^{\infty} (1 - \delta_i)^{t-1} I_{i,T-t} = S_{i,T-1}(1 - \delta_i) + I_{i,T} \tag{A5}$$

If one assumes that the flow of capital services from each asset type i (K_i) is proportional to the average of the stock available at the end of the current and the prior period ($S_{i,T}$ and $S_{i,T-1}$), one can aggregate capital service flows from these asset types as a translog quantity index to:

$$\Delta \ln K = \ln K_T - \ln K_{T-1} = \sum_i \bar{v}_i [\ln S_{i,T} - \ln S_{i,T-1}] \tag{A6}$$

where weights are given by the average shares of each component in the value of capital compensation $\bar{v}_i = \frac{1}{2}[v_{i,T} + v_{i,T-1}]$ and $v_{i,T} = p_{i,T} S_{i,T} / \sum_i p_{i,T} S_{i,T}$.

The estimation of the compensation share of each asset, v_i is related to the user cost of each asset. The user cost approach is crucial in any analysis of the contribution of ICT capital to growth, because the annual amount of capital services delivered per euro of investment in ICT is much higher than that of an euro invested in, say, buildings. While an ICT asset may typically be scrapped after five years, buildings may provide services for decades. ICT assets have a high user cost due to high depreciation and declining prices. For example, the user cost of IT-machinery is typically 50 to 60% of the investment price, while that of buildings is less than 10%. Therefore one euro of IT capital stock gets a heavier weight in the growth decomposition than one euro of building stock. This different weight on capital services is picked up by using the rental price of capital services, $p_{k,t}^K$, which reflects the price at which the investor is indifferent between buying or renting the capital good for a one-year lease in the rental market. In the absence of taxation the equilibrium condition can be rearranged, yielding the familiar cost-of-capital equation:

[45] An important implicit assumption made here is that the services by assets of different vintages are perfect substitutes for each other.

$$p_{k,t}^K = p_{k,t-1}^I r_t + \delta_k p_{k,t}^I - [p_{k,t}^I - p_{k,t-1}^I] \tag{A7}$$

with r_T representing the nominal rate of return, δ_k the depreciation rate of asset type k, and $p_{k,T}^I$, the rate of inflation in the price of asset type k.[46] This formula shows that the rental fee is determined by the nominal rate of return, the rate of economic depreciation and the asset specific capital gains.

The nominal rate of return is determined *ex post* (endogenous approach). It is assumed that the total value of capital services for each industry equals its compensation for all assets. This procedure yields an internal rate of return that exhausts capital income and is consistent with constant returns to scale. This nominal rate of return is the same for all assets in an industry, but is allowed to vary across industries, and derived as a residual as follows:

$$r_{j,t} = \frac{p_{j,t}^K K_{j,t} + \sum_k [p_{k,j,t}^I - p_{k,j,t-1}^I] S_{k,j,t} - \sum_k p_{k,j,t}^I \delta_k S_{k,j,t}}{\sum_k p_{k,j,t-1}^I S_{k,j,t}} \tag{A8}$$

where the first term $p_{j,t}^K K_{j,t}$ is the capital compensation in industry j, which under constant returns to scale can be derived as value added minus the compensation of labor.

Growth of labor services

As for capital, the productivity of various types of labor, such as low- versus high-skilled labor, will differ across these types. Standard measures of labor input, such as number of persons employed or hours worked, will not account for such differences. Hence it is important that measures of labor input take account of the heterogeneity of the labor force in measuring productivity and the contribution of labor to output growth. In the growth accounting approach, these measures are called labor services, as they allow for differences in the amount of services delivered per unit of labor. It is assumed that the flow of labor services for each labor type is proportional to hours worked, and workers are paid their marginal productivities. Then the corresponding index of labor services input L is given by

$$\Delta \ln L_t = \sum_l \bar{v}_{l,t} \Delta \ln H_{l,t} \tag{A9}$$

where $\Delta \ln H_{l,t}$ indicates the growth of hours worked by labor type l and weights are given by the period average shares of each type in the value of labor compensation. In this way, aggregation takes into account the changing composition of the labor force. We cross-classify labor input by educational attainment, gender and age (to

---

[46] The logic for using the rental price is as follows. In equilibrium, an investor is indifferent between two alternatives: earning a nominal rate of return r on an investment q, or buying a unit of capital collecting a rental p and then selling it at the depreciated asset price $(1 - \delta)q$ in the next period. Assuming no taxation the equilibrium condition is: $(1 + r_T)q_{i,T-1} = P_{i,T} + (1 - \delta)q_{i,T}$, with P as the rental fee and q_i the acquisition price of investment good i (Jorgenson and Stiroh, 2000, p. 192). Rearranging yields a variation of the familiar cost-of-capital equation: $P_{i,T} = q_{i,T-1}r_T + \delta q_{i,T-1} - [q_{i,T} - q_{i,T-1}]$, which when dividing the rental fee by the acquisition price of the previous period transforms into equation (A4).

proxy for work experience) into 18 labor categories (respectively $3 * 2 * 3$ types). Typically, a shift in the share of hours worked by low-skilled workers to medium- or high-skilled workers will lead to a growth of labor services which is bigger than the growth in total hours worked. We refer to this difference as the labor composition effect.[47]

Series on hours worked by labor types are not part of the core set of national accounts statistics put out by NSIs, not even at the aggregate level. Also, there is no comprehensive international database on skills which can be used for this purpose. Previous cross-country studies relied on rough proxies of skills such as distinguishing production versus non-production workers as in Griffith, Redding and van Reenen (2004) or combined a wide variety of disconnected sources such as in Nicoletti and Scarpetta (2003). More in-depth country studies such as Koeniger and Leonardi (2007) use consistent data for wages and employment by skill from one particular source. This is also the strategy followed in EU KLEMS. For each country covered, a choice was made for the best statistical source for consistent wage and employment data at the industry level. In most cases this was the labor force survey (LFS), which in some cases was combined with a earnings survey when wages were not included in the LFS. In other instances, an establishment survey, or social-security database was used.[48] Care has been taken to arrive at series which are consistent over time. This involved significant additional effort, as most employment surveys are not designed to track developments over time, and breaks in methodology or coverage frequently occur.

Level accounting set-up

Comparing productivity levels across countries is in many ways analogous to comparisons over time. However, while one typically compares productivity in one year with productivity in the previous year, there is no such natural ordering of countries. Therefore the comparison should not depend on the country that is chosen as the base country. There are various index number methods that can be used to make multilateral comparisons. We use the method suggested by Caves, Christensen and Diewert (1982). This index mirrors the Törnqvist index approach used in our growth accounting, but all countries are compared to an artificial 'average' country (AC). This average country is defined as the simple average of all N countries in the set. For example, a multilateral index of capital service input in country c is given by:

$$\ln\frac{K_c}{K_{AC}} = \sum_j \bar{v}_j \ln\frac{S_{j,c}}{S_{j,AC}} \qquad (A10)$$

---

[47] This difference is also known as 'labor quality' in the growth accounting literature (see e.g. Jorgenson, Ho and Stiroh 2005). However, this terminology has a normative connotation which easily leads to confusion. For example, lower female wages would suggest that hours worked by females have a lower 'quality' than hours worked by males. Instead we prefer to use the more positive concept of 'labor composition'.

[48] See Timmer *et al.* (2007a).

with $\bar{v}_j = \frac{1}{2}[v_{j,c} + v_{j,AC}]$ and $v_{j,c}$ the share of asset type j in total nominal capital compensation in country c, $v_{j,AC} = 1/N\sum v_{j,c}$ the average compensation share of capital asset j over all countries N and $S_{j,AC} = 1/N\sum S_{j,c}$, the average stock of asset j. This mirrors equation (A6). Similar indices can be constructed for labor services inputs and intermediate inputs. Gaps in multi factor productivity levels can be derived by subtracting the compensation-weighted relative inputs from relative output as follows (industry and time subscript suppressed for convenience):

$$\ln\frac{A_c^Y}{A_{AC}^Y} = \ln\frac{Y_c}{Y_{AC}} - \bar{v}^X \ln\frac{X_c}{X_{AC}} - \bar{v}^K \ln\frac{K_c}{K_{AC}} - \bar{v}^L \ln\frac{L_c}{L_{AC}} \qquad (A11)$$

with v's the input shares in gross output averaged between country c and the average country AC. A comparison between two countries, say Germany and the US, can be made indirectly: by first comparing each country with the average country and then comparing the differences in German and US levels relative to the average country.[49]

Output and input PPPs

A level accounting approach to output and productivity comparisons has not been widely applied, which is primarily due to the lack of adequate industry-specific PPPs for output and inputs. PPPs are needed to adjust output and inputs for differences in relative price levels between countries. This is true, even when countries have a common currency unit, such as the euro. For example, when the price of a haircut is 10 euro in Portugal against 15 euro in Germany, the Portuguese price level is 67% of that in Germany and this should be taken into account.[50] This price adjustment is often done by means of GDP PPPs (Purchasing Power Parities) which reflect the average expenditure prices in one country relative to another. GDP PPPs are widely available through the work of the OECD and Eurostat. However, it is well-recognized that the use of GDP PPPs, which reflect expenditure prices of *all* goods and services in the economy, can be misleading when used to convert industry-level output. For example, Bernard and Jones (2001) stated that '... research is needed to construct conversion factors appropriate to each sector and that research relying on international comparisons of sectoral productivity and income should proceed with caution until these conversion factors are available' (p. 1169). Until recently, no comprehensive set of industry-level PPPs was available. As an alternative, some studies resorted to the use of 'adjusted' expenditure prices as a proxy for prices for industry output (see e.g. Nicoletti and Scarpetta, 2003). In this paper we make use of a new and comprehensive

---

[49] Note that the same assumptions as for the growth accounts underlie the level accounts. In particular the assumption of constant returns to scale might be less plausible when comparing countries rather than developments over time. This might be important if one wants to argue that low productivity in services in Europe is in part driven by lack of economies of scale. This can only be tested through a parametric exercise which is outside the scope of this paper. If economies of scale are important at the country level then the measured productivity levels of small countries are underestimated.

[50] Engel and Rogers (2004) found a significant dispersion in prices in the euro area countries, even after introduction of the euro.

dataset of industry PPPs for 1997, in combination with a benchmark set of Supply and Use tables. PPPs for value added are constructed by double deflation of gross output and intermediate inputs within a consistent input–output framework. In addition, relative price ratios for labor and capital input are developed. For a full discussion of the new industry output PPPs, the reader is referred to Timmer, Ypma and van Ark (2007b). For the integration of gross output PPPs and the derivation of input PPPs in a level accounting framework, details are spelled out in Inklaar and Timmer (2007b). Below we only present the most important elements of our methodology.

PPPs for gross output are defined from the producer's point of view and are at basic prices, which measures the amount received by the producer for a unit of a good or service produced. These PPPs have partly been constructed by way of unit value ratios for agricultural, mining, manufacturing and transport and communication services. For other industries, PPPs are based on specific expenditure prices from Eurostat and the OECD, which are allocated to individual industries producing the specific item. The value was adjusted from expenditure to producer level with relative transport and distribution margins and by adjusting for differences in relative tax rates. Margins and tax rates were derived from benchmark supply and use tables for 1997. This set of gross output PPPs for 1997, covering 45 industries at (roughly) 2-digit industry level, has been made transitive across countries by applying the multilateral EKS-procedure for a total of 26 countries.[51] For this study the gross output PPPs were then aggregated to the 26 market industries used in this study.

Intermediate input PPPs should reflect the costs of acquiring intermediate deliveries, hence they need to be based on purchasers' prices. Assuming that the basic price of a good is independent of its use, we can use the same gross output PPP for a particular industry, after adjustment for margins and net taxes, to deflate all intermediate deliveries from that industry to other industries. The aggregate intermediate input PPP for an industry is then derived by weighting its intermediate inputs at the gross output PPPs from the delivering industries. Imports are separately identified for which exchange rates are used as PPP, hence assuming no price differences across countries for imported commodities.

To obtain PPPs for capital and labor input, we follow the methodology outlined by Jorgenson and Nishimizu (1978). The PPP for capital services is based on the expenditure PPP for investment from Eurostat and the OECD, adjusted for differences in the user costs between countries. The user cost of capital input depends on the rate of return to capital, the depreciation rate and the investment price change. These data are taken from the capital accounts discussed above. The procedure to obtain a PPP for labor is more straightforward than for capital as it simply involves aggregating relative wages across different labor types using labor compensation for each type as weights. For this purpose we only distinguish between two labor categories: workers

---

[51] These include 25 OECD countries and Taiwan.

with a university degree or higher, and those without. This limited number of skill types is due to difficulties in matching schooling systems across the various countries.

APPENDIX 3. CRUDE AND SOPHISTICATED MFP MEASURES

The growth accounting methodology has been theoretically motivated by the seminal contribution of Jorgenson and Griliches (1967) and put in a more general input–output framework by Jorgenson, Gollop and Fraumeni (1987).[52] However, the empirical implementation of this methodology for European countries has been scarce. Despite the publication of an OECD handbook on productivity measurement (Schreyer, 2001), which is based on the growth accounting methodology, national statistical institutes (NSIs) have been slow in adopting this methodology and to date, only one European NSI, i.e. Statistics Denmark, has published MFP-measures on a regular basis.[53] The OECD and the Groningen Growth and Development Centre maintain MFP series for aggregate OECD economies, but not at the industry level with the exception of a single study by Inklaar et al. (2005) including four European countries (France, Germany, the Netherlands and the United Kingdom).[54] Because of the lack of useful statistics, various scholars have put together ad-hoc databases mostly for the purpose of one single study. The estimates were often based on the OECD Structural Analysis database, STAN (and its predecessor the International Sectoral Database–ISDB) which provides industry-level series on output, aggregate hours worked and aggregate capital stock for a limited group of countries and years. However, MFP measures based on these aggregate concepts of inputs can be seriously biased as will be shown in this appendix. This is unfortunate, given the increased demand and use of industry-level growth accounting statistics for evaluating a wide range of policy areas, including for example outsourcing and international trade, educational policies, investment tax credits and innovation policies. More broadly, MFP statistics are used to study the effects of regulation of product-, labor- and capital-markets on economic growth and inequality. Finally, MFP measures are a crucial ingredient in growth projections used by central banks to set monetary targets.[55]

In Table A2 we indicate that using more sophisticated input measures is not only conceptually appealing, but also leads to measures of MFP which can be radically different from cruder measures which have been used in previous studies. The first column in Table A2 indicates 'crude' MFP growth rates averaged over the period 1995–2004 for each country. The crude measure is calculated by subtracting the weighted growth in persons engaged and growth of the capital stock from growth in

[52] See Jorgenson (1995) and Hulten (2001) for an overview.

[53] Several European NSIs are experimenting with growth accounting statistics, including Statistics Netherlands, Statistics Sweden, Statistics Finland and ISTAT (the Italian NSI).

[54] For OECD series, see www.oecd.org/dataoecd/27/39/36396940.xls. For GGDC series, see www.ggdc.nl/dseries/growth-accounting.shtml, described in Timmer and van Ark (2005).

[55] See e.g. Koeniger and Leonardi (2007), Nicoletti and Scarpetta (2003), Griffith et al. (2004), Vandenbussche et al. (2006) and Jorgenson, Ho and Stiroh (2007).

Table A2. Sensitivity of MFP growth in market services to different input and output measures, averaged across industries, average 1995–2004

	(1) Crude estimate	(2)	(3)	(4)	(5)	(6) = sum (1) to (5) Prefered estimate
			Effect of accounting for:			
		Changes in average hours worked	Changes in labor composition	Changes in capital composition	Value added/ gross output ratio	
Austria	0.2	0.0	−0.2	−0.1	0.1	−0.1
Belgium	0.6	0.0	−0.3	−0.7	0.4	−0.1
Denmark	0.6	−0.2	−0.3	−1.0	0.4	−0.4
Finland	1.9	0.1	0.1	−0.1	−0.8	1.3
France	0.9	0.4	−0.4	−0.1	−0.4	0.5
Germany	0.1	0.7	0.0	−0.1	−0.2	0.4
Italy	−0.5	0.2	−0.1	0.2	0.2	−0.1
Netherlands	1.7	0.4	0.0	−0.2	−0.9	0.9
Spain	−0.6	0.0	−0.4	−0.2	0.7	−0.6
UK	1.5	0.3	−0.4	−0.3	−0.5	0.5
US	2.0	0.1	−0.3	−0.2	−0.6	1.0

Notes: Column (1), labelled 'Crude', calculates MFP growth by subtracting the (cost-share weighted) growth in persons engaged and the capital stock from growth of value added at constant prices. Figures show average MFP growth for the nine market services for the period 1995–2004. Column (2) shows the effect of accounting for changes in average hours worked by persons engaged. Column (3) shows the effect of accounting for changes in the composition of the workforce (distinguishing workers based on education, age and gender). Column (4) shows the effect of accounting for changes in the composition of capital (distinguishing six types of capital assets). Both composition adjustments recognize that workers with higher wages and capital assets with higher user costs should have a higher marginal product. Column (5) shows the effect of accounting for differences in the use of intermediate inputs. Column (6), labelled 'Preferred', calculates MFP growth by subtracting the (cost-share weighted) growth in hours worked by different types of workers, different types of capital and intermediate inputs from growth of gross output at constant prices. It is equal to the sum of columns (1) through (5).

Source: Calculations by authors on EU KLEMS database, March 2007 (http://www.euklems.net), described in Timmer *et al.* (2007).

value added volumes.[56] This crude measure is used for example by Vandenbussche, Aghion and Meghir (2006) and Färe *et al.* (2006). In the remaining columns, the ingredients for an adjustment of the MFP measure are constructed in a sequential procedure. Each column shows the additional effect on MFP growth rates by taking into account an improvement in a particular input measure. Subsequently, we show the effects of taking into account changes in average hours worked (as e.g. in Nicoletti and Scarpetta, 2003), changes in labor composition (as e.g. in Griffith, Redding and van Reenen, 2004; Cameron, Proudman and Redding, 2005), changes in capital

[56] An additional issue for the growth accounting decomposition not discussed so far, is the calculation of the weights in equations (A2) and (A3). As each input should be weighted by its share in total costs, most studies typically take the compensation of employees as the weight for labor input. However, the labor input weight should also reflect the costs of labor for self-employed. Especially for industries with a large number of self-employed such as retailing, hotels and restaurant and some business services, the share of self-employed can be up to 15 percent. We adjust labor compensation by the ratio of total persons engaged over employees, implicitly assuming that self-employed have a wage similar to employees. The weight of capital is defined as gross value added minus our measure of labor compensation. This will include taxes on production.

composition and accounting for intermediate inputs. By summing up the MFP effects from the four adjustments, our preferred estimate in the last column of Table A2 is derived from the crude MFP estimate.[57]

The overall adjustments made to the crude MFP estimate vary considerable across countries and we find no clear cross-country pattern in the bias. Our preferred estimate is up to 1.0 percentage point lower than the crude estimate for Denmark, the UK and the US, but up to 0.4% higher in Italy and Germany. For example, while on the basis of the crude measures annual US MFP growth is 1.9% higher than in Germany, our preferred estimate indicates a growth advantage of 0.6%. However, although no clear biases can be detected in the overall combined adjustments, the individual component adjustments often have predictable effects. Accounting for changes in hours worked (column 2) leads to higher MFP growth rates in all countries (except Denmark) as hours worked per worker are still declining across Europe. The adjustments for changes in labor composition are often negative, as there is a general shift towards higher-skilled and more experienced workers. The most important adjustment is the shift from a capital measure based on aggregate stocks to capital services. As shown in the main text, the importance of short-lived ICT assets relative to non-ICT assets has increased over time. Consequently, capital service input growth rates are higher than capital stock growth rates in all countries (except for Italy). The final adjustment from a value added based MFP measure to a gross output based MFP measure shows no effect in a particular direction. If value added volume growth is measured as a weighted growth rate of gross output and intermediate input volumes, MFP measured for gross output and MFP as measured for value added are proportional to each other depending on the ratio of gross output over value added as the factor of proportion.[58] This factor will differ across countries, and over time. For example, there is a general tendency towards using more intermediate inputs, especially business services, as firms outsource many of the standardized service activities. This leads to an increase in the ratio of intermediates over gross output which should be accounted for. As can be seen from column (5), this adjustment differs across countries without a clear pattern.

Obviously, our preferred measure is still imperfect as it does not deal with other adjustments which are needed such as changes in capital capacity utilization (which is especially important for short-run analysis), imperfect competition, intra-industry deliveries and intangible capital. The latter refers to the need for including intangible capital measures such as R&D knowledge and organizational capital into the input measures. These adjustments are beyond the scope of the current study, but point to avenues for further research (see e.g. Corrado, Hulten and Sichel (2006) on the measurement of intangibles).

---

[57] Note that the preferred MFP estimate in this table differs from the one shown in Table 6. While the MFP measure shown here is based on the gross output basis, the one in Table 6 is on a value added basis, see main text.

[58] See Bruno (1984), Jorgenson, Gollop and Fraumeni (1987) or Schreyer (2001) for an extensive discussion.

Table A3. Multi-factor productivity leaders by industry in 1980, 1995 and 2004

Industry	Rank	1980	1995	2004
Motor trade	1st	BEL	BEL	BEL
	2nd	DNK	FRA	GBR
	3rd	FRA	GBR	NLD
Wholesale trade	1st	BEL	GER	GER
	2nd	GER	BEL	NLD
	3rd	FIN	DNK	FIN
Retail trade	1st	DNK	DNK	DNK
	2nd	BEL	GER	GER
	3rd	GER	FRA	FRA
Hotels and restaurants	1st	FRA	GER	AUT
	2nd	GER	AUT	GER
	3rd	DNK	US	US
Transport and storage	1st	NLD	NLD	NLD
	2nd	US	US	US
	3rd	FRA	FRA	FRA
Post and telecommunications	1st	GBR	GBR	GBR
	2nd	US	FRA	FRA
	3rd	BEL	BEL	GER
Financial intermediation	1st	ITA	ITA	ITA
	2nd	US	NLD	BEL
	3rd	ESP	FRA	DNK
Business services	1st	US	US	US
	2nd	ESP	DNK	BEL
	3rd	ITA	GER	DNK
Social and personal services	1st	NLD	DNK	FRA
	2nd	AUT	GER	NLD
	3rd	DNK	NLD	GER

Source: Calculations based on EU KLEMS database, March 2007 (http://www.euklems.net), See Appendix 2.

APPENDIX 4. ROBUSTNESS ANALYSIS

Available at http://www.economic-policy.org

REFERENCES

Acemoglu, D., P. Aghion and F. Zilibotti (2006). 'Distance to Frontier, Selection, and Economic Growth', *Journal of the European Economic Association*, 4(1), 37–74.

Aghion, P. and R. Griffith (2005). *Competition and Growth. Reconciling Theory and Evidence*, Cambridge, MA: MIT Press.

Aghion, P. and P. Howitt (2006). 'Joseph Schumpeter Lecture: Appropriate Growth Policy: A Unifying Framework', *Journal of the European Economic Association*, 4(2–3), 269–314.

Alesina, A., S. Ardagna, G. Nicoletti and F. Schiantareli (2005). 'Regulation and Investment', *Journal of the European Economic Association*, 3(4), 791–825.

Baily, M.N. and J.F. Kirkegaard (2004). *Transforming the European Economy*, Washington DC: Institute for International Economics.

Basu, S., J. Fernald, N. Oulton and S. Srinivasan (2004). 'The Case of the Missing Productivity Growth: Or, Does Information Technology Explain Why Productivity Accelerated in the United States but not in the United Kingdom?' in M. Gertler and K. Rogoff (eds.), *NBER Macroeconomics Annual*, Cambridge, MA: MIT Press, pp. 9–63.

Baumol, W. and W.G. Bowen (1966). *Performing Arts: The Economic Dilemma*, New York: Twentieth Century Fund.

Baumol, W. (1967). 'Macroeconomics of Unbalanced Growth: The Anatomy of Urban Crisis', *The American Economic Review*, 57(3), 415–426.

Bernard, A. and C.I. Jones (1996). 'Comparing Apples to Oranges: Productivity Convergence and Measurement Across Industries and Countries' *American Economic Review*, 86(5), pp. 1216–1238.

— (2001). 'Comparing Apples to Oranges: Reply' *American Economic Review*, 91(4), 1168–69.

Black, S.E. and L.M. Lynch (2005). 'Measuring Organizational Capital in the New Economy', *IZA Discussion Paper Series 1524*, Bonn: IZA.

Blanchard, O.J. (2004). 'The Economic Future of Europe' *Journal of Economic Perspectives*, 18(4), 3–26.

Bloom, N. and J. van Reenen (2006). 'Measuring and Explaining Management Practices Across Firms and Nations', forthcoming in *Quarterly Journal of Economics*, also available as *NBER Working Paper 12216*.

Bosworth, B.P. and Triplett, J.E. (2007). *The 21st Century Productivity Expansion is STILL in Services*, revised version of paper presented at AEA meeting 2006, March 2007.

Boylaud, O. and G. Nicoletti (2000). 'Regulation, Market Structure and Performance in Telecommunications', *OECD Economics Department Working Paper 237*, Paris: OECD.

Bruno, M. (1984). 'Raw Materials, Profits, and the Productivity Slowdown', *Quarterly Journal of Economics*, 99(1), 1–30.

Brynjolfsson, E. and L.M. Hitt (2003). 'Computing Productivity: Firm-level Evidence', *Review of Economics and Statistics*, 85(4), 793–808.

Cameron, G., J. Proudman and S. Redding (2005). 'Technological Convergence, R&D, Trade and Productivity Growth', *European Economic Review*, 49, 775–807.

Caves, D.W., L.R. Christensen and W.E. Diewert (1982). 'Multilateral Comparisons of Output, Input and Productivity using Superlative Index Numbers', *Economic Journal*, 92, March, 73–86.

Colecchia, A. and P. Schreyer (2002). 'ICT Investment and Economic Growth in the 1990s: Is the United States a Unique Case? A Comparative Study of Nine OECD Countries', *Review of Economic Dynamics*, 5, 408–42.

Conway, P. and G. Nicoletti (2006). 'Product Market Regulation in the Non-Manufacturing Sectors of OECD Countries: Measurement and Highlights', *OECD Economics Department Working Paper 530*, Paris: OECD.

Conway, P., D. De Rosa, G. Nicoletti and F. Steiner (2006). 'Regulation, Competition and Productivity Convergence', *OECD Economics Department Working Paper 509*, Paris: OECD.

Corrado, C.A., C.R. Hulten and D.E. Sichel (2006). 'Intangible Capital and Economic Growth', *NBER Working Paper 11948*, Cambridge, MA: NBER.

Crafts, N. (2006). 'Regulation and Productivity Performance', *Oxford Review of Economic Policy*, 22(2), 186–202.

Crespi, G., C. Criscuolo, J. Haskel and D. Hawkes (2006). 'Measuring and Understanding Productivity in UK Market Services', *Oxford Review of Economic Policy*, 22(2), 186–202.

Daveri, F. and O. Silva (2004). 'Not only Nokia: What Finland Tells Us about New Economy Growth', *Economic Policy*, 19(38), 117–163.

De Long and J. Bradford (1988). 'Productivity Growth, Convergence, and Welfare: Comment', *American Economic Review*, 78(5), 1138–1154.

Engel, C. and J.H. Rogers (2004). 'European Product Market Integration after the Euro', *Economic Policy*, 19(39), 347–384.

European Commission (2004). *The EU Economy 2004 Review, European Economy. No 6. 2004.* Luxembourg: Office for Official Publications of the EC.

Eurostat (2001). *Handbook on Price and Volume Measures in National Accounts*, Luxembourg: Office for Official Publications of the EC.

Färe, R., S. Grosskopf and D. Margaritis (2006). 'Productivity Growth and Convergence in the European Union', *Journal of Productivity Analysis*, 25(1), 111–141.

Foster, L., J. Haltiwanger and C.J. Krizan (2006). 'Market Selection, Reallocation, and Restructuring in the US Retail Trade Sector in the 1990s', *Review of Economics and Statistics*, 88(4), 748–758.

Fraumeni, B.M. (1997) 'The Measurement of Depreciation in the US National Income and Product Accounts', *Survey of Current Business*, July, 7–23.

Freeman, R.B. and R. Schettkat (2005). 'Marketization of Household Production and the EU–US Gap in Work', *Economic Policy*, 20(41), 6–50.

Garibaldi, P. and P. Mauro (2002). 'Employment Growth: Accounting for the Facts', *Economic Policy*, 17(1), 67–113.

Griffith, R., R. Harrison and H. Simpson (2006). 'Product Market Reform and Innovation in the EU', *CEPR Discussion Paper 5849*, London: CEPR.

Griffith, R., S. Redding and J. van Reenen (2004). 'Mapping the Two Faces of R&D: Productivity Growth in a Panel of OECD Industries', *Review of Economics and Statistics*, 86(4), 883–895.

Griliches, Z. (1992). *Output Measurement in the Service Sectors*, (ed.), *NBER, Studies in Income and Wealth*, Volume 56, Chicago: University of Chicago Press.

— (1994). 'Productivity, R&D, and the Data Constraint', *American Economic Review*, 84(1), 1–23.

Gust, C. and J. Marquez (2004). 'International Comparisons of Productivity Growth: The Role of Information Technology and Regulatory Practices', *Labour Economics*, 11(1), 33–58.

Hopenhayn, H.A. (1992). 'Entry, Exit, and Firm Dynamics in Long Run Equilibrium', *Econometrica*, 60(5), 1127–1150.

Horrigan, M., D. Bathgate and R. Swick (2006). 'Services Producer Price Indices: Past, Present, and Future', paper presented at the NBER/CRIW Summer Institute, July 17–19, 2006, see http://www.nber.org/CRIW/.

Hulten, C.R. (2001). 'Total Factor Productivity: A Short Biography', in C.R. Hulten, E.R. Dean, and M.J. Harper (eds.) *New Developments in Productivity Analysis*, Studies in Income and Wealth, vol. 63, Chicago: The University of Chicago Press, pp. 1–47.

Inklaar, R., M. O'Mahony and M.P. Timmer (2005). 'ICT and Europe's Productivity Performance; Industry-level Growth Account Comparisons with the United States', *Review of Income and Wealth*, 51(4), 505–36.

Inklaar, R. and M.P. Timmer (2007a). 'Of Yeast and Mushrooms: Patterns of Industry-level Productivity Growth', *German Economic Review*, 8(2), 174–187.

— (2007b). 'International Comparisons of Industry Output, Inputs and Productivity Levels: Methodology and New Results', *Economic Systems Research*, 19(3), 343–363.

— (2007c). 'Accounting for Growth in Retail Trade: An International Productivity Comparison', forthcoming in *Journal of Productivity Analysis*.

Inklaar, R., M.P. Timmer and B. van Ark (2007). 'Mind the Gap! International Comparisons of Productivity in Services and Goods Production', *German Economic Review*, 8(2), 281–307.

Jorgenson, D.W. (1995). *Productivity, Volume 1: Postwar US Economic Growth*, Cambridge, MA: MIT Press.

Jorgenson, D.W. and Z. Griliches (1967). 'The Explanation of Productivity Change', *Review of Economic Studies*, 34(3), 249–83.

Jorgenson, D.W. and M. Nishmizu (1978). 'US and Japanese Economic Growth, 1952–1974: An International Comparison', *Economic Journal*, 88(352), 707–26.

Jorgenson, D.W., F.M. Gollop and B.M. Fraumeni (1987). *Productivity and US Economic Growth*, Cambridge, MA: Harvard Economic Studies.

Jorgenson, D.W. and K.J. Stiroh (2000). 'Raising the Speed Limit: US Economic Growth in the Information Age', *Brookings Papers on Economic Activity*, 2000:1, 125–211.

Jorgenson, D.W., M. Ho and K.J. Stiroh (2005). 'Growth of US Industries and Investments in Information Technology and Higher Education', in C.A. Corrado, J. Haltiwanger and D.E. Sichel (eds.) *Measuring Capital in the New Economy*, Chicago: University of Chicago Press.

— (2007). 'A Retrospective Look at the US Productivity Growth Resurgence', *Federal Reserve Bank of New York Staff Report, no. 277*, NY: Fed Reserve Bank.

Koeniger, W. and M. Leonardi (2007). 'Capital Deepening and Wage Differentials: Germany versus US', *Economic Policy*, 22(49), 71–116.

Kox, H. and A. Lejour (2005). 'Regulatory Heterogeneity as Obstacle for International Services Trade', *CPB Discussion Papers 49*, Netherlands Bureau for Economic Policy Analysis, www.cpb.nl.

Krueger, A. and M. Lindahl (2001). 'Education for Growth: Why and for whom?' *Journal of Economic Literature*, 39(4), 1101–1136.

Losch, M. (ed.) (2006). *Deepening the Lisbon Agenda: Studies on Productivity, Services and Technologies*, Vienna: Austrian Federal Ministry of Economics and Labour.

Mason, G., B. O'Leary and M. Vecchi (2007). *Cross-country Analysis of Productivity and Skills at Sector Level*, Report to Sector Skills Development Agency, London: National Institute of Economic and Social Research (mimeo).

Melitz, M.J. (2003). 'The Impact of Trade on Intra-Industry Reallocations and Aggregate Industry Productivity', *Econometrica*, 71(6), 1695–1725.

Nicoletti, G. and S. Scarpetta (2003). 'Regulation, Productivity and Growth: OECD Evidence', *Economic Policy*, 36, 9–72, April.

OECD (2004). *The Economic Impact of ICT. Measurement, Evidence and Implications*, Paris: OECD.

— (2007). *OECD Economic Surveys: Italy*, Issue 12, Paris: OECD.

O'Mahony, M. and B. van Ark (eds.) (2003). *EU Productivity and Competitiveness: An Industry Perspective Can Europe Resume the Catching-up Process?* Luxembourg: Office for Official Publications of the European Communities.

O'Mahony, M. and M. Vecchi (2005). 'Quantifying the Impact of ICT Capital on Output Growth: A Heterogeneous Dynamic Panel Approach', *Economica*, 72, 615–33.

Sapir, A., P. Aghion, G. Bertola, M. Hellwig, J. Pisani-Ferry, D. Rosati, J. Viñals and H. Wallace (2004). *An Agenda for a Growing Europe: The Sapir Report*, Oxford: Oxford University Press.

Schettkat, R. and L. Yokarini (2006). 'The Shift to Services: A Review of the Literature', *Structural Change and Economic Dynamics*, 17(2), 127–47.

Schreyer, P. (2001). *Measuring Productivity – OECD Manual. Measurement of Aggregate and Industry-Level Productivity Growth*, Paris: OECD.

— (2002). 'Computer Price Indices and International Growth and Productivity Comparisons', *Review of Income and Wealth*, 48(1), 15–31.

Sichel, D.E. (1997). 'The Productivity Slowdown: Is a Growing Unmeasurable Sector the Culprit?' *Review of Economics and Statistics*, 79(3), 367–370.

Stiroh, K.J. (2002). 'Information Technology and the US Productivity Revival: What Do the Industry Data Say?' *American Economic Review*, 92(5), 1559–1576.

— (2004). 'Reassessing the Impact of IT in the Production Function: A Meta-Analysis and Sensitivity Tests', forthcoming in *Annales d'Economie et de Statistique*.

Temple, J. (2000). 'Growth Regressions and What the Textbooks Don't Tell You', *Bulletin of Economic Research*, 52 (3), 181–205.

Temple, J.R.W. (1998). 'Robustness Tests of the Augmented Solow Model', *Journal of Applied Econometrics*, 13(4), 361–375.

Timmer, M.P. and B. van Ark (2005). 'Does Information and Communication Technology Drive EU–US Productivity Growth Differentials?' *Oxford Economic Papers*, 57(4), 693–716.

Timmer, M.P., M. O'Mahony and B. van Ark (2007a). *The EU KLEMS Growth and Productivity Accounts: An Overview*, mimeo, University of Groningen & University of Birmingham, March.

Timmer, M.P., G. Ypma and B. van Ark (2007b). 'Industry-of-Origin Prices and Output PPPs: A New Dataset for International Comparisons', *GGDC Research Memorandum*, GD–82 Groningen Growth and Development Centre, www.ggdc.net.

Triplett, J.E. and B.P. Bosworth (2004). *Productivity in the US Services Sector; New Sources of Economic Growth*, Washington DC: Brookings Institution.

— (2006). '"Baumol's Disease" Has Been Cured: IT and Multifactor Productivity in US Services Industries', in D.W. Jansen (ed.), *The New Economy And Beyond. Past, Present and Future*, Cheltenham: Edward Elgar.

Triplett, J.E. (2006). *Handbook on Hedonic Indexes and Quality Adjustments in Price Indexes. Special Application to Information Technology Products*, Paris: OECD.

van Ark, B., R. Inklaar and R.H. McGuckin (2003). 'ICT and Productivity in Europe and the United States, Where Do the Differences Come From?' *CESifo Economic Studies*, 49(3), 295–318.

van Ark, B., M. O'Mahony and M.P. Timmer (2008). 'European Growth: The End of Convergence', forthcoming in *Journal of Economic Perspectives*.

Vandenbussche, J., P. Aghion and C. Meghir (2006). 'Growth, Distance to the Frontier and Composition of Human Capital', *Journal of Economic Growth*, 11, 97–127.

Wang, J.C., S. Basu and J. Fernald (2004). 'A General-Equilibrium Asset-Pricing Approach to the Measurement of Nominal and Real Bank Output', *FRB Boston Series, paper no. 04–7*, NY: Fed Reserve Bank.

Wölfl, A. (2003). 'Productivity Growth in Service Industries: An Assessment of Recent Patterns and the Role of Measurement' *OECD/STI Working Paper Series, 2003/7*, Paris: OECD.

Erratum

In the printed issue of Economic Policy 52, the following error was published. On the outside front cover of the journal the article titles read:

school tracking
EASTERLY

... and ...

foreign aid
BRUNELLO & CHECCHI

The titles here had been incorrectly swapped over and didn't match the correct authors. The correct titles should have read:

foreign aid
EASTERLY

... and ...

school tracking
BRUNELLO & CHECCHI

We apologize for this error.

Economic Policy January 2008 pp. 195 Printed in Great Britain
© CEPR, CES, MSH, 2008.

Blackwell
Publishing

Blackwell Publishing
9600 Garsington Road
Oxford OX4 2DQ UK

Tel: +44 (0) 1865 776868
Fax: +44 (0) 1865 714591

The Scandinavian Journal of Economics

Edited by: Nils Gottfries and Espen R. Moen

The Scandinavian Journal of Economics is one of the oldest and most distinguished economics journals in the world. It publishes research of the highest scientific quality from an international array of contributors in all areas of economics and related fields. The *Journal* features theoretical and empirical articles in all fields of economics, book reviews, comprehensive surveys of the contributions to economics of the recipients of the Alfred Nobel Memorial Prize in Economics, and a special issue each year on key topics in economics.

Online Early Now you can access fully finished, peer-reviewed articles from *The Scandinavian Journal of Economics* online before the print issue is published. This enables you to access information faster without having to wait for the delivery of the entire issue. All Synergy *OnlineEarly* articles can be cited using the Digital Object Identifier (DOI), which continues to allow links to the article even when it has been assigned to an issue. To view OnlineEarly material from *The Scandinavian Journal of Economics* go to: **www.blackwell-synergy.com/loi/sjoe** and click on the sun icon.

For more information visit

www.blackwellpublishing.com/sjoe

Or visit **www.blackwell-synergy.com/loi/sjoe** for more information about accessing the journal online.

Register FREE at Blackwell Synergy and you can:

- Receive tables of contents e-mail alerts directly to your desktop with links to article abstracts
- Search across all full text articles for key words or phrases
- Access free sample issues from every online journal
- Browse all journal table of contents and abstracts, and save favourites on your own custom page.

Published quarterly, ISSN 0347-0520

NEW

Blackwell Reference Online

A major new online academic reference resource - for students, teachers and researchers.

Blackwell Publishing's acclaimed reference titles in economics are now available online through **Blackwell Reference Online** - a vast online library giving instant access to the most authoritative and up-to-date scholarship across the humanities and social sciences.

Blackwell Reference Online provides:

❖ access to the titles from the renowned **Blackwell Companions to Contemporary Economics** series.

❖ seamless integration of content, simple navigation and useful research tools.

❖ sophisticated content classification by subject, person, period, key topic and place to enable the user to find information quickly and easily.

With unbeatable functionality, undergraduate and graduate students, lecturers, and researchers will find **Blackwell Reference Online** an invaluable learning and teaching resource and an indispensable addition to any university library.

Blackwell
Reference Online

To find out more about **Blackwell Reference Online**, visit
www.blackwellreference.com